The Third Space and Chinese Language Pedagogy

The Third Space and Chinese Language Pedagogy presents the Third Space as a new frame through which foreign language pedagogy is conceptualized as a pedagogy of negotiating intentions and expectations in another culture.

The field of Chinese as a foreign language (CFL) in the past decades has been expanding rapidly at the beginning and intermediate levels, yet it is lacking in scholarship on the true advanced level both in theory building and research-supported curriculum and material development. This book argues that it is time for CFL to go beyond merely satisfying the desire of gazing at the other, whether it is curiosity about the other or superiority over the other, to focusing on learning to work with the other. It reimagines the field as co-constructing a transcultural Third Space where learners are becoming experts in negotiating intentions and expectations in another culture. It presents a range of research-based CFL pedagogical scholarship and practices especially relevant to the advanced level and to the goal of enabling learners to go past fans or critics to become actors/players in the game of cross-lingual and intercultural cooperation.

Xin Zhang is an assistant professor of Chinese language and intercultural communication and co-director of the Third Space Lab at Duke Kunshan University, where she coordinates the Chinese as a Second Language program. Her research interests center around second language acquisition, Chinese language pedagogy and intercultural communication manifested in language teaching, program building and teacher training. She is the co-author of *Perform Guangzhou: A Course in Intermediate to Advanced Spoken Mandarin*.

Xiaobin Jian is an associate professor of Chinese in the Department of East Asian Languages and Literatures at The Ohio State University. He specializes in language pedagogy, negotiation and presentation in cross-lingual and cross-cultural context, program design and material development aiming at training non-native learners at the true advanced level in domain-specific and culturally authentic context. In addition to publishing articles on early Chinese tradition and contemporary Chinese behavioral culture, he is the author/co-author of the five-volume Kaleidoscope series and the multi-volume Perform China series (two volumes published with two more volumes forthcoming and several more in planning).

Contents

List of figures vii
List of tables viii
List of contributors ix
Acknowledgments xi

Introduction: Third Space and Chinese language pedagogy: possibilities of and paths to cross-lingual and cross-cultural cooperation 1
XIN ZHANG AND XIAOBIN JIAN

1 **Negotiating a co-constructed multilingual and transcultural Third Space** 7
XIAOBIN JIAN

2 **Native speaker effects, C2 receptivity of learner and co-construction of Third-Space personae: a pedagogy of target culture expectation** 26
XIN ZHANG

3 **Negotiating intentions in intercultural conversational interactions: excusing oneself from a family gathering** 45
BING MU

4 **Striving for the Third Space: an American professional's experiences in Chinese workplaces** 68
ZHINI ZENG

5 **Establishing domain expertise in the Third Space: constructing language learning motivation to perform beyond proficiency** 99
JUNQING (JESSIE) JIA

6	**Online forum as Third Space? CFL learners' experiences on an online knowledge-sharing community** ZHINI ZENG	117
7	**Why we perform** GALAL WALKER	139
	Index	159

Figures

3.1	Social moves that the host and the guest adopt in a family gathering	58
3.2	The development of the guest's intention to leave	59
6.1	Percentages of three different types of responses from Chinese	127

Tables

3.1	Students' demographic information	52
6.1	Data collected from curriculum-based Zhihu activities at upper-intermediate level	123
6.2	Data collected from extracurricular Zhihu activities at advanced level	124
6.3	Examples of three types of responses received from Chinese Zhihu users	125
6.4	Representative successful and unsuccessful cases for focal data analysis	126

Contributors

Junqing (Jessie) Jia is an assistant professor of Chinese in the Department of East Asian Languages and Literatures at Hamilton College. She received her doctorate in Chinese language pedagogy from The Ohio State University in 2017. Her research focuses on understanding sustainable foreign language learning motivation and creating motivating experiences in the classroom and beyond.

Xiaobin Jian is an associate professor of Chinese in the Department of East Asian Languages and Literatures at The Ohio State University (OSU). He received his doctorate in Chinese literature from OSU in 1998 and worked as assistant professor and then associate professor at The College of William and Mary for almost 20 years. In 2012, he returned to OSU and has been teaching in its graduate program of pedagogy of Chinese language and culture and its graduate program of advanced Chinese language and culture (OSU Chinese Flagship). He specializes in language pedagogy, negotiation and presentation in cross-lingual and cross-cultural context, program design and material development aiming at training non-native learners at the true advanced level in domain-specific and culturally authentic context. In addition to publishing articles on early Chinese tradition and contemporary Chinese behavioral culture, he is the author/co-author of the five-volume *Kaleidoscope* series and the multi-volume *Perform China* series (two volumes published with two more volumes forthcoming and several more in planning).

Bing Mu is an assistant professor of Chinese in the Department of Modern and Classical Languages and Literatures at the University of Rhode Island. Her research foci include Chinese language pedagogy, intercultural communication and competence, study abroad and pedagogical material development. She is the co-author of *Action! China: A Field Guide to Using Chinese in the Community*.

Galal Walker (PhD, Cornell) is a professor of Chinese in the Department of East Asian Languages and Literatures, and the Director of the National East Asian Languages Resource. In 2003 he was the first US recipient of the China Language and Culture Friendship Award, presented by the People's Republic of China Ministry of Education. In 2010, the People's Government of the City of Qingdao awarded him the Qindao Award for his contributions to the social and economic life of the city. In 2012, he was awarded the Walton Lifetime Achievement Award by the Chinese Language Teachers Association (CLTA) and honored at a special session at the MLA Annual Convention in Boston (January 2013), where he became the 2012 recipient of the Association of Departments of Foreign Languages (ADFL) Award for Distinguished Service to the Profession. The ADFL award honors members of the profession who have attained a national or international reputation for distinguished service to teaching and scholarship in foreign languages.

Zhini Zeng is an assistant professor of the Chinese Flagship program at the University of Mississippi. She received her BA in teaching Chinese as a foreign language (2009) from the Shanghai International Studies University and her MA and PhD in Chinese language pedagogy (2015) from The Ohio State University. Having taught a wide range of courses in Chinese language, literature and culture at all levels, her expertise includes developing pedagogical materials and designing performance-based curriculum and study-abroad programs, foreign language assessment and teacher training. Her current research focuses on coaching advanced-level CFL learners to demonstrate domain expertise in the target-language professional community. In addition to publishing several articles in these areas, she is the author of *Perform Chun Cao: A Multimedia Advanced Chinese Course*, an advanced-level pedagogical material utilizing an authentic Chinese novel to develop students' oral and written narrative skills, and the co-author of *Perform Guangzhou*, a multimedia pedagogical material training intermediate-advanced CFL learners to engage with the local community in Guangzhou, China, through a series of authentic performances.

Xin Zhang is an assistant professor of Chinese language and intercultural communication and co-director of the Third Space Lab at Duke Kunshan University. Her research interests center around second language acquisition, Chinese language pedagogy and intercultural communication manifested in language teaching, program building and teacher training. She has directed intensive study-abroad Chinese programs, including the Critical Language Scholarship program, and has received several awards for her projects from the Chinese Language Teachers Association, the Five Colleges of Ohio Consortium, the National Federation of the Modern Language Teachers' Association and the National Council of Less Commonly Taught Languages in the United States. She is the co-author of *Perform Guangzhou: A Course in Intermediate to Advanced Spoken Mandarin*.

Acknowledgments

The making of this volume dates back to the Symposium on Interdisciplinary Approaches to East Asian Languages Pedagogy organized by Xin Zhang and Mari Noda (The Ohio State University), which gathered all the contributors in Columbus in February 2018. The symposium was sponsored by an Ohio-Five Mellon Language Enrichment Grant, Five Colleges of Ohio, East Asian Studies at Oberlin College and Department of East Asian Languages and Literatures at The Ohio State University. We wish to thank the following individuals for supporting the symposium that precipitated this volume: Hsiu-Chuang Deppman (Oberlin College), Danial Hartnett (Kenyon College), Sarah Stone (Five Colleges of Ohio), Galal Walker (The Ohio State University), as well as the then graduate and undergraduate students on the symposium organizing committee (Miki Arakaki, John Bundschuh, Ramzy Lakos, Cong Li, Kai Liang, David Lo, Hiromi Tobaru, Adam Work, and Anni Zong).

Two joint presentations by Galal Walker and Xiaobin Jian were critical to the early stage of our effort to re-establish basic assumptions for Chinese language pedagogy through the framework of Third Space: "A Chinese Language Pedagogy for the 21st Century: Basic Assumptions" at Institute for Chinese Studies Lecture Series, February 19, 2016, The Ohio State University; and "Performed Culture: Negotiating 'Self' and 'Other' in the Third Space" at International Symposium on Language Communication and Civilization Dialogue, June 29, 2017, Oxford University. Presentations and discussions taking place at the following two occasions were also enlightening and informative to the further explorations of the possibilities of and paths to negotiating a cooperative and productive Third Space as relevant to the field of Chinese as a foreign language (CFL): Xiaobin Jian's presentation of "Co-constructing a Multilingual and Transcultural Third Space" at The 9th International Conference of Intercultural Communication, November 26, Wuhan University and Mari Noda chaired panel "Constructing 'Self' in East Asian Languages and Cultures: Negotiating the Third Space" at Association for Asian Studies 2019 Annual Conference, March 23, 2019, Denver.

We would like to thank the editorial staff at Routledge and Apex CoVantage for their support and attention to detail. In particular we are indebted to Andrea Hartill, senior publisher, Claire Margerison, senior editorial assistant, Ellie Auton, editorial assistant, and Autumn Spalding, project manager.

Acknowledgments

In different stages of conceptualizing and putting together the current volume, we benefited enormously from the generous comments and feedback from anonymous outside reviewers as well as Jianhua Bai (Kenyon College) and Don Snow (Duke Kunshan University). We are especially grateful to Galal Walker for his life-long work, mentorship and inspiring contributions to the field of East Asian language pedagogy, which we aspire to follow.

All the contributors have made editing this volume a pleasant journey. Our deep gratitude is with each of them for their insightful input, graceful acceptance of feedback, and sustained commitment to the volume despite the interruption of the Covid-19 pandemic on their personal and professional life. It is our distinct privilege to present this volume, and we hope the readers will enjoy all contributions as much as we do.

Xin Zhang and Xiaobin Jian

Introduction

Third Space and Chinese language pedagogy: possibilities of and paths to cross-lingual and cross-cultural cooperation

Xin Zhang and Xiaobin Jian

Focusing on Chinese as a foreign language (CFL), this edited volume responds to the need of rethinking the goals of foreign language (FL) education in relation to the urgent call for greater global cooperation despite and because of the overwhelming challenges we are experiencing. At the time the chapters in this volume were being drafted, the COVID-19 pandemic was reaching every corner of the world and impacting the lives of millions of people regardless of their national, ideological, cultural and linguistic backgrounds. This reminds us once again that human well-being depends on shared experience and cooperation among all people across all real or perceived boundaries. The re-conceptualization of Third Space and the discussions of its practice in CFL as presented in this volume are all informed by and based on the objective of exploring the possibilities of and paths to constructive and productive cross-lingual and cross-cultural cooperation.

Entering the third decade of the 21st century, it is long overdue that the goal of FL or CFL education should go beyond satisfying the desire of cultural gazing at the other to focusing on the need of productively working with the other. Programmatically developing foreign language (L2) learners' capacities of expertly negotiating intentions and expectations in another culture (C2) should be imagined as necessary and possible objectives instead of merely being ideals or afterthoughts. With shift at this level, researchers and practitioners in the field have faced difficult conceptual and pedagogical challenges. These challenges include, on the one hand, the conceptualization of if and how such intercultural encounters take place, the diversified roles and power dynamics involved and its emergent and co-constructive nature; and on the other hand, the pedagogical decisions about how to optimize learning in preparing L2 learners for such engagements in a sustainable way, if that goal is in fact attainable. We are not alone in having grappled with such questions, although many of the discussions have remained largely divided within the traditional parameters of "scholarship" and "pedagogy." With the current volume, we intend to initiate an open discussion, with an aim to connect readers from both groups.

Responding to these challenges, this volume explores the conceptualization of a constructive and cooperative *Third Space* with substantial empirical studies examining various aspects and factors involved in constructing such a space. We conceptualize cross-lingual and intercultural interaction should and can open up a new field, a Third Space, where different cultures converge, contest and cooperate; where expectations for the actors and interpretations of their actions do not entirely or constantly conform to the assumptions and norms of one culture but are dynamic and fluid, motivated by specific goals of the interaction in question and negotiated among involved actors; and where the cooperative interactions of the actors' emerging multilingual and transcultural personae are made possible by, and in turn, continue to co-construct the multilingual and transcultural Third Space that is continuously becoming (Jian, this volume). This volume presents to its targeted audience—scholars, graduate students and practitioners in the field of foreign language pedagogy—a new conceptual frame to redefine the field as about enabling learners of foreign languages to become experts in negotiating *intentions* and *expectations* in another culture, that is, experts in co-constructing a Third Space.

We have attempted and will continue to respond to these difficult questions: Are cultural differences essential elements objectively embedded in cultures or they are goal-based constructions conditioned by needs and situations? How can learners learn to change from not being consciously aware of the other culture to being able recognizing cultural differences to being capable to negotiate cultural boundaries? How can we go beyond training learners to just "get the message across" to helping them to learn to construct multilingual transcultural personae? If one speaking another language and performing another culture should be basic to this Third Space, what will be the challenges to sustaining such performances? In co-constructing a mutually beneficial Third Space, how should one respond to contradictions and contentions? How can learners learn to recognize target culture expectations? Should we train them to "meet" these expectations or to "negotiate" these expectations? Do the learners need to learn to "meet/negotiate" the target culture expectations of its native speakers or the target culture expectations of non-native speakers? Is intention what the speaker has in mind, what the audience recognize, or it is negotiated and emergent from interactions conditioned by who is speaking to whom for what purpose? How do global professionals negotiate a Third Space at work by creatively appropriate the target language as one's own use? What will involve in developing advanced-level learners' capacities to operate between languages when negotiating domain expertise with members of the target community? It is only possible as well as meaningful if learners can commit to long-term learning and working in cross-lingual and intercultural context. And it is crucial to explore how to construct motivation that goes beyond fulfilling curiosity about another culture to developing capacity of working in another culture with domain expertise and ability to establish and achieve common goals with counterparts in that culture. If online communities brought about by seemingly boundary-breaking new technologies should not be simply imagined as an unproblematic Third Space, how may deliberate acts of recognizing conflicts and strategic engagement through mutual paths lead to eventual transcendence of dichotomy?

These are hard questions without easy answers. They are necessary to respond to if the FL and CFL enterprises want to remain relevant and meaningful in the 21st century. The chapters in this volume provide research-based first-round discussions and welcome more questions and more explorations from all concerned.

In particular, the seven chapters in this volume revisit, problematize and advance the existing Third Space literature and, in doing so, offer pedagogical suggestions and practices in the context of CFL education at the advanced level. We highlight the following threads of notions and key areas of examinations.

Third Space as emergent and co-constructed

Several chapters reflect critically on the interactions between advanced CFL learners and native Chinese within the sphere of Third Space often explored as an in-between place of hybridity, explanation, invention and resignification under various labels (MacDonald, 2019), such as third culture (Useem, 1963; Useem, Useem, & Donoghue, 1963), third place (Kramsch, 1993), and third space (Bhabha, 1994). Considering cultural boundaries as goal-oriented constructions conditioned by needs and situations, Jian's Chapter 1 problematizes the counterproductive self-centered assumption of different cultures as different stages of the same culture as well as the equally counterproductive static dichotomy of "self" and "the other." He argues that—constructing the Third Space of the 21st century—it's time to go beyond comparative cultures, intercultures or cross-cultures to focus on critically and programmatically exploring the possibilities of and paths to trans-cultures based on shared experience and negotiated cooperation. The chapter also problematizes the illusion of being multicultural under monolingual condition and contends that the Third Space of the 21st century is necessarily multilingual and characteristically one performing the language/culture of the other. Mu's Chapter 3 showcases how intercultural communication between a foreigner and a native speaker is, just like interpersonal communication, by nature cooperative, coordinated and emergent. Using discourse analysis, her study examines a classroom performance that approximated a real-life scenario of "a foreign guest excusing oneself from a Chinese family gathering" between an American advanced CFL learner and two native Chinese speakers. Her observation is that the CFL learners' engagement level with native speakers varies at different points of negotiating their intentions due to a (perceived) sporadic lacking in Chinese linguistic and cultural capacities. This led her to the conclusion that L2 learners and native speakers shoulder different weights during intention negotiation (in the Third Space).

Similarly, other chapters in this volume also subscribe to the non-static view of Third Space as a dynamic and co-constructed engagement of all parties involved towards shared goals. Grounded in an ecological view of language learning, in Chapter 2 Zhang proposes that L2 learners have to navigate an "emergent and ever-changing . . . agent(learner)-environment dynamics" in a Third Space via developing effective *Third Space personae*. In Chapter 5, Jia states that a co-constructed Third Space should benefit all parties in both tangible and emotional/psychological ways. In Chapters 4 and 6, Zeng argues that Third Space be seen as a "deliberate engagement, which involves a cooperative effort" and as a "negotiation of what one chooses to be in the specific context [while] seeking the optimal way to meet the expectations from players from the other side." Naturally, as seen in these accounts, in conceptualizing Third Space as co-constructed between participants in the context of foreign language learning, one cannot avoid the questions of identity, roles and relations of dominance, which lead to the next point of examination.

Third Space personae

Speaking a foreign language at a sophisticated level inevitably involves making conscious (or in fewer occasions, unconscious) choices of codes to shape one's ways of being in relation to others in that moment. Taking on the issues of identity in the context of CFL learning and intercultural communication between advanced CFL learners and native Chinese speakers, the chapters in this volume build upon Walker's (2000) proposal of using *persona*—"what an individual allows an audience to know about him or her" (cited in Shepherd, 2005, p. 262)—as an alternative to the term *identity*. Persona, which is observable, contingent and constantly evolving, is particularly suitable for discussing the negotiation of images of the Self and the Other in a Third Space.

Zhang's Chapter 2 explores *native speaker effects*, that is, real-life effects produced by the ideologies of the "native speaker" (Doerr, 2009), which manifest in the asymmetrical power relations between CFL learners and native speakers of Chinese. She proposes a new model for FL education that recognizes this delicate and dynamic relation of dominance by repositioning at the center of L2 instruction how well L2 learners are received by people they interact with based on C2 expectations. Zhang argues that "a Third-Space persona is most effective in resulting in fruitful intercultural engagement if it emerges from proper recognition of situated C2 expectations and participation in negotiating various levels of expectation . . . leading toward a shared goal." CFL learners of all levels, with the advanced learners in particular, benefit from trainings that help them recognize what is culturally expected of them as "non-native speakers and cultural outsiders (or insiders, in the case of heritage learners)" and develop strategies for using these expectations to their own advantage.

Echoing the sentiment that L2 learners need to recognize the "boundaries of transgression and the target-society expectations so as to co-construct a desirable [T]hird [S]pace for both parties," Zeng's (Chapter 4) case study of an American CFL learner's experiences in a Chinese workplace reports in rich detail how the L2 learner strategically negotiates who he choose to be with his counterparts in the C2 workplace and the complex set of expectations for a global professional he had to navigate in forming his Third Space personae. By collecting and analyzing Chinese counterparts' perception of the CFL learners' performance, Zeng's empirical study reminds us that it is imperative to recognize the unequal power relations between native and non-native speakers precisely because the CFL learners have to deal with the native speaker effects in their real-life Third Space encounters.

In Chapter 7, Walker cites a narrative of a young American CFL learners' adventure in China as an example of common American-in-China failures due to a lack of *consciousness* of "alternative way[s] to make meaning." He argues that for L2 learners who intend to communicate with peoples from another culture, developing this new functional consciousness of how the new culture prefers the learners to behave and to use the L2 requires training. Walker proposes that in helping CFL learners to develop successful personae when communicating in Chinese social contexts, from an early stage L2 learners' awareness should be directed away from their own *identity* and on to their Chinese audiences. In the same vein, analyzing CFL learners' participation in a Chinese online knowledge-sharing community, Zeng's Chapter 6 reveals that "sticking to the 'self' and ignoring the 'other'" results in an unsuccessful attempt to engage and sustain the Third Space.

Domain expertise

Another thread that underlies the chapters in this volume is *domain expertise*. Developing capacities of using an L2 to converse about knowledge in one's disciplinary domain should be of particular interest to advanced L2 learners who wish to function professionally in another culture. Drawing on empirical data examining advanced CFL learners' motivation at different stages of their Chinese learning journey, Jia's Chapter 5 argues that establishing domain expertise through negotiating a Third Space with native speakers helps advanced CFL learners sustain their learning motivation. From the perspective of understanding motivation as a complex process, Jia suggests that an advance-level CFL curriculum should build in trainings of developing domain knowledge in L2, achieving shared goals with C2 counterparts, and visualizing a successful professional self as major motivating strategies. Both of Zeng's chapters in this volume chose Chinese professional spaces, one physical and one online, as her research sites where advanced CFL learners' articulation of their domain knowledge in Chinese are observed and judged by their Chinese counterparts. On the one hand, Zeng's findings confirm that high language proficiency combined with demonstration of expertise contribute significantly to the successful engagement with the Chinese audience. On the other hand, her studies show that a Third Space cannot be sustained without acknowledging and addressing the intentions and expectations of all parties in a specific community of practice.

Pedagogical manifestations in CFL

In examining the diversified pedagogical manifestations of the Third Space, the seven chapters offer conceptual reflections and empirical studies in direct reference to the CFL pedagogical model (Zhang, Chapter 2), program design (Jia, Chapter 5, and Walker, Chapter 7) and instructional practices (Mu, Chapter 3 and

Zeng, Chapter 6), with a focus on the advanced levels. As this volume is rooted in the field of Chinese language pedagogy with the aim of informing language teaching and learning, we hope to break the traditional divisions of "research" and "practice" and engage a wider readership of practitioners to explore the practical aspects of this volume.

References

Bhabha, H. K. (1994). The commitment to theory. In *The location of culture* (pp. 18–40). New York: Routledge.

Doerr, N. M. (Ed.). (2009). *The native speaker concept: Ethnographic investigations of native speaker effects*. Berlin: Mouton de Gruyter.

Kramsch, C. J. (1993). *Context and culture in language teaching*. Oxford: Oxford University Press.

MacDonald, M. N. (2019). The discourse of "thirdness" in intercultural studies. *Language and Intercultural Communication, 19*(1), 93–109. https://doi.org/10.1080/14708477.2019.1544788

Shepherd, E. (2005). *Eat Shandong: From personal experience to a pedagogy of a second culture*. Columbus, OH: National East Asian Languages Resource Center at The Ohio State University.

Useem, J. (1963). The community of man: A study in the third culture. *Centennial Review, 7*(4), 481–498.

Useem, J., Useem, R. H., & Donoghue, J. (1963). Men in the middle of the third culture: The roles of American and non-western people in cross-cultural administration. *Human Organization, 22*(3), 169–179.

Walker, G. (2000). Performed culture: Learning to participate in another culture. In R. D. Lambert & E. Shohamy (Eds.), *Language policy and pedagogy* (pp. 221–236). Amsterdam: John Benjamins. https://doi.org/10.1075/z.96.14wal

1 Negotiating a co-constructed multilingual and transcultural Third Space

Xiaobin Jian

Introduction: possibilities of and paths to a constructive and productive Third Space?

Human history can be characterized as a history of cooperation among more and more groups of people with diverse traditions and practices, although "cooperation" is by no means always benign, voluntary or mutually beneficial but more likely involves negotiation, manipulation and/or coercion (Tomasello, 2014; Harari, 2015). As we are entering the third decade of the 21st century, where *glocal* (global-local) is a fact of life and "one world one civilization" is more than just an idea, cooperation among people speaking different languages in different cultures is not only inevitable but desirable. It is with this understanding of the world we are in and the future to which we are heading that rethinking the goals and approaches of the enterprise of foreign language pedagogy, with special attention to the field of Chinese as a foreign language (CFL), becomes necessary and urgent. Simply satisfying the desire of gazing at the other, curiosity about the other (seeing/hearing something about them) or superiority over the other (telling/showing them what to do) are no longer enough or meaningful as programmatic objectives—we need to go beyond these assumed and often unquestioned outcomes to focus on meeting the call of learning to cooperate with the other. To this end, it is time to further explore the conceptualization of Third Space with special focus on the possibilities of and paths to the constructive and productive cross-lingual-cultural interactions taking place in a negotiated and co-constructed multilingual and transcultural space.

Spatializing what happens when differences meet (self meets the other, old meets new, etc.) presents the advantage of catching and further exploring the complexity of hybridity inevitable in these meetings, such as Bourdieu's generative "habitus," a "structuring structure" where the more durable "primary habitus" confronts the more amenable "secondary habitus" (Bourdieu, 1984, p. 166; Bourdieu & Passeron, 1977, pp. 42–45); Bhabha's "space of translation," where negotiated construction of an object "that is new, neither the one nor the other" (Bhabha, 1994, p. 37); Derrida's "being-elsewhere," an undefinable space where and only where the monolingual/multilingual paradoxically exist (Derrida, 1998, pp. 39–43); Panikkar's "terra nullius (no man's land)" where a utopia of interculturality "situated between two (or more) cultures" and "must kept silent" (Panikkar, 2000, p. 2); Sinha's "blended space" where blending as microgenesis takes place within the collaborative micro-community (Sinha, 2005, p. 1551); Jullien's "écart," a constructed dynamic space in between two sides where shared imagination and conceptualization may take place (Jullien, 2013, p. 373); and, perhaps most influential to the field of foreign language education, Kramsch's potentially subversive "third place," where foreign language learners may turn "multilingual social actors" through their "resignifying practice" (Kramsch, 2009, pp. 103, 115, 200).

Focusing on the possibilities of and paths to a constructive and productive Third Space, cross-lingual and cross-cultural interactions should and can open up a new field, where different cultures converge, contest and cooperate; where expectations for the actors and interpretations of their actions do not entirely or constantly conform to the assumptions and norms of one culture but dynamic and fluid, motivated by specific goals of the interaction in question and negotiated among involved actors; and where the cooperative interactions of the actors' emerging multilingual and transcultural personae are made possible by, and in turn, continue to co-construct the multilingual and transcultural Third Space that is continuously becoming.

From feeling "only-one" to seeing "obvious-two" to doing "not-two": inter-cultural? Transcultural?

Although it seems unquestionably outdated, the subconsciousness of "my culture is the only culture" or "my culture is the only culture that matters" is still part of the reality in every culture. To the extent that the other culture's presence cannot be simply overlooked, the subconsciousness of "theirs is but an inferior version or earlier stage of ours" may kick in. Operating under such subconsciousness in cross-lingual and cross-cultural interactions, the higher foreign language proficiency level the learners have, unfortunately, the more likely "communication breakdowns" and misconceptions about each other will occur as language and/or behavioral mistakes, inevitable in non-native environments, will likely be interpreted as intended offenses. It therefore should be argued strongly that developing learners' awareness of and sensitivity towards other cultures remains a major issue for foreign language programs to consider (Walker, Chapter 7 of this volume).

More complicated, more problematic and more consequential is the conceptualization of the "obvious-two." As well intended as they may be (ill intended is beyond the scope of this study), those from the perceived dominant culture tend to exoticize the other side as "the other" (they are so different from us), hoping to normalize differences but often ending up further abnormalizing the other. For examples, see Arthur Smith's study on Chinese behavior culture (Smith, 1894) and Richard Nisbett's study on how Asians think (Nisbett, 2003), both offering neatly contrasted but nearly static perceptions of "the other"; those from the perceived marginalized culture tend to exoticize the self as "the other" (we are so different from them), hoping to redefine the self's place in its own right but often ending up further isolating the self, such as Ji Xianlin's belief that the East's holistic "combining two into one 合二为一 heerweiyi" culture will replace the West's analytic "dividing one into two 一分为二 yifenweier" culture and save the 21st century for humanities (Ji, 1992); and Cao Shunqing's argument that the Eastern civilization and the Western civilization are two qualitatively different entities—"异质文明 *yizhi wenming*" (Cao, 2016). Finally, paradoxically, those tend to romanticize the other are more likely driven by what they see the self is not than by what the other is, such as the ahistorical presentation of "the Chinese way of thinking" by Francois Jullien (Jullien, 2000) and the equally ahistorical presentation of "the American way of life" by Lin Da (Lin, 2015). It is not uncommon for those of us who live and work regularly between cultures to hear disappointments that the "the other" is not as the other as they are supposed to be—for example, upon arriving China, some American learners of Chinese are surprised that the Chinese are not behaving the Chinese way while some Chinese who work with the American learners of Chinese are dismayed that the Americans are not American enough. Indeed, the popularity of the two-color-schemed (red and blue) and simplistically contrasted graphic series *East Meets West* (Liu, 2016) further demonstrates that developing critical reception towards static ahistorical generalizations of cultural differences should become a serious concern of foreign language programs.

Consider the case of "Steven quitting learning Chinese." According to his Chinese teacher's published account, Steven (who has a Chinese name 史力文 Shi Liwen) was the all-agreed most hard-working and most talented top student in Yale University's Chinese language program during the years he was in Yale and he quitted learning Chinese after two summer study-abroad trips to China—that is, he quitted learning the language after actually interacting with the native people in their native cultural environment (Su, 2007).[1] The reasons for Steven's quitting are so complex and so revealing that it is worth discussing more about it here. According to this published nonfiction narrative, Steven already wanted to quit after his first summer in China because he felt his Chinese language partners/roommates kept reminding him how great Chinese culture was and how short the US history was. The fact that they wanted him to learn a Chinese song named *Our Great China* really provoked him: "Can you imagine what effects it would have if America had a song named *Our Great USA?*" he asked, and he declared in English: "I am sick of it!" (Su, 2007, pp. 109–110). However, he managed to continue learning this time. When Steven returned to Yale from his second summer study-abroad trip to China, he calmly informed his Chinese teacher (平静道出), in his smooth and Beijing-accented Chinese (一口滑溜的充满卷舌音的京片子) that he had decided to quit learning Chinese. He explained: "I am not kidding you. I already know how I can pass off and drift through in China, and I am not bad at doing this at all" (The Chinese word "混 *hùn*" with fourth tone is used here as a verb to mean "pass off," "drift along"). He went on to express his frustration: "I have never thought I could have become such a . . . jerk, that's right, a jerk!" (The same Chinese word "混 *hún*" with second tone is used here as part of the noun "混蛋 *húndàn*" to mean "a jerk," "a bastard"). Responding to his teacher's surprise, he came up with an English word "fake" to further explain:

> As long as you learn how to fake and get used to all kinds of faking, that'll be it. . . . you first lie ("骗 *piàn*") to yourself and then you lie to others. . . . you lie to yourself that you are not that "Steven" and you change to this "Shi, Li, Wen," and then you are free to fake. . . . you can fake for whatever reason, the Chinese

love to hear flattering words, I'll then say flattering words to them; if they say they don't like Americans, I'll say I am a Uighur from Xinjiang; if they want to learn something about America, I'll then say I am a Yale student. This is called "oily" ("油 *yóu*") in Beijing speech, and I, this "Shi, Li, Wen," is pretty oily now.

Steven finally sincerely told his teacher (诚恳道出): "I have discovered that the better Chinese language I have the less respect I have towards it and it seems getting more and more so this way; if I continue to learn, the result can only be that I will become disrespectful to both the Chinese language and China." With an unusually calm tone of voice (口气却异常平静), Steven declared: "So, I've decided to quit Chinese." It is worth noting that towards the end of the narrative, it was indicated that the teacher noticed Steven's Chinese sounded very fluent and effective (流畅达意) (Su, 2007, pp. 111–112).

It is clear that Steven was keenly (painfully?) aware that there are "us" and "them," but it is unclear if he saw "them" as the wrong/bad version of "us" that should be left behind, or if he thought "them" as a "qualitatively different entity" impossible to penetrate and to work with. He just didn't seem to be able to pass the "obvious-two" stage and move on to the next step. Indeed, just recognizing differences alone will not lead to productive cross-cultural conversation; dwelling on the differences and overly exoticizing, romanticizing or stereotyping the other often end up strengthening the division rather than bringing about the cooperation between "us" and "them." A constructive and productive Third Space can only be emerging from the state that is beyond "obvious-two" after seeing them, as the Chinese Buddhist tradition may call it, the state of "无二 *wuer*" (no-two). Raimon Panikkar once warned that, to speak of "interculturation" or "mutual fecundation,"

> We must seek a middle way between the colonial mentality which believes that we can express the totality of the human experience through the notions of a single culture, and the opposite extreme which thinks that there is no communication possible between diverse cultures, and which should then condemn themselves to a cultural apartheid in order to preserve their identity.
> (Panikkar, 2000, p. 5)

We may add that this type of condemning oneself to a "cultural apartheid" could happen to anyone just by staying on seeing "obvious-two," regardless of whether that person is from a perceived dominant culture or from a perceived marginalized culture.

The acts of 反 *fan* (return, reverse), 不二 *buer* (don't see/do "two") and 物化 *wuhua* (transformation of things): the Daoist and Buddhist practices

If the term "middle way" sounds too cliché to have real impact on bringing about "mutual fecundation," let us introduce to the dialog some considerations from the Chinese tradition, namely, the acts of 反 *fan* (return, reverse), 不二 *buer* (don't see/do "two") and 物化 *wuhua* (transformation of things).

A quick glance on some of the most well-known texts from the Daoist tradition, such as the 《老子》 *Laozi*[2] and the 《庄子》 *Zhuangzi*,[3] one will find relative dualism seemingly everywhere: Birth relative to and contrasting with death, good relative to and contrasting with evil, beautiful relative to and contrasting with ugly, hard relative to and contrasting with soft, tall relative to and contrasting with short, and so forth. Upon close reading, one can argue that the motive of the recognition of all these relative dualistic contrasts is the desire to transcend them instead of dwelling on them. It starts with a remarkable critical reflection on the act of recognizing differences. The first line of the second chapter of the *Laozi* is widely quoted but often-misinterpreted: "天下皆知美之为美斯恶矣" (Yang, 2014, p. 8). The commonly accepted interpretation of this line, "When people see somethings as beautiful, other things become ugly" (Mitchell, 1988, p. 2) takes the pronoun "斯 *si*" (this, it) to refer to "other things" and thus makes the expression to reflects a relative dualism the *Laozi* attempts to transcend. In the original text, the pronoun refers to what has been stated before it, that is, the act of recognizing the beautiful as beautiful, and the expression should be read as "When all under the heaven knows the beautiful as beautiful—this is ugly" (Lau, 1963, p. 6; I modified Lau's English translation to reflect the original text's sentence structure more closely). It is a dialectical thinking process, on the one hand realizing that recognitions of the interdependence between differences is necessary, and on the other hand being sensitive about the limitations and possible negative affects embedded in such recognitions. In this context, the Daoist idea of "反/返 *fan*" (reverse, return) may provide a new perspective to contemplate approaches to move beyond the stage of recognizing contrasting differences. The *Laozi* states very clearly that "反者道之动 Reversing is the movement of the Dao" (Yang, 2014, p. 184), and that it metaphorically illustrates the ideal as "复归于婴儿 return to being a baby" (Yang, 2014, p. 123). Being a baby, presumably, one will not discriminate and will not stuck with divisions of things. "我独泊兮其未兆如婴儿之未孩 I alone am inactive and reveal no signs, like a baby not yet become a child" (Yang, 2014, pp. 81–82).[4] Keep in mind that it is "return to being a baby" and not "stay being a baby"; in other words, one can only begin to transcend differences after recognizing them. Indeed, in the same section it talks about "return to being a baby," the *Laozi* advises its readers to "知其雄守其雌 know what is masculine but keep what is feminine," "知其白守其黑 know what is white but keep what is black" and "知其荣守其辱 know what is glorious but keep what is humiliating" (Yang, 2014, pp. 123–126). Perhaps continuously exchanging positions and performing actions corresponding to those positions is the next step after seeing "obvious-two."

The Chinese Buddhist deliberation about what one can do so that one may enter the Gate of Nondualism (不二法门 *buer famen*) sheds additional light on this issue and can be pondered together with the Daoist anxiety of passing beyond the dualist contrasts seemingly everywhere. As recorded in chapter nine of the 《维摩诘经》 (*The Vimalakirti Sutra*),[5] a group of Buddhist bodhisattvas (菩萨 *pusa*), enlightened divines in Buddhism, got together to explore how one could do "不二 *buer*" (don't do/see "two") so that one could live a life of "无二 *wuer*" (not "two") as they were all keenly aware of the suffering caused by the seemingly overwhelming dualistic perception of the world. One by one, each of the 31 bodhisattvas presented a case of dualistic perception and a possible path to go beyond it. Let's take a closer look at these two presentations:

> 普守菩萨曰: "我、无我为二, 我尚不可的, 非我何可得? 见我实性者, 不复起二, 是为入不二法门。
>
> (Lai & Gao, 2010, p. 146)

> The bodhisattva Universal Guardian said: "'I' and 'not-I' form a dualism. But when one cannot grasp even 'I,' how can one grasp 'not-I'? One who has seen into the true nature of 'I' will no longer give rise to these two concepts, and in this way enter the gate of nondualism."
>
> (Watson, 1997, p. 106)

> 华严菩萨曰: "从我起二为二, 见我实相者, 不起二法。若不住二法, 则无有识, 无所识者, 是为入不二法门。"
>
> (Lai & Gao, 2010, p. 151)

> The bodhisattva Flower Garland said, "From the concept of 'self' rises the concept of two things, [self and other,] which creates a dualism. But one who see into the true form of the self will not give rise to the thought of two things. And if one does not dwell in the thought of two things, then one will be without consciousness and without anything one is conscious of, and in this way may enter the gate of nondualism."
>
> (Watson, 1997, p. 109)

The key move here is to de-centralize and de-stabilize the "I" so that one will not have a taken-for-granted starting point against which everything else will be compared, contrasted and judged. Without a static point of view to grasp, the division between the one and the other may begin to lose and their respective positions may be exchanged. In other words, the act of "不二 buer" or don't see/do "two" may lead to the state of "无二 wuer" or no-"two."[6]

Let us end this section with one of the most celebrated dreams in the Daoist tradition as it is told in the *Zhuangzi*:

> 昔者庄周梦为蝴蝶, 栩栩然胡蝶也。自喻适志与, 不知周也。俄然觉, 则蘧蘧然周也。不知周之梦为胡蝶与, 胡蝶之梦为周与? 周与胡蝶, 则必有分矣。此之谓物化。
>
> (Zhuangzi, 2019, p. 22)

> Once upon a time Zhuang Zhou dreamed that he was a butterfly, a butterfly flitting about happily enjoying himself. He didn't know that he was Zhou. Suddenly he awoke and was palpably Zhou. He did not know whether he was Zhou who dreamed of being a butterfly or a butterfly dreaming that he was

Zhou. Now, there must be a difference between Zhou and the butterfly. This is called the transformation of things.

(Zhuangzi, 2019, p. 22; English translation by Victor Mair)

Does Zhuangzi here seem to be arguing that on the one hand divisions and differences between the one and the other are unavoidable and should be fully recognized, while on the other hand they can be transcended through exchanging the identities (personae?) and performance between the one and the other, albeit it takes place in the context of a dream?

Boundaries and differences as goal-oriented constructions: the 21st-century perspectives

Based on cutting-edge neuroscience research, Lisa Feldman Barrett in her pathbreaking discussion on how emotions are made (Barrett, 2017) argues strongly that categories and concepts are goal-based constructions realized through interplays of brain, body and culture and they are not context-free "discoveries" of objective "elements" that are already completed and out there independent from the subjects. For example, you see color strips in a rainbow, not because the color strips objectively exist in the rainbow—a rainbow is a continuous spectrum of light with no borders or bands, but because your eyes have been trained to see them with the learned color concepts. "Your brain automatically uses these concepts to group together the wavelengths in certain ranges of the spectrum, *categorizing* them as the same color. Your brain downplays the variations within each color category and magnifies the differences between the categories, causing you to perceive bands of color" (Barrett, 2017, p. 84, emphasis in original). Furthermore, concepts of categories or prototypes are not fixed but dynamically constructed and re-constructed "on the fly" based on needs and situations in question instead of "perceptual features" of similarities or differences. For example, the concept of "Things That Can Protect You from Stinging Insects" includes a wide range of instances of the category and they are very flexible based on, again, specific needs and situations (Barrett, 2017, pp. 91–92). Of course, your construction of concepts is flexible as it is not free in any sense but constrained by "storm of predictions" in your brain which in turn is constrained by your past experience.

> Your brain weights its predictions based on probabilities; they compete to explain what caused your sensations, and they determine what you perceive, how you act and what you feel in this situation. Ultimately, the most probable predictions become your perception.
>
> (Barrett, 2017, p. 93)

Barrett's discussion on goal-based construction of categories and concepts in a way speaks to the Daoist and Buddhist anxieties and deliberations of recognizing divisions and then transcending them—changing needs and changing situation should lead to changing positions or changing point of departure for re-constructing/transcending the divisions. This is informative to the exploration of a constructive and productive Third Space in foreign language pedagogy at least in these three aspects: (1) Instead of being objective "realities" that are fixed, perceived cultural differences are constructed categories and concepts that can (and will) be re-constructed, so while developing learners' awareness about other cultures' expectations remains a major task for foreign language programs, switching the focus from "meeting expectation" to "negotiate expectation" should be in order and should be a major task for advanced-level curriculums. (2) The construction and re-construction of cultural differences are continuous and flexible in accordance to specific needs and situations, so cultivating learners' sensitivity toward context and ability to handle dynamic and continuous negotiation should also be in order in advanced-level curriculums. (3) Constructing and re-constructing cultural perceptions may seem to be done "naturally" or "automatically," but they are constrained by predictions which in turn are constrained by past experiences; so it should be the core concern of foreign language programs to develop the appropriate past experiences for the learners to prepare them to make appropriate predictions in the future—in other words, "remembering the future," as Walker and Noda so aptly coin it (Walker & Noda, 2000).

It will be interesting to re-examine here a couple of popular East-West cultural dichotomies, namely, the East's "indirect" vs. West's "direct" and the East's "collectivism" vs. the West's "individualism." Indeed, the presentation of flattened and static impressions of "cultural traits" offers a quick grasp of perceived cultural differences seemingly too overwhelming to approach. However, as comfortable and satisfying as these perceptions may be when one is merely gazing at cultures, they are far too simplistic to be productive when one needs to work across cultures. In practice, we often find that in some areas and under some circumstances the generalization for each culture can be exchanged and used for the other culture. The East (say, the Chinese) can be far more direct than the West (say, the Americans) depending who is interacting with whom and on what kinds of matters, and the Americans more indirect and more circumlocutory than the Chinese if the situations and needs call for it. Likewise, although the generalization of "Chinese collectivism" has become some sort of conventional wisdom about China, influential Chinese thinkers such as Liang Qichao, Sun Zhongshan and Lu Xun have from time to time presented an opposite description: "一盘散沙 *yipansansha*" or "a batch of loose sands!" (Liang, 1901; Sun, 1924; Lu, 1933). What is at issue here is not which perception is right and which is wrong, or which is closer to the "truth." The meaningful questions to ask should be under what circumstances and for what purpose these perceptions of "cultural differences" were generated; whether or not they were effective in that context; and whether or not it will be productive if we just use them today for the tasks we have at hand. We nonetheless should be especially alert about all those neatly contrasted dichotomous "cultural differences" which are constructions constrained by specific goals and context but often being presented as "discoveries" of independently existing "characteristics" embedded in the cultures being contrasted. The irony is that, more often than not, simple impressionistic perceptions about the other likely reflect more about how one sees one's own culture than an "objective" description of the other culture.

Continuous re-constructing perceptions and concepts about one's own and the other cultures in the context of cross-lingual and cross-cultural interaction will lead to the emergency of various degrees of hybridity. In this sense, a Third Space is not about if we want to have it but it will be there regardless if we want it. What concerns us here is if and how we can approach negotiating a constructive and productive Third Space. Discussing language in novels, Bakhtin once attempted to make distinctions between "organic hybrid" and "intentional hybrid" to explore the productive impacts hybridity may bring about. "Organic hybridity" refers to the "unintentional, unconscious hybridization" taking place "in the historical life and evolution of all languages" (Bakhtin, 1981, p. 358) where "the mixture remains mute and opaque, never making use of conscious contrasts and oppositions" (Bakhtin, 1981, p. 360). "Intentional hybridity," on the other hand, involves "two linguistic consciousness." As Bakhtin stresses:

> Thus there are always two consciousnesses, two language-intentions, two *voices* and consequently two accents participating in an intentional and conscious artistic hybrid . . . the important activity is not only (in fact not so much) the mixing of linguistic forms—the markers of two languages and styles—as it is the collision between different points of views on the world that are embedded in these forms. Therefore an intentional artistic hybrid is a *semantic hybrid*; not semantic and logical in the abstract (as in rhetoric), but rather a *semantics that is concrete and social*.
> (Bakhtin, 1981, p. 360, emphasis in original)

The "intentional Third Space" we are exploring is a multilingual and transcultural space where cooperation between cultures may be possible through negotiation, where the interplays of different voices (points of views and presentations of them) should be fully recognized with the aim of going beyond collision constructively and productively, and where what defines being constructive and productive does not automatically conform to one culture only but conditioned by the particular play's negotiated shared goals and negotiated shared expectations for players. It is worth noting here the conceptual distinction between a "multicultural space" and a "transcultural space," where the former tolerates the co-existence of different cultures and the latter encourages the exchange between these cultures and the transcendence beyond their differences. Discussing "critical transculturalism," Kraidy contrasts multiculturalism and transculturalism: "The former establishes boundaries of recognition and institutionalization between cultures; the latter underscores the fluidity of these boundaries" (Kraidy, 2005, p. 150).

The Chinese philosopher Zhao Tingyang and the French anthropologist Alain Le Pichon in their year-long (2014–2015) correspondences took pains to differentiate "inter-subjectivity," "cross-subjectivity," "relational subjectivity," "conjunctive subjectivity" and "trans-subjectivity" in order to explore the possibility of and approach to a "reciprocal knowledge" (Zhao & Le Pichon, 2017). Imagining "travels" to each other, where the East travels to the West and the West travels to the East, Le Pichon laments: "The problem is that, in this languages and cultures all being 'globalized' era, where is 'East' and what is 'Eastern Culture'? Where is 'West' and what is 'Western culture'? We seem to have lost directions" (Zhao & Le Pichon, 2017, p. 27). Could such a "problem" turn out to be the beginning of the next journey? For even in the past when clean-cut boundaries between the East and West were presumably "out there," they were nothing but constructions responding to various objectives of the time. Perhaps the time has come for us to see through and work beyond these imagined divisions, starting with the "radical epoche" Le Pichon evokes. Constructing a series of contrasted East-West differences may have been (or still is) useful for certain purposes under certain circumstances, but de-constructing the contrasts and no longer feeling clear and confident about the divisions and boundaries is the very first step towards constructing a transcultural Third Space.

The differences between a "Third Space" and a "Third Culture" should also be noted here: "Third Space" imagines a condition under which continuous transcultural experiences may be possible, while "Third Culture" imagines the realization of a transculture, or as Kramsch calls it, "a culture 'of a third kind'" (1993, p. 235). In other words, the former refers to the one and the other acting *transculturally* enabled by the condition they are in while the latter is presumably the result of such interactions. Focusing on conceptualizing a transcultural condition, a Third Space, allows more opportunities to explore what is involved in a cross-cultural negotiation and cooperation and in a transcultural experience and how foreign language pedagogy may respond to them; focusing on conceptualizing a transculture, a "third culture," may lead to seeing cultures as definable entities and to attempt to create a "new culture" and to cultivate "thirdness" of the learners and turn them into a "Third Person"—an elusive mission that is neither possible nor meaningful for foreign language programs to take on.

Third Space as a cultural utopia and Third Space as a social practice: from "a space of a voiceless" to "a space of a single voice" to "a space of many voices" to "a space of one speaking the other's language"

When Panikkar contemplates "interculturality" as a *terra nullius* (no man's land) in between cultures, he immediately realizes that this space, not occupied by any determined culture, can only be a utopia that is voiceless.

> The very moment that I open my mouth to speak, I am obliged to use a concrete language, and thus I am completely in a particular culture: I am on a land which already belong to someone. I am in my culture, cultivating my land, speaking my language.
>
> (Panikkar, 2000, p. 3)

This type of paradox about the power and limitation of silence and the power and limitation of sounding out is also present in some "stories" passing down through the Chinese tradition. For example, this paradox is present in the account about how the poet Tao Yuanming (365?–427 CE) played his stringless instrument 琴 *qin* (zither) whenever he felt the urge to express himself musically (". . . 畜素琴一张, 无弦, 每有酒适, 辄抚弄以寄其意," Shen, 488). Chinese scholars have been debating forever what caused the poet to play a stringed musical instrument that has no string attached to it. Some speculate that he simply did not know how to play music, while others argue that he realized the greatest expressive potential when playing music without making any particular sound (Mo, 2012).[7] Another example, the paradox is also present in the account of the aforementioned deliberation by a group of Buddhist bodhisattvas of how one may enter the Gate of Nonduality. After 31 bodhisattvas, one after another, voiced their respective opinions on the subject matter, according to the account they turned to Manjushri, the head of the group, for an answer. Manjushri replied that the way to enter the Gate of Nondualism should be "无言无说, 无示无识 without words, without explanations, without purport, without cognition" (Lai & Gao, 2010, p. 154; Watson, 1997, p. 110). At the end of the event, the same question was presented to the founder of the sect, Vimalakirti. "At that time, Vimalakirti remained silent and did not speak a word. Manjushri sighed and said: 'Excellent, excellent! Not a word, not a syllable—this truly is to enter the gate of nondualism!'" (Watson, 1997, pp. 110–111). Why are all these presumably enlightened thinkers so anxious and suspicious about utilizing language to think and to express their thoughts? It seems they are painfully aware of the fact that without language they will not be able to conduct and communicate their thinking, as well as the fact that with language their thinking and the communication of it will be framed, constrained or "sidetracked." To borrow a pair of terms for a paradox observed by Lakoff and Johnson in their pathbreaking study of metaphor, while an utterance may very well brilliantly "highlight" some aspects of the topic at hand, it at the same time necessarily and inevitably "hides" other aspects (Lakoff & Johnson, 1980, p. 10) In the context of cross-lingual and cross-cultural communication, if no one speaks, there will be hardly any meaningful exchange; as soon as someone speaks, it signifies the occupation of the space by a culture because at any given moment one can only speak a language that is embedded with cultural perspectives, points of views and presentation traditions, and it risks jeopardizing the construction of a transcultural Third Space. How, if possible, can we break this conundrum?

The *Laozi/Dao De Jing*'s construction and representation of the concept of "道 *Dao*," the "ultimate truth," demonstrate an effective response to this "highlight/hide" paradox (Jian, 1991). The word used to represent the concept "道 *Dao*" highlights the idea of "path, way," but at the same time it hides other important qualities of the concept, for example, that it is generating without dominating; it is encompassing without discriminating; it is evolving, growing and returning; it is a great dark void that can only be felt and admired at the same time; it is tens of thousands of natural and everyday life objectives that can be firmly grasped and so forth. It is in this sense we understand a discourse on the Dao should begin with a warning: "道可道非常道 The Dao that can be spoken of is not the eternal Dao"[8] (Yang, 2014, p. 2). Throughout the discourse, in addition to the metaphor of "a path," the Dao is also metaphorically expressed as "water" that is soft and always flows to the lower place and eventually penetrates everything, "a living organism" that can grow, give birth to others, die and be reborn, "a dark hole" that is big and void and so forth. When Qian Zhongshu comments on the *Zhuangzi*'s seemingly endless metaphorical expressions for the one concept of Dao, he argues that may prevent the readers from being confined within what one particular metaphor highlights: "星繁而月失明, 连林则独树不奇 a myriad of stars makes the moon lose its brightness, and in a forest a tree will not seem unusual" (Qian, 1979, p. 14). It is in this sense we understand one of the most apparent "contradictions" in the *Laozi*: It proclaims that "those who know don't speak and those who speak don't know" (知者不言, 言者不知, Yang, 2014, p. 245), and therefore the sage "practice[s] teaching without speaking" (行不言之教, Yang, 2014, p. 11 and p. 197), while it goes on to deliberate the Dao with more than 5,000 words in 81 chapters! The multiple perspectives from which the Dao is constructed and presented in fact are contradicting as well as complementing each other, so each has its function, none will have exclusive ownership and all together contribute to the conceptualization of the Dao (Jian, 1991, pp. 281–282).

While the construction and presentation of the Dao in *Laozi/Dao De Jing* demonstrates how multiple perspectives may work together within one cultural tradition, the aforementioned correspondences between Zhao and Le Pichon offer a peculiar and intriguing case study, very informative albeit unsatisfying as to how multiple perspectives may work across cultures. In this case, how did a Chinese philosopher who did not know French and a French anthropologist who did not know Chinese communicate with one another? It was through a "metalanguage," or in Zhao's word, a "fake global language" (伪球语 *weiqiuyu*)—English! Accepting the fact that they don't have other options but to take up the challenge of communicating in this "fake global language," Zhao quoted a Spanish anthropologist who once quipped to him, in his hard to understand English, that "English is not a world language, only bad English is," and then lamented: "I admitted our bad English is hurting this language, on the other hand, it is also hurting our thoughts" (Zhao & Le Pichon, 2017, p. 21). Agreeing with Zhao that it was truly regrettable and helpless that they had to communicate with each other in this poor, crude, overbearing and impolite (贫瘠而蹩脚, 霸道而无礼) "fake global language," Le Pichon nonetheless offered a rather interesting take on the situation: The non-native language could function as a screen or a filter to make the space between them as if it were a "no man's land" (无人区) not contaminated by a particular culture, because when they spoke a non-native language they would need to depart from their respective cultural backgrounds and meet each other in the "common area" (普遍领域) (Zhao & Le Pichon, 2017, p. 32). Seeing the transcultural potentials come with all speaking a non-native language is indeed very insightful, but all who speak the one and same super-language, be it real or fake, will nonetheless make the transcultural space questionable as it will be conditioned by certain cultural perspectives and presentations that come with that language. Moreover, at a practical level, this super-language will almost certainly be English, whose dominating power has the potential to "correct" and "modify" other marginalized languages/cultures into its own frame. It is indeed problematic to imagine a multicultural, cross-cultural or transcultural experience under a monolingual condition, regardless of whether this single language is native to one of the parties involved or if it is non-native to all.[9]

If a "no voice" space can only have unrealized (and unrealizable?) potential of becoming a transcultural Third Space, and a "single voice" space will always be conditioned by a particular culture and counterproductive to the construction of a transcultural Third Space, it is time for us to consider a "multiple voices" space where different cultures may enter and interact in their respective languages without having to first go through a one-for-all language/culture filter. A 21st-century Third Space, a sustainable transcultural Third Space, must be characteristically multilingual and co-constructed. If we don't want "multiple voices" to be stuck in the stage of simply coexisting without meaningful interactions, and we don't want these interactions to be sanitized and constrained by (mistakenly) assumed "objective" translations into one of the languages involved or into a super "common" language, we need to go beyond the "multicultural under monolingual" illusion and find ways to create a space where each can speak the other's language, perform the other's culture and negotiate and co-construct a transcultural experience—that's the call for a 21st-century foreign language pedagogy.

The dynamics between "message" and "messenger": multilingual personae as emergent

When it comes to the pedagogy of "one speaking the other's language," there is a peculiar tension between the field's overwhelming attention to the training of "getting message across" and, to borrow an expression from conventional wisdom, "it's not what you said, but how you said it" counts the most in cross-lingual and cross-cultural interactions.[10] It should be further argued that the perception of "how you said it" is interdependent of the perception of "who you are." In this sense, the exploration of the dynamics between "message" and "messenger" is long overdue. As someone who travels frequently between languages, religions and cultures, Panikkar offers this keen observation:

> In the dialogical dialogue the partners is not an object of a subject merely putting forth some objective thoughts to be discussed, but a you, a real you and not an it/ I must deal with you and not merely with your thoughts, and of course, vice versa, You yourself are a source of understanding. . . . We never have an encounter of pure ideas. We always have an encounter of two (or more) persons.
>
> (Panikkar, 1999, p. 30)

Framing the communication between cultures as an interaction between persons encourages us to go beyond code-switching to explore the complex of what really accounts for "getting a message across," as a person is far more than a code-generating machine and/or a message carrier. There can be two ways to explore the person-in-cross-cultural interaction issue: One is to understand the another-culture-person through shared experience in that culture; the other is to construct dynamic goal-based multilingual transcultural personae functioning in such interactions.

Recall the case of Steven, who quit learning Chinese despite being the best student in an elite institution's Chinese program. It seems the fact that his Chinese experiences disgust him has a lot to do with the perceived "faking" and "lying" by the other and his anxiety of becoming a type of person he despises. Reading the account by his teacher, we know that although Steven was physically in China for two summers, his segregated living and educational arrangements did not provide him the opportunities to develop shared experiences with the people he intended to communicate with. His perceptions about what people in that culture said and wanted and about what he needed to say and do in order to get by in that culture seem to only come from his judgment of the messages he received from his familiar perspectives; in fact, the entire narrative did not mention whether or not he had made any individual person-to-person connection at all. If we do not see people of another culture as real persons living in real context and do not have shared experience with them, we will by default see them merely as generators or carriers of some cultural indicators or messages and easily (comfortably) evaluate what we received from the standing points of our own culture. In re-thinking the dynamics between "message" and "messenger," let us bring some 2,000-year-old wisdom into the consideration. The 《论语》 *Lunyu* or *The Analects of Confucius*[11] presents a well-known two-word response from Confucius when asked about "Wisdom": "Understand people" (知人) (Ruzang, 2005, p. 48). How? "See how he operates, observe what path he follows, examine what he is satisfied with, and how can a man remain inscrutable? How can a man remain inscrutable?" (视其所以, 观其所由, 察其所安, 人焉瘦哉? 人焉瘦哉?) (Ruzang, 2005, pp. 4–5; English translation by Raymond Dawson. Dawson, 2008, p. 7).

The other side of the coin is the construction of multilingual and transcultural personae in such interactions. It is crucial to differentiate "identity" and "persona": The former is a self-imagination of who one is based on, what one prefers in one's mind; while the latter is a public perception of who one is based on, what one does in interaction. It is also important to recognize that the construction of persona will not be done once and for all, but it is a continuous process conditioned by continuous needs and situations. A Third-Space foreign language pedagogy should focus on helping learners develop capacities to recognize needs and situations in question as well as capacities to construct and present a multilingual and transcultural persona constructive to the intended cooperation. To this end, "performance" is a much more productive concept than "faking" or "lying" (Walker, Chapter 7 of this volume). As Trevor Noah so vividly puts it:

> I became a chameleon. My color didn't change, but I could change your perception of my color. If you spoke to me in Zulu, I replied to you in Zulu. If you spoke to me in Tswana, I replied to you in Tswana. Maybe I didn't look like you, but if I spoke like you, I was you.
>
> (Noah, 2016, p. 35)

Beyond cognitive? Major challenges call for critical reflections and extensive researches

The Analects presents a rather insightful three-level differentiation regarding one's relationship with what one is learning/doing: "know it" (知之), "like it" (好之), "enjoy it" (乐之) (Ruzang, 2005, p. 21). Thus far, most of what we have explored here is at the first level (the cognitive), and we talk about another language and another culture as objects of inquiry, something we need to learn to deal with or to find way to work with. We utilize game metaphor and concepts such as "persona," "play" and "performance" to overcome anxieties and frustrations caused by senses of "identity," "being oneself" and "sincere action" and have avoided touching upon issues related to the other two levels (aesthetics and values). Perhaps questions about "like it" or "enjoy it" are beyond the consideration and capacity of a foreign language pedagogy? If so, how far can learners go in performing another language/culture if they only operate at the cognitive level and see that language/culture merely as something to be handled? In fact, in our program we regularly encounter among the advanced-level learners (those who have long-term experience of researching and working in Chinese) the frustration of being tired of "playing games" and "performing" instead of "being." Could such frustrations be more complex than simple "performance fatigue" or unsophisticated conception about self and the other? As fluid and shaky as they may be, the ideas of "identity," "being oneself" and aesthetic and affectional attachment have real impacts on how one thinks and acts and avoiding confronting them can only get us this far, perhaps not far enough to co-construct a Third Space. In the aforementioned correspondences between Zhao and Le Pichon, Zhao at one point takes issues with Habermas's "ideal speech situation," as it only focuses on the mutual understanding of the "minds" and ignores the mutual acceptance of the "hearts." To Zhao, dialogues between the minds, regardless how fully and how reasonable they may be, will not necessary lead to the conciliation of the different pursuits of the hearts—thus the concept of trans-subjectivities and transcultures remains problematic (Zhao & Le Pichon, 2017, pp. 23–24). It is not by coincidence that, in cross-cultural interactions, those from cultures perceived dominant are more focused on studying and evaluating the other, while those from cultures perceived marginalized are more anxious about being accepted and appreciated.

Time has come for foreign language pedagogy to rethink its mission in terms of unprecedented need for cooperation among people of different languages/cultures. Programmatically developing learners' capacities in negotiating a co-constructed multilingual and transcultural Third Space is the first and necessary step.

Notes

1 This nonfiction narrative was published in Chinese. English translations are my own.
2 The 《老子》 *Laozi/Lao Tzui*, or 《道德经》 *Dao De Jing/Tao Te Ching* in its canonized title, is a collection of verse-like text purportedly composed by Laozi (6th century BCE?), about whose life very few facts are known. The earliest extant version of the text is written on hundreds of bamboo slips excavated from a Chun Tomb in modern-day

Guodian, Hubei, and dated around the mid- to late Warring States period (second half of the 4th century BCE), while the most widely used version in the past 2,000 years has been the 王弼 Wang Bi edition completed during the first half of the 3rd century CE.
3 The 《庄子》 *Zhuangzi/Chuang Tzu* is a collection of text attributed to Zhuangzi/Zhuang Zhou (late 4th century to early century BCE). While some revealing stories about Zhuanzi's life have been passed down through the centuries, the authorship of the *Zhuangzi* text has been speculated and debated by generations of scholars. It has been generally accepted that the *Zhuangzi* is a work of a group of authors rather than one author, that it began to circulate no later than 1st century BCE and that the most widely used 郭象 Guo Xiang edition was completed between the late 3rd century and the early 4th century BCE.
4 English translation of this line adapted from D. C. Lao (Lau, 1963, p. 24) with minor modification to reflect the choice of word in the original text.
5 《维摩诘经》 *The Vimalakirti Sutra* was one of the most important texts in the Mahayana Buddhist tradition and was extremely influential to the development of 禅 *chan*/Zen Buddhism. It is not clear exactly when, where and how the original text was composed, but it is believed that shortly after that the earliest Chinese translation of the *Sutra* was completed in 188 CE. The most widely used version of the *Sutra* has been the sixth Chinese translation by Kumarajiva (Chinese name 鸠摩罗什) in 406 CE.
6 It is worth noting here the irony that these early Buddhist expressions for non-discriminatory worldviews later would have become everyday life expressions (成语 *chengyu*, four-character idioms) to mean the opposite. For example, while in Buddhist tradition "独一无二 *duyiwuer*" means to embrace everything as a whole without dividing it into two, in everyday life it is used to boast "the only one" (that matters, that is good). Similarly, while in Buddhist tradition "不二法门 *buerfamen*" refers to the gate of non-dualism, in everyday life it is often used to promote certain approach as "the only way" (that matters, that is good).
7 An interesting modern comparison to this "musical expression without sound" argument can be found in the famous "4′33″," a soundless musical work by composer John Cage. It was first performed in New York on August 29, 1953, by pianist David Tudor, who sat in front of a piano for 4 minutes and 33 seconds without making any sound; it presumably would make people listen better and allow more sounds come into being in more diverse and spontaneous ways. (See Alex Ross, "Searching for Silence," *New Yorker*, October 4, 2010. Retrieved from https://www.newyorker.com/magazine/2010/10/04/searching-for-silence, accessed June 9, 2020.)
8 The other early Daoist text, the *Zhuangzi*, also states: "道不可闻，闻而非也；道不可见，见而非也；道不可言，言而非也。知形形之不形呼？道不当名。The Dao cannot be heard, for what is heard is not the Dao; the Dao cannot be seen, for what is seen is not the Dao; the Dao cannot be spoken, for what is spoken is not the Dao. Do you know the formlessness of that which gives form to form? The Dao does not corresponding to any name" (Zhuangzi, 2019, p. 202; English translation by Victor Mair. I made a modification by replacing "Way" with "Dao.").
9 It will be very interesting to learn more about the process of how these correspondences were constructed. Did Zhao and Le Pichon each compose his letter directly in English? Or did they compose their respective letters in their respective native language and then translate them into English? Did each of them translate his letter by himself, or did someone else do the translations? The published texts for all these correspondences are all in Chinese, and my presentation of them here is my interpretation of these Chinese texts, so it has already gone through several language/culture filters.
10 It has been argued that this is also true in the context of "same language same culture" communication, as Mehrabian in his research attempted to demonstrate what could account for the reception of the intended message: Words 7%, tone of voice 38% and body language 55%. Mehrabian, A., & Wiener, M. (1967). "Decoding of inconsistent communications." *Journal of Personality and Social Psychology*, 6(1), 109–114. https://

doi.org/10.1037/H0024532; Mehrabian, A., & Ferris, S. R. (1967). "Inference of attitudes from nonverbal communication in two channels." *Journal of Consulting Psychology*, *31*(3), 248–252. https://doi.org/10.1037/H0024648.
11 While 孔子 Confucius's lifetime (551–479 BCE) is relatively clear, the compilation date for the text presenting his teaching and life titled 《论语》 *The Analects* has been the subject of debate for generations. It is generally believed that the disciples of Confucius began to compile the text soon after the Master's death, and several generations of disciples continued the work until it took the current form. While the earliest extant (incomplete) version of the text was found in the bamboo slips inside a Han tomb in modern-day Dingzhou, Hebei, and dated around 200 BCE, the most widely used version has been the one edited and annotated by 何晏 He Yan (195–249 CE).

References

Bakhtin, M. M. (1981). *The dialogical imagination: Four essays*. English translation by Cary Emmerson and Michael Holquist. Austin: University of Texas Press.
Barrett, L. F. (2017). *How emotions are made: The secret life of the brain*. Mariner Book. Boston, MA: Houghton Mifflin Harcourt.
Bhabha, H. K. (1994). *The location of culture*. London and New York: Routledge.
Bourdieu, P. (1984). *Distinction: A social critique of the judgment of taste*. English translation by Richard Nice. London and New York: Routledge.
Bourdieu, P., & Passeron, J.-C. (1977). *Reproduction in education, society and culture*. English translation by Richard Nice. London and Los Angeles: Sage.
Cao, S. 曹顺庆. (2016). 跨文明文论的异质性、变异性及他国化研究 (Heterogeneity, variation and domestic appropriation of cross-civilization literary theories). 深圳大学学报 (社会科学版) *Journal of Shenzhen University (Humanities and Social Sciences)*, *2*(2016), 2–16.
Dawson, R. (2008). Translated. *Confucius: The Analects*. Oxford: Oxford University Press.
Derrida, J. (1998). *Monolingualism of the other or the prosthesis of origin*. English translation by Patrick Mensah. Stanford, CA: Stanford University Press.
Harari, Y. N. (2015). *Sapiens: A brief history of humankind*. New York: HarperCollins.
Ji, X. 季羡林. (1992). 21世纪：东方文化的时代 (21st century: The era of oriental culture). 文明 *Civilizations*, *3*(2002), 8. (First published in 文汇报 *Wenhuibao*, March 10, 1992.)
Jian, X. 简小滨. (1991). 《老子》中'道'的比喻系统 (The metaphorical fields of the 'Dao' in *Laozi*). In S. Jingyao 孙景尧 (Ed.), 《沟通》 *Connecting* (pp. 258–285). Nanning: 广西人民出版社 Guangxi People Publishing House.
Jullien, F. (2000). *Detour and access: Strategies of meaning in China and Greece*. English translation by Sophie Hawkes. New York: Zone Books.
Jullien, F. (2013, September–December). Congratulation letter from Paris. Chinese translation by Esther Lin. *Journal of Chinese Philosophy*, *40*(3–4), 371–376.
Kraidy, M. M. (2005). *Hybridity, or the cultural logic of globalization*. Philadelphia, PA: Temple University Press.
Kramsch, C. (1993). *Context and culture in language teaching*. Oxford: Oxford University Press.
Kramsch, C. (2009). *The multilingual subject*. Oxford: Oxford University Press.
Lai, Y. 赖永海, & Gao, Y. 高永旺. (Eds.). (2010). 《维摩诘经》 *The Vimalakirti Sutra*. Beijing: 中华书局 Zhonghua Book.
Lakoff, G., & Johnson, M. (1980). *Metaphors we live by*. Chicago: University of Chicago Press.
Lau, D. C. (1963). Translated. *Lao Tzu Tao Te Ching*. New York and London: Penguin Books.

Liang, Q. 梁启超. (1901). 十种德性相反相成议 (On the ten types of virtues, in contrast and complementary). In 《饮冰室合集》 *Collections from the Ice-Drinker's Studio* (Vol. 1, Section 5, p. 44). 中华书局 (1988年版) Zhonghua Book (1988 ed.). Beijing: 中华书局 Zhonghua Book.

Lin, D. 林达. (2015). 《近距离看美国》 (*Observing America close-up*). Beijing: 生活. 读书. 新知三联书店 SDX Joint.

Liu, Y. (2016). *East meets west* (English & Chinese, ed.). Cologne, Germany: Taschen.

Lu, X. 鲁迅. (1933). "沙" ("Sands"). Originally published in 《申报月刊》 *Shenbao Monthly*, August 15, 1933, Volume 2 #8. 《鲁迅全集》 *Complete Works of Lu Xun* (Vol. 4, p. 549). 人民文学出版社 (1996版) People's Literature Press (1996 ed.). Beijing: 人民文学出版社 People's Literature Press.

Mitchell, S. (1988) Translated. *A new English version of Tao Te Ching*. New York: Harper & Row.

Mo, L. 莫砺峰. (2012, February 4). 陶渊明的无弦琴 (Tao Yuanming's stringless zither). 文汇报 *Wenhuibao*, p. 7.

Nisbett, R. (2003). *The geography of thought: How Asians and Westerners think differently . . . and why*. New York: Free Press.

Noah, T. (2016). *Born a crime: Stories from a South African childhood*. New York: Spiegel & Grau.

Panikkar, R. (1999). *The intra-religious dialogue* (Rev. ed.). New York: Paulist Press.

Panikkar, R. (2000). Religion, philosophy and culture. English translation by Robert Vachon. *Polylog: Forum for Intercultural Philosophy*, *1*, 1–24. Retrieved October 3, 2017, from *Polylog: Themes and Focus* http://them.polylog.org/1/fpr-en.htm

Qian, Z. 钱钟书. (1979). 《管锥篇》 *Limited views: Essays on ideas and letters*. Beijing: 中华书局 Zhonghua Book.

Ruzang bianzuan yu yanjiu zhongxin 儒藏编纂与研究中心 (Editorial and Research Center of Confucian Canon). (2005). 《儒藏 (四书类论语属)》 *The Confucian Canon: The category of Sishu and the volume of Lunyu*. Beijing: 北京大学出版社 Peking University Press.

Shen, Y. 沈约, 《宋书. 隐逸》卷九十三列传第五十三 *The history of song-the biography of the hermits* (Vol. 93, Biography 53). Retrieved June 2, 2020, from 《中国哲学书电子化计划》 *Chinese Text Project* https://ctext.org/wiki.pl?if=gb&chapter=890874&remap=gb

Sinha, C. (2005). Blending out of the background: Play, props and staging in the material world. *Journal of Pragmatics*, *37*, 1537–1554.

Smith, A. (1894). *Chinese characteristics*. New York, Chicago and Toronto: Fleming H. Revell.

Su, W. 苏炜. (2007). 史力文为什么中止了学中文? (Why did Steven Quit learning Chinese?). 《上海文学》 *Shanghai Literature*, *3*, 107–112.

Sun, Z. 孙中山. (1924). 《民权主义》 *Principle of democracy*. Retrieved June 6, 2020, from 近代 中国 ModernChina.org, http://modernchina.org/6202.html

Tomasello, M. (2014). *A natural history of human thinking*. Cambridge, MA: Harvard University Press.

Walker, G., & Noda, M. (2000). Remembering the future: Compiling knowledge of another culture. In D. Birckbichler & R. M. Terry (Eds.), *Reflecting on the past to shape the future*. National Textbook Company.

Watson, B. (1997). *The Vimalakirti Sutra: From the Chinese version by Kumarajiva*. New York: Columbia University Press.

Yang, B. 杨丙安. (2014). Annotated.《老子古本合校》*Early editions of the Laozi*. Beijing: 中华书局 Zhonghua Book.

Zhao, T. 赵汀阳, & Le Pichon, A. (2017). 你是利玛窦那样的人吗—关于一神论的系列通信之一 (Are you someone like Matteo Ricci—#1 of a series of correspondences on Monotheism). Translation to Chinese by 王惠民 Wang Huimin.《江海学刊》*Jianghai Journal*, *2*, 21–32.

Zhuangzi (Bilingual Edition)《庄子》(双语本) . (2019). Wuhan: 长江出版传媒崇文书局 *Changjiang publishing media group Chungwen books*. Columbus, OH: The Ohio State University Foreign Language Publications.

2 Native speaker effects, C2 receptivity of learner and co-construction of Third-Space personae
A pedagogy of target culture expectation

Xin Zhang

Introduction

The past few decades have witnessed an unprecedented increase in intercultural communication (both in quantity and intensity) among individuals and organizations of different cultural backgrounds, practices, beliefs and value systems. Boundaries between countries and cultures are becoming increasingly blurred as the ever-growing global economy, along with the recent Covid-induced virtual collaboration, strengthens the interdependent side of the power restriction among entities in the international marketplace. What this means to foreign language education is that more foreign language students need to be capable of functioning at higher levels in professional settings to engage in extended and sustainable professional relationships. They must be able to go beyond the "expressing myself" mindset and be ready to negotiate complex situations in the target-culture (C2)-dominated Third Space where interpretations of intentions and actions are negotiated, conflicting interests reconciled and delicate power relations settled.

The key question to educators is clear: How to train foreign language learners to effectively negotiate intentions in the target language while handling the delicate power relations between the native and non-native speakers at a professional level. Foreign language (FL)/second language (SL) program goals in the 21st century should be redefined to address this pressing need in the current global economic context.

This chapter overviews the need and rationale of proposing a new model for FL/SL pedagogy that foregrounds *target culture expectations* of foreign/second language (L2) learners held by native speakers of the language. The new model is premised on two interconnected but often overlooked concepts in FL/SL education: *Native speaker effects* and *C2 receptivity of learner.* Native speaker effects are real-life effects of the conceptual opposition of "native" and "non-native" speakers on people's perception and practice in daily encounters. I argue that insufficient attention on the native speaker effects in FL/SL teaching has led to ignorance of the C2 receptivity of the learner, that is, how well L2 learners' performance is received by their native-speaking counterparts.

A pedagogy of C2 expectation is preoccupied with (1) raising awareness of the effects of language ideologies regarding the native/non-native power dynamics on individual L2 learners and their learning experience and (2) cultivating effective Third-Space personae, defined in this chapter as the aspects of one's personal attributes and information revealed in a given Third Space, which take advantage of how L2 learners are received in situated C2 encounters.

Native speaker effects

Central to engaging in a foreign culture at the most sophisticated level are the asymmetrical power relations between "native speakers" (NS) and "non-native speakers" (NNS), a dichotomy that stems from language ideologies of the "native speaker" as a folk concept. Pennycook (1994, p. 176) divides the concept of "native speaker" into three ideological premises: (1) National language is linked to a nation-state, and hence holding citizenship makes one a "native speaker" of the national language; (2) language is a bonded, homogeneous system spoken by a homogeneous group of "native speakers"; and 3) "native speakers" as having complete competence in all aspects of their first language. In addition to the three premises, native speakers are assumed to hold a superior/privileged status (*nativespeakerism*). This last premise feeds into a NS-NNS dichotomy based off of the view that certain varieties of language are more "correct" and "desirable" than others.

Researchers have problematized these language ideologies surrounding the concept of "native speakers" (see Doerr, 2009, for an overview), disputing the validity of those based on the binary opposition of "native" and "non-native" speakers and its related premises. Kubota (2009), for instance, argues that the privileged status of "native speakers" is not purely based on their linguistic attributes but also their racial and politico-economic profiles. Yet, it is imperative to recognize that such beliefs, despite their conceptual fallacy, have concrete real-life implications on people's linguistic practices and perceptions of others. Doerr (2009) proposes that research of "native speakers" shifts its focus from grouping individuals in terms of their linguistic practices (e.g., imposing the native/non-native binary) to examining native speaker effects, that is, "effects produced by the ideologies of the 'native speaker'" (2009, p. 15), on people's daily life as they interact under various relations of dominance. Building on Doerr's proposition, the following sections bring attention to the need of investigating native speaker effects in foreign/second language teaching and learning.

Native speaker effects in FL/SL teaching and learning

In the realm of FL/SL education, there is a tendency in the ideology and pedagogical practices that holds *nativespeakerism* as the default for language learning and teaching. As pointed out by Gill (2011), "the figure of the native speaker has long been instrumental in defining the apparently common-sense linguistic boundaries of authentic belonging, in relation to which the non-native speaker has been positioned" (p. 273).

Challenges of the rationale behind *nativespeakerism* and how such an ideology is manifested on the empirical level have been raised in the past two decades. In foreign language education, the debate centers around the authenticity and legitimacy associated with nativespeakership. Specifically, scholars have questioned the use of the monolingual "native speaker's" idealized competence as the benchmark for defining and assessing L2 teaching and learning (Firth & Wagner, 1997; Hall, Cheng, & Carlson, 2006; Larsen-Freeman, 2014; The Douglas Fir Group, 2016; Ortega, 2013; Zuengler & Miller, 2006). Kramsch (1993) broke new ground by adopting the concept of a *third place* to question the traditional NS/NNS dichotomy in foreign/second language learning. Yet despite such efforts, in the majority of FL/SL classrooms, the "authentic and ideal" notion of the "native speaker" continues to hold sway, affecting crucial hiring decisions and pedagogical practices. This reality calls for serious research attention on the native speaker effects in FL/SL educational contexts and on incorporating insights that come out of such investigation in pedagogical practices.

In examining the native speaker effects, extensive research has been focused on the relations of dominance between NS and NNS foreign language teachers (Relaño-Pastor & Fernández-Barrera, 2019; Houghton & Rivers, 2013; Pérez Andrade, 2019; Tuchiya, 2016; Weekly, 2018) and between native foreign language teachers/guests who occupy the space of authority and non-native foreign language learners in class activities (Doerr & Sato, 2011). Very few studies of FL/SL teaching focus on examining the manifestation of native speaker effects in FL/SL learning and intercultural encounters to inform FL/SL pedagogical practices (Zeng, Chapter 4 in this volume.)

Native speaker effects on C2 expectations

Expectation is a powerful element in human communication, and perhaps even more so in intercultural contexts. Communication functions on the basis of a shared understanding between interlocutors about what one intends and what one takes the other to intend. What interlocutors *take* each other to intend most of the time is influenced by what we *expect* each other to intend. L2 learners enter an intercultural interaction with interlocutors from another culture, carrying a pre-existing judgment about who they are, which aspects of their identity are relevant in the immediate context, and consequentially what courses of action they are likely to take to manifest the underlying intentions that make the most sense given the information available. This expectation of the "other" is emergent as it continues to be shaped throughout the interaction, yet at the same time it is predominantly rooted in prior knowledge gained through socialization with particular individuals in that particular culture.

Gumperz (cited in Young, 1994) argued that one cannot assume communication between a competent foreigner and a native is the same as that between two "native speakers". Agar (1994) asserts that the nature of the interactions L2 speakers face is fundamentally different from those of natives since they are consciously or subconsciously treated differently in C2 contexts. To a certain extent, "native speakers" react to what they expect of the NNS interlocutors based on existing ideologies formulated about these individuals at both the micro and the macro levels. In this chapter, I use the concept of *target culture expectation* to describe the aggregated expectations toward "non-natives" shared by groups of individuals from the target culture community (Zhang, 2016).

This native speaker effect on C2 expectations is predominantly rooted in the mentality of the natives as the self-perceived "rightful owners" of their language. Regardless of whether this "ownership" is real or simply imagined, it has actual, concrete influences on their perception and evaluation of the L2 learners' language usage. The asymmetrical power relation between native and non-native speakers has been captured in various manifestations, including testimonies of L2 learners themselves describing the pleasure derived from successfully "passing for a native," as well as the frustrating *Schadenfreude* of "native speakers" who are "eager to detect the slightest trace of a [foreign] accent, real or imagined" (Kramsch, 2010, p. 93). The stereotypical expectation that "non-native speakers" perform incompetence and embody foreignism derives from the same ideology that places "native" and "non-native speakers" at two opposite ends of the power dynamic.

Native speaker effects in CFL/CSL: C2 expectations of "foreigners" in mainland China

Traditionally governed by the jus sanguinis principle ("heritage by blood lineage"), Chinese culture presents an interesting case for analyzing how individuals, both CFL/CSL learners and Chinese natives, contextualize and utilize the NS/NNS binary in institutionalized discursive practices that cite native speaker effects as meaningful. To further justify the need of recognizing and addressing native speaker effects in FL/SL teaching and learning, this section illustrates how this ownership mentality is manifested in the Chinese conceptualizations of NNS and its root in a strong discourse of homogeneity of Chinese. Among the Chinese discourses of NNS or "foreigners," which represent a diverse demographic background, *laowai* (老外, 'foreigner') and *huayi* (华裔, 'foreign citizens of Chinese ancestry'; 'heritage Chinese speakers') are chosen for the analysis with a focus on the Chinese expectations of these groups' use and appropriation of Chinese language in juxtaposition with ideological dichotomies such as NS versus NNS and in-group versus out-group.

Laowai

Laowai is the widely adopted moniker of *waiguoren* (外国人, 'foreigner') used by mainland Chinese to refer to non-Chinese westerners, for the most part, not merely non-Chinese nationals (Ilnyckyj, 2010; Stanley, 2012; Mao, 2015). Mao's (2015) study of Chinese usage of *laowai* shows that Chinese people use ethnicity-based physical dissimilarity to distinguish *laowai* (e.g., Caucasians and people of African descent) and other non-Chinese (e.g., East Asians). The most stereotypically constructed image of *waiguoren* or *laowai* is someone who is white and English speaking (Henry, 2013; Mao, 2015; Liu & Self, 2019). A close second, according to Mao (2015), is someone of African descent. This reliance on race or ethnicity, reflected in physical appearance (e.g., skin color and physique), is grounded in the jus sanguinis principle of nationality law and a shared public discourse on family that foregrounds patrilineal descent and blood lineage.

The asymmetric power dynamic between the native and non-native manifested in the mainlanders' ownership mentality fuels the stereotypes of *laowai* as an oversimplified and homogeneous ethnic label in mainland China. But different from other cases of ethnic labeling that result in stereotypes of immigrants as "the alien, inferior, threatening, unwelcomed and even unwanted *Other*" (Liu & Self, 2019) in other cross-cultural interactions (Liu, 2007; Hecht, Warren, Jung, & Krieger, 2005), the labeling of *laowai* seems more amiable: An exotic being who is perhaps ignorant and incompetent in regard to Chinese language and cultural knowledge but in general welcomed and even wanted.

What are the expectations mainland Chinese have of *laowai*'s Mandarin capacities? A typical assumption is that it is impossible for foreigners to have equal or better Chinese linguistic skills than native speakers. Zhang (2016) investigated native Chinese perception of white American CSL speakers' idiom usage in comparison with the same idiom usage by native Chinese speakers. The study reveals that native Chinese speakers have lower expectations of non-native Chinese speakers in terms of using 成语 *chéngyǔ* (four-character Chinese idioms). The lowered standard was implied in Chinese natives' acceptance of no use of *chengyu* as the norm for a "foreigner" in contrast with their explicit expectation for a "native speaker" to properly employ *chengyu* in the same contexts. When these *laowai* exceed this lowered expectation by pulling off a *chengyu* usage in formal contexts, native Chinese were pleasantly surprised and considered the foreigners as exceptionally competent communicators with impressive Mandarin skills. Yet non-native Chinese speakers who intentionally transgress the conventional use of *chengyu* (e.g., wordplay) are perceived as making learner mistakes, even when they do so in exactly the same way native Chinese speakers "creatively use the *chengyu* to achieve certain stylistic effects."

Zhang's study reveals a very particular set of C2 expectations of how well *laowai* can and should function linguistically and culturally using *chengyu*. *Chengyu* is clearly not the only linguistic index that points to the veiled C2 expectations of a "non-native speaker's" inferior Chinese capacities and legitimacy. *Laowai* in China who use Chinese in their daily routine and professional settings report that they are constantly positioned as inferior and incompetent when they speak Chinese by particular C2 expectations.

Jesse Appell, an American comedian and founder of the US-China Comedy Center based in Beijing, has performed 相声 *xiàngsheng* (traditional Chinese crosstalk comedy) and Chinese standup in China since 2012. He often jokes on stage about how little Mandarin Chinese nationals expect him to speak. When he meets a Chinese person for the first time, no matter what his first words are, the response is always the same compliment on his Mandarin proficiency: "Your

Chinese is so good!" Liu and Self's study (2019) on the unnoticed stereotyping of American expatriates in mainland China also points out that the Western expatriates labeled *laowai* are usually deemed as culturally and linguistically incompetent outsiders, regardless of the their individual experience and investment. "I feel like no matter how great I speak Chinese, I am always going to be *laowai*, and lumped with the other group of people who speak shitty Chinese, to be honest," commented a frustrated subject (Liu & Self, 2019, p. 9).

These testimonies echo the sentiment of being treated as the cultural, linguistic and ethnic *Other* (Ilnyckyj, 2010; Conceison, 2004; Stanley, 2012; Mair, 2014; Hessler, 2001; Birks, 2012; Liu & Self, 2019), shared by many foreigners living in China. Unfortunately, in most cases this was seldom addressed in CLS classrooms and becomes an issue only after foreign learners of Chinese arrive in China.

Huayi as heritage Chinese speakers

A heritage language (HL) speaker is a heterogeneous category that encompasses varied levels of proficiency in oral skills and literacy and of inheritance and affiliations to the heritage culture. Individual heritage Chinese speakers can be mapped onto two partially overlapping spectrums of ethnic affiliation and linguistic competence (Li & Duff, 2008; Fishman, 2001; Wiley, 2001). An ethnically Chinese speaker might speak fluent Mandarin but may or may not be fully literate in Chinese or even be able to read a single Chinese character. A third- or fourth-generation Chinese American who didn't grow up speaking Mandarin (or Cantonese) can still feel closely affiliated to Chinese culture or claim an ethnic inheritance.

Yet outside the circles of scholars whose research specifically centers on HL and experienced instructors who have taught diversified groups of heritage language learners, the HL speaker is often reduced to a homogeneous label. Heritage Chinese speakers often encounter assumptions of who they should be and how well they should speak Chinese that are wildly different from C2 expectations of those labeled *laowai*.

Mochimocha (alias), an American subject of Chinese descent in Liu and Self's (2019) study of American expatriates in Mainland China, described her encounter with the local ideologies of who are foreigners and who are not.

> I don't encounter this label [*laowai*] here as much as my white American friends or African American friends. They [Chinese people] don't consider me as *laowai*, especially when I am alone. I only encounter this label when I am with my American friends who don't have [a] Chinese face. Chinese people would use *laowai* to address us as a group. Even so, I still feel they [Chinese people] mean my American friends who don't have the Chinese look, not me.
> (p. 7)

Having a salient Chinese blood lineage, an essential characteristic for being Chinese (Liu, 2015; Dikötter, 1997, 2015), heritage Chinese speakers are often considered by local Chinese people as part of the in-group. With the inclusion, which many foreign expatriates of non-Chinese descent felt they were deprived of, comes obligation. Mochimocha encountered social expectations of having to act in certain ways, including being told by her local Chinese relatives that "she must understand certain Chinese customs because she is Chinese" (Liu & Self, 2019, p. 10).

Mochimocha's story is not a single case. The 2015 documentary *All Eyes and Ears* captured an interaction between US Ambassador Jon Huntsman's adopted Chinese daughter Gracie Mei and two Chinese staff, a Chinese male and an elderly Chinese lady, working at the US embassy.

Chinese male:	那她会说中文呢. [So she can speak Chinese.]
Chinese old lady:	她就会说这一句, 别的她听不懂 [That's the only (Chinese) sentence] she can speak. She can't understand anything else.
Chinese old lady:	Do you speak Chinese?
Gracie Mei:	A little bit.
[*Gracie Mei's monologue*:	I wish I spoke fluent Chinese. I feel embarrassed when people think I might be fluent because of how I look. But at the same time, I remind myself that [being] an American in China gives me certain advantages. I am afraid to speak the truth.]

Gracie Mei's monologue echoes similar experiences shared by many heritage learners who grow up attending overseas Chinese schools in their childhood. Francis, Archer, and Mau's (2009) study shows that British-Chinese complementary school attendees of Chinese descent are influenced by and embody the ideology that Chinese heritage language competence is essential to their ethnic identity. The young respondents used words such as "ashamed," "embarrassing," and "disgrace" to describe how they would feel about not being able to speak Chinese as a Chinese person. Mau's (2013) study of young people of Chinese heritage who couldn't speak Chinese fluently also reveals the idealized expectation of knowing one's heritage language shared within many Chinese communities. A respondent articulated the perceived disapproval of their limited Chinese language abilities by older generations of Chinese descendants:

> Sometimes if you meet um, like some old aunties and things, they'll sort of look at you and shake their heads, and the older people tend to, quite, they think it's sort of, there's something quite wrong with me for not being able to (speak Chinese), and a lot of people think it's very strange (p. 265).

What the Chinese heritage speaker encounters in mainland China, unlike *laowai* who are more than often positioned on the "out-group" end of the self-other spectrum, are expectations closely tied to their heritage language capacities based off of their "in-group" membership, sanctioned and approved by the existing members of Chinese society, the "native speakers." Somehow, irrelevant to the individual's upbringing and subjectivity, heritage speakers of Chinese are assumed to have the obligation to learn or speak Chinese, if it is not already "hard-wired" with knowledge and expertise in their home language. In other words, they are "expected to perform 'Chineseness' as constructed within the imagined community, including re/production of Chinese language" (Francis, Mau, & Archer, 2014, p. 213).

Conflicting expectations: the danger of a single persona in the Third Space

The alarming message underlying these accounts of C2 expectations of foreigners in mainland China is not just that such C2 expectations, in conflict with their self-perceived identity and goals, are causing frustration to the Chinese language learners. What is more problematic is that many of these CLS/CFL learners were unaware of, and unprepared to handle, the conflicting expectations until they had to experience them after arriving in China. Some end up going through a painful identity dissonance or developing a negative impression of their experience. Phil, a subject in Stanley's study (2012, p. 221), pointed out that some foreigners come to China expecting that they would be treated as "heroes helping China," while in reality they end up feeling like, in Stanley's words, "puppets made to dance to Chinese tune."

> [They are] disappointed that their "China adventure," which was about individualism and adventure for them, and [about] "giving" the Chinese their "Westernness" has been co-opted into a system in which the primacy of the individual is much diluted.
> (Phil, email 19/06/2009)

If CSL/CFL learners go to China with ill-informed expectations, whether it is the borderline neo-colonialist, in Stanley's words, "white people's burden in 'helping' China," or "foreigner's right to run amok in China to their own ends" (2012, p. 222), they inevitably will experience their own powerlessness in Chinese discourse. The fixation on a monocultural position of "this is who I am and how I do things as a(n) _____ (the base culture one identifies with) person" in intercultural contexts has a connotation of condescension that leads nowhere in establishing oneself in the target culture.

FL/SL learners need to be made aware of the danger of holding on to a single persona in Third-Space encounters. Persona is the aspect of personal attributes publicly *presented* and *perceived*. As functional members of societies, we all have multiple personae when engaging different groups of people, who also make conscious or unconscious choices of codes to "actively create and recreate their worlds and themselves" (Lantolf, 1993, p. 232). Speaking a second/foreign language inevitably involves making the same kind of choices of language and styles to match a desired persona revealed in that moment, which is mediated by L2 speakers' varying positions in the society (e.g., as a *laowai*, a professional, a woman) and other's expectations of them foregrounded in a particular Third-Space encounter.

Stanley (2012, p. 209) offers a peek into the range and complexity of Third-Space personae some CFL/CSL learners keep as a foreign professional teaching English in China:

> Foreign teachers need a complex set of skills including a larger-than-life, "bubbly" classroom persona, game-playing/entertainment skills, and the ability to manage the "soft-focus" of classroom dynamics that create a harmonious atmosphere. In addition, they need a certain amount of Chinese knowledge and humility, an ability to perform stereotypical "foreignness," and some willingness to be ridiculed as "foreign idiots."

C2 receptivity of learner as an ignored concept in CFL/CSL

The collection of studies, testimonies and anecdotes in the previous sections are by no means exhaustive of the C2 expectation subgroups of CFL/CSL learners encounter in Chinese speaking communities. Instead, the shared sentiments lend themselves to cautioning FL/SL educators of the need to take into serious consideration native Chinese interlocutors' readiness and willingness to receive a learners' Chinese performance favorably.

Language pedagogues have recognized C2 expectations toward foreign/second language learners that originated from the NS ownership mentality laid out in previous sections as an important factor in foreign language education. Almost two decades ago, Walker and Noda (2000) already asserted the necessity of assessing foreign language learners' performance against the expectations of the target culture:

> We can't be content to observe the understanding and performance of our learners, even if they seem to reflect the assumptions of the target culture. We must also evaluate the receptivity of their performance in the target culture. It should not be enough that they have conveyed their intentions or comprehend another person's intentions successfully. We need to be concerned with how the persons with whom they interact view the success of the communication. Only when our students are made aware of the reactions of their interlocutors in the classroom and beyond will their memory of the future serve them well.
> (pp. 47–48)

Yet receptivity of learners' L2 performance in the target culture is seldom positioned at the center of Chinese as a FL/SL teaching. The default benchmark of the instruction and assessment has always been the homogeneous and mysterious "native speaker of Chinese," failing to account for what it means to be a "native speaker of Chinese" and who has access to which part of the "nativeness/ Chineseness" constructed within the imagined Chinese community.

Current mainstream practices adopted in most CFL/CSL classrooms are predominantly oriented toward linguistic accuracy and, to certain extent, pragmatic competence as defined in a monolingual sense. Seldom do they equip learners with readily available strategies for handling the native speaker effects on their in-China experience. Learners often have to develop interpretation and strategies on their own when certain C2 expectations clash with their base-cultural instinct. Caucasian learners of Chinese frequently encounter an overly enthusiastic compliment on their Chinese skills regardless of their actual proficiency, which might easily be interpreted as patronizing or even alienating. Heritage learners unprepared for the expectations for them to perform "Chineseness" are likely to feel disempowered and frustrated by the unequal responses received from Chinese interlocutors that distinguish themselves from their peers who "don't look Chinese."

If as foreign language instructors we claim to value authenticity in textbooks and reading materials because it gets language learners ready for what they eventually have to deal with in reality, why should we hide learners from authentic C2 expectations in language classrooms? C2 receptivity of learners deserves to be repositioned at the center of L2 teaching. The understanding of C2 expectations needs to be contextualized within the delicate power relation in which L2 learners are often assigned a subordinated "non-native" position. The rationale behind highlighting the receptivity of L2 learners is not to urge them to give up autonomy and conform to the sociocultural norms of C2, but rather to point to the alternative. That is, L2 learners can negotiate tactfully to reject their marginalized position or even reposition themselves into a powerful position. Concrete awareness of and consequentially actionable strategies in response to anticipated C2 expectations are what L2 classrooms should equip learners with.

A pedagogy of C2 expectations

The following section proposes a pedagogy of C2 expectations as a new model for foreign language education. This new model is less preoccupied with training learners to "replicate" the linguistic system of the "native speakers." Instead, it views the goal of learning a foreign language as the construction of desirable and effective Third-Space personae, which make use of the part of nativeness that is accessible to NNS to negotiate their intentions effectively.

Theoretical grounding

A pedagogy of C2 expectations is grounded in an ecological approach to the study of language learning. This approach conceptualizes second language acquisition (SLA) as a form of second language socialization (SLS) (Douglas Fir Group, 2016; Steffensen & Kramsch, 2017). It compares the relation of language learners to their learning/sociocultural environment to the relationship of living organisms (or agents) and their physical environment. Such an ecological perspective focuses less on how individual learners use inner cognitive capacities to "acquire" or "develop" a second linguistic system. Instead it is preoccupied with the dynamic and complex agent (learner)-environment interaction from which learning emerges. Like a monkey "learned" to use a tool to crack open a nut after finding a fist-sized stone in the woods, from an ecological point of view, learning a second/foreign language is an emergent phenomenon prompted by the symbolic and non-symbolic affordances (the proper-sized stone) available to the learner in the environment. Learning happens as L2 learners make use of what is offered in the learning environment, both inside and beyond the classroom to participate in, adapt to, and consequently shape the environment.

In particular a pedagogy of C2 expectations contributes to two lines of discussions in response to some of the challenges and criticisms toward an ecological approach to the study of SLA and SLS (see Steffensen & Kramsch, 2017).

SL/FL learning as forming emergent Third-Space personae

First, a pedagogy of C2 expectations subscribes to the ecological view of agent (learner) identities as dynamic and "emerging in the interplay between local interaction and large-scale sociocultural and natural dynamics" (Steffensen & Kramsch, 2017, p. 25). Taking this one step further, a pedagogy of C2 expectations conceptualizes the goal of learning a second/foreign language as forming desirable and effective Third-Space personae rather than becoming "native speakers."

Walker (2000) defines persona as "what an individual allows an audience to know about him or her" (cited in Shepherd, 2005, p. 262). Not only can one's personae vary considerably from one situation to another, it can change quickly in the moment-by-moment unfolding of real-time interactions. The notion of Third-Space personae dismisses the stable and structuralist connotation of identity and instead foregrounds the emergent and ever-changing nature of the agent(learner)-environment dynamics individual L2 learners have to navigate in a Third Space. Such a pedagogy therefore takes its starting point in learners' "microecological orbits" (Goffman, 1964), such as concrete encounters within the target culture that is personally meaningful and relevant to the learner.

Third-Space personae as neither native nor non-native

Second, the construct of Third-Space personae transcends the dichotomous opposition between learner and environment, highlighting the co-constructive roles environment and subjectivity both play in the formation of learners' Third-Space personae. A pedagogy of C2 expectation is preoccupied with both how learners adapt to the non-native language and target culture expectations and how that environment (e.g., native speakers and situated C2 expectations) in turn changes as a result of L2 learners' actions. Therefore, such a pedagogy directly responds to the theoretical challenges for an ecological approach to second language research that concerns the "subjectivity and integrity of the language learner" (Steffensen & Kramsch, 2017) in socializing NNS into NS discourses. Subscribed to the Third-Space framework of conceptualizing intercultural communication as opening up a space that is neither dominated by participants' native culture (C1) nor by C2 in a static and holistic sense a pedagogy of C2 expectations supports L2 learners in maintaining a negotiated "third place that is neither native nor nonnative" (Kramsch, 2010) but are based on the emergent C2 expectations in various relations of dominance among the interlocutors.

Four proposals of a pedagogy of C2 expectation

FL learning journey as playing the game of C2 expectations

A game is a useful analogy for conceptualizing the role of C2 expectations in FL/SL teaching and learning. A game contains a few defining elements, including a clearly defined goal, a set of rules agreed on among participants, and a scoring system for determining successful and unsuccessful performance. To claim that one plays a game, it is minimally assumed that the players know what is allowed and what is prohibited, what is the purpose of playing, and what indicates winning and losing.

Following the vein of studies that conceptualize games as a primary means by which members of a culture construct shared social reality (Walker & Noda, 2000; Shepherd, 2005; Jian & Shepherd, 2010), a pedagogy of C2 expectations reintroduces the notion of an *expectation game*. It conceptualizes the foreign/second language learning career as participating in a succession of games of negotiating sets of C2 expectations. A game of expectations is not a new concept. Political campaigns and product launches hinge on the successful anticipation and manipulation of voters' and customers' expectations in order to gain votes and earn profits. In these cases, winning the game doesn't solely depend on how well the political candidate performs or how advanced the products are, but mostly on how well the *players'* performances measure up to the expectations of the *judges* given the particular circumstances. Unlike the scoring systems of most games that are based on explicitly laid-out and objective rubrics, the game of expectations bestows authority on a target population to decide what is "correct, appropriate and desired."

"Judges" and "players"

In aiming at success in playing the expectations games of the target culture, a foreign/second language learner needs to be made aware of how language ideologies regarding the native/non-native speaker dichotomy affect people's practices and perceptions (Doerr, 2009). The native speaker effects that L2 learners need to recognize, in particular, are rooted in the mentality of native speakers who grow up socialized in Chinese culture. They see themselves as "judges" who possess self-perceived ownership of Mandarin Chinese. The underlying ideology is that "native speaker" status automatically bestows one with (1) a high level of competence in using the language and (2) the authority to make a judgment about the legitimacy of language usage. The reverse side of this is the stereotypical profiling of "non-native speakers" as various types of deficient speakers with underdeveloped Chinese language skills in relation to "the natives."

A critical understanding of this general power difference between "judges" and "players" is crucial to identifying emergent expectations in any given context. The foreigners' testimonies have presented cases of such native speaker effects on L2 learning as players engage in the Third Space. Chinese language learners should be prepared to be automatically perceived as the embodiment of different "foreigner" stereotypes. These collectively constructed stereotypes, whether labeled as the "out-group" *laowai*, for those whose physical features stand out in the target-culture environment, or as the "in-group" *huayi* are activated each time individual L2 speakers enter the presence of target culture members. It is helpful, if not absolutely necessary, for learners to be equipped with knowledge about how they might be perceived and their situated expectations when dealing with a particular C2 community. Developing psychological and behavioral strategies in response to anticipated encounters that are potentially frustrating in the target culture also reduces the chances of misunderstandings, disappointment or embarrassment. Therefore it is necessary for pedagogical materials and teachers to present ample examples of good game players as well as opportunities to analyze and practice. These models will serve as affordances or instruments of language socialization for L2 learners to observe, memorize, imitate and appropriate in developing proper visions of themselves as welcomed "*waiguoren*" or "*huayi*" members in the Chinese-speaking community.

For those who are highly invested in establishing themselves in Chinese speech communities, there are practical values in stepping up their Chinese expectations game. Demonstration of knowledge and behaviors that are conventionally desirable in C2 indexes (1) a certain level of Chinese language competency in operating in Chinese culture, which removes the anticipation of heavy accommodation burden, and (2) L2 learners' intention to establish common ground with native Chinese interlocutors by taking on the values and conventions of Chinese culture. Both lead to L2 learners being recognized as serious game players, which is an imperative foundation to effectively navigate the ideologies, intentions and expectations in L2.

Winning the game: co-construction of effective Third-Space personae

Third-Space personae are co-constructed. Failing to recognize this mutually constitutive nature of the agent (learner)-environment dynamics leads to less effective (if at all) Third-Space personae. At one end of the continuum, foreign learners of Chinese, revealing nothing but their base-culture self to Chinese interlocutors and rationalizing their actions as staying truthful to oneself, face the risk of foreignism and cultural imperialism. At the other end, a fluent non-heritage learner of Chinese who strives to achieve nativeness, even with the best intentions possible and no matter how good they are at impersonating Chinese natives, most likely won't be perceived as such. They are subject to different sets of expectation and therefore are playing different games.

Instead, a Third-Space persona is most effective in resulting in fruitful intercultural communications if it emerges from proper recognition of situated C2 expectations and participation in negotiating various levels of expectation (both that of themselves and that of the C2) leading toward a shared goal. An expectation game is not a zero-sum game. Winning instead is defined as achieving a mutually beneficial state in the long run. In the context of developing a repertoire of effective Third-Space personae, it means an evolving balance-keeping between performing the "foreignness" and "nativeness" to strategically manage the expectations of the C2 interlocutors.

Performed "foreignness" and borrowed "nativeness"

L2 learners' Third-Space personae are emergent and evolving as they navigate different types of situations and as they gradually grow and (hopefully) become more adept at handling each scenario. If political candidates can switch their discourse and even the way of carrying themselves to appeal to different demographic groups of voters, L2 learners shouldn't think any less of themselves as players of expectation games.

Playing along the expected "foreignness" isn't always a passive act of weakness. Sometimes it is a conscious move of strategic expectation management and a move of repositioning oneself in a more powerful position that helps learners score in the game in the long run. In some cases, learners might want to retain the expectations of the native Chinese "judges" slightly above the minimum performance that admits them into the game. In this way their chances of outperforming the expectations is much higher than when native Chinese judges' held high expectations to begin with. Other times, that foreignness presented in a persona, juxtaposed against an array of other interconnected factors, changes the power relation in a particular context and gives more capital as a form of power to the marginalized "non-native." Kramsch (2010) points out that language learners are multilinguals who do not merely abide by the order of the target culture; they should retain an "outsideness that enables [them] to play with various objective and subjective meanings" (p. 189). Shepherd (2005) also suggests that

> the person who learns how to interact with the target culture on its terms while maintaining some semblance of his or her individual identity with a trace of "foreignness," or who is able to forge an accepted identity within the new culture, seems less likely to be rejected by the group.
>
> (p. 197)

In place of aiming to achieve "native Chineseness," it is also recommended that L2 learners strategically make use of the portion of "ownership" native speakers are willing to share to create desirable and effective Third-Space personae. This also means being aware of the fact that there is a portion of linguistic and cultural conventions that is seldom accessible to the out-group. Zhang's (2016) study of native Chinese perception of *chengyu* usage by both native and L2 speakers of Chinese shows that only native execution of certain performances, such as humorous use of *chengyu* in casual settings, is endorsed by native Chinese judges.

Retaining the right amount of "foreignness" and recognizing the emergent boundaries between accessible and inaccessible "nativeness" seem to be daunting tasks that take a significant period of socialization in a foreign culture. FL teachers and programs can help mitigate such concerns by starting to foster learners' awareness of C2 expectations and to afford the collection of memories of performing in situated Third-Space encounters from the very beginning stage of a foreign language curriculum. Being able to identify *situated* C2 expectations means that L2 learners have a good grasp of the rules of the game they are playing. And knowing how to perform in relation to the target culture's varying expectations in a manner that best negotiates one's own intentions is what distinguishes a good player from an average one.

Conclusion and implications

As shown in this chapter, there are multiple rationales behind the proposal to reposition native speaker effects and the C2 receptivity of learners at the center of the learning and teaching of Chinese as a Second/Foreign Language. Perhaps the most striking one is the gap between the lack of readiness in CFL/CSL research and teaching practice to prepare learners for real-life C2 expectations and learners' reported powerlessness and frustration in their encounters with the embodiment of Chinese discourses that cite the NS-NNS dichotomy as meaningful. A pedagogy of C2 expectations is proposed as a new model for foreign language programs with goals of training FL/SL learners to recognize and act on what is culturally expected of them as "non-native speakers" of the language. Such a new model offers a way forward that connects theory-building, educational practice and research projects.

Theoretical contribution

From a theoretical perspective, a pedagogy of C2 expectations contributes to an ecological approach to FLE. It expands the narrow view of the L2 leaning environment beyond classrooms to complex agent (learner)-environment systems in which L2 learners make use of affordances, whether it is a textbook or a member of the C2 community, to develop individual competence and to navigate their own reality. Such a model conceptualizes L2 teaching as fostering awareness of and providing guidance for using and shaping the rich affordances learners encountered in the C2 community as a Third Space. L2 learners develop awareness of and strategies to position themselves not as incompetent "non-native speakers" of their L2 but rather multilingual subjects who are socializing into a Third Space, capable of recognizing what is expected of them by the C2 community and taking advantage of that expectation to achieve their own agenda. In doing so, L2 learners create and maintain Third-Space personae that are "neither native nor non-native" but are based on the emergent C2 expectations in various relations of dominance among the interlocutors.

Pedagogical suggestions

From a teaching perspective, a pedagogy of C2 expectations encourages language practitioners and programs to embrace practices that are grounded in the concrete real-life encounters between L2 learners and their counterparts in the C2.

Observable performances make good basic units of analysis and learning for foreign/second language education (Walker, Chapter 7 of this volume), as they are personal, relevant and local. Performance-oriented foreign language teaching approaches, such as the Performed Culture Approach (Walker, 2000; Walker & Noda, 2000; Christensen & Warnick, 2006), and pedagogical materials and activities that utilize concepts, such as Performance Watch (Noda, Ramdeen, Luft, & Mason, 2018; Chai, Cornelius, & Mu, 2018; Zhang, Forthcoming), present one way of doing so. By bridging many oppositions in the traditional model, including language versus culture, inside versus outside of the classroom, in-country versus study-abroad environments, and textbook versus real-life language uses, such practices prepare foreign language learners for navigating the evolving landscape of the Third Space in the future.

Future research

Lastly, from the perspective of research implications, the proposal of a new C2 expectation-oriented model encourages foreign language teacher-researchers to conduct studies and projects examining how the native speaker affects FL/SL learners and its pedagogical implications. Two types of studies utilizing methodologies such as ethnography and discourse analysis to investigate real-life intercultural interactions are valuable in particular: (1) Ones that capture *situated acts of intentions* between FL/SL learners (NNS) and members of the target speech community (NS), that is, the way people's performance—behavior and linguistic practices—embodies, registers and materializes ideologies of the native speaker (Althusser, 1971); and (2) ones that examine how FL/SL learners "submit, utilize, counter, and context" (Doerr, 2009, p. 17) language ideologies of the native speaker in the Third Space. The former informs us of what learners are likely to encounter in particular intercultural contexts, while the latter suggests actionable strategies and offers a lens to capture and understand an authentic learner experience. The insights gained from such studies deserve a wider readership, if not direct involvement, among language teachers, pedagogical material developers and FL/SL program designers.

References

Agar, M. (1994). *Language shock: Understanding the culture of conversation*. New York: William Morrow.

Althusser, L. (1971). *Lenin and philosophy and other essays*. New York: Monthly Review Press.

Birks, Y. (2012). *Encounters with Westerners: Understanding the Chinese construction of the Western other*. Unpublished master's thesis, University of Ottawa.

Chai, D., Cornelius, C., & Mu, B. (2018). *Action! China: A field guide to using Chinese in the community = Ti yan ri zhi: Zhong wen shi di ying yong zhi nan* (1st ed.). New York: Routledge.

Christensen, M. B., & Warnick, J. P. (2006). *Performed culture: An approach to East Asian language pedagogy*. Columbus, OH: National East Asian Languages Resource Center, The Ohio State University.

Conceison, C. (2004). *Significant other: Staging the American in China*. Honolulu: University of Hawai'i Press.
Dikötter, F. (Ed.). (1997). *The construction of racial identities in China and Japan: Historical and contemporary perspectives*. London: Hurst.
Dikötter, F. (2015). *The discourse of race in modern China* (2nd ed.). Oxford: Oxford University Press.
Doerr, N. M. (Ed.). (2009). *The native speaker concept: Ethnographic investigations of native speaker effects*. Berlin: Mouton de Gruyter.
Doerr, N. M., & Sato, S. (2011). Modes of governmentality in an online space: A case study of blog activities in an advanced level Japanese-as-a-Foreign-Language classroom. *Learning, Media and Technology*, *36*(1), 69–83. https://doi.org/10.1080/17439884.2010.509547
The Douglas Fir Group. (2016). A transdisciplinary framework for SLA in a multilingual world. *Modern Language Journal*, *100*(S1), 19–47. https://doi.org/10.1111/modl.12301
Firth, A., & Wagner, J. (1997). On discourse, communication, and (some) fundamental concepts in SLA research. *Modern Language Journal*, *81*(3), 285–300. https://doi.org/10.1111/j.1540-4781.1997.tb05480.x
Fishman, J. A. (2001). 300-plus years of heritage language education in the United States. In J. K. Peyton, D. A. Ranard, & S. McGinnis (Eds.), *Heritage languages in America: Preserving a national resource* (pp. 81–98). Washington, DC: Center for Applied Linguistics/Delta Systems.
Francis, B., Archer, L., & Mau, A. (2009). Language as capital, or language as identity? Chinese complementary school pupils' perspectives on the purposes and benefits of complementary schools. *British Educational Research Journal*, *35*(4), 519–538. https://doi.org/10.1080/01411920802044586
Francis, B., Mau, A., & Archer, L. (2014). Chapter 10. Speaking of identity?: British-Chinese young people's perspectives on language and ethnic identity. In X. L. Curdt-Christiansen & A. Hancock (Eds.), *AILA Applied Linguistics Series* (Vol. 12, pp. 203–218). Amsterdam: John Benjamins Publishing Company. https://doi.org/10.1075/aals.12.11fra
Gill, M. (2011). Authenticity. In J.-O. Östman & J. Verschueren (Eds.), *Handbook of pragmatics highlights* (Vol. 9, pp. 46–65). Amsterdam: John Benjamins. https://doi.org/10.1075/hoph.9.03gill
Goffman, E. (1964). The neglected situation. *American Anthropologist*, *66*(6_PART2), 133–136. https://doi.org/10.1525/aa.1964.66.suppl_3.02a00090
Hall, J. K., Cheng, A., & Carlson, M. T. (2006). Reconceptualizing multicompetence as a theory of language knowledge. *Applied Linguistics*, *27*(2), 220–240. https://doi.org/10.1093/applin/aml013
Hecht, M. L., Warren, J. R., Jung, E., & Krieger, J. L. (2005). A communication theory of identity: Development, theoretical perspective, and future directions. In *Theorizing about intercultural communication* (pp. 257–278). Thousand Oaks, CA: Sage Publications.
Henry, E. S. (2013). Emissaries of the modern: The foreign teacher in urban China. *City & Society*, *25*(2), 216–234. https://doi.org/10.1111/ciso.12017
Hessler, P. (2001). *River town: Two years on the Yangtze* (1st ed.). New York: HarperCollins.
Hope, V. (2015). *All eyes and ears* [Documentary].
Houghton, S., & Rivers, D. J. (Eds.). (2013). *Native-speakerism in Japan: Intergroup dynamics in foreign language education*. Bristol: Multilingual Matters.
Ilnyckyj, R. A. (2010). *Learning as laowai: Race, social positioning*. Unpublished master's thesis, University of British Columbia.

Jian, X., & Shepherd, E. (2010). Playing the game of interpersonal communication in Chinese culture: The "rules" and the moves. In W. Galal (Ed.), *The pedagogy of performing another culture*. Columbus, OH: National East Asian Languages Resource Center.

Kramsch, C. J. (1993). *Context and culture in language teaching*. Oxford: Oxford University Press.

Kramsch, C. J. (2010). *The multilingual subject: What foreign language learners say about their experience and why it matters* (Reprint). Oxford: Oxford University Press.

Kubota, R. (2009). Rethinking the superiority of the native speaker: Toward a relational understanding of power. In M. D. Neriko (Ed.), *"Native speakers" revisited: Multilingualism, standardization, and diversity in language education* (pp. 233–247). Berlin: Mouton de Gruyter.

Lantolf, J. P. (1993). Sociocultural theory and the second-language classroom: The lesson of strategic interaction. In J. E. Alatis (Ed.), *Strategic interaction and language acquisition: Theory, practice and research* (pp. 220–233). Washington, DC: Georgetown University Press.

Larsen-Freeman, D. (2014). Another step to be taken—Rethinking the end point of the interlanguage continuum. In Z. Han & E. Tarone (Eds.), *Language learning & language teaching* (Vol. 39, pp. 203–220). Amsterdam: John Benjamins. https://doi.org/10.1075/lllt.39.11ch9

Li, D., & Duff, P. A. (2008). Issues in Chinese heritage language education and research at the postsecondary level. In A. W. He & Y. Xiao (Eds.), *Chinese as a heritage language: Fostering rooted world citizenry* (pp. 13–32). Honolulu: University of Hawai'i, National Foreign Language Resource Center.

Liu, S. (2007). Living with others: Mapping the routes to acculturation in a multicultural society. *International Journal of Intercultural Relations*, *31*(6), 761–778. https://doi.org/10.1016/j.ijintrel.2007.08.003

Liu, S. (2015). *Identity, hybridity and cultural home: Chinese migrants and diaspora in multicultural societies*. New York: Rowman & Littlefield.

Liu, Y., & Self, C. C. (2019). Laowai as a discourse of othering: Unnoticed stereotyping of American expatriates in Mainland China. *Identities*, 1–19. https://doi.org/10.1080/1070289X.2019.1589158

Mair, V. (2014, April 9). Laowai: The old furriner. *Language Log*. Retrieved from http://languagelog.ldc.upenn.edu/nll/?p=11626

Mao, Y. (2015). Who is a laowai? Chinese interpretations of laowai as a referring expression for non-Chinese. *International Journal of Communication*, 2119–2140.

Mau, A. (2013). *On not speaking "much" Chinese: Identities, cultures and languages of British Chinese pupils*. PhD dissertation, University of Roehampton.

Noda, M., Ramdeen, Y. I., Luft, S. D., & Mason, T. (2018). *Action! Japan: A field guide to using Japanese in the community*. New York: Routledge.

Ortega, L. (2013). SLA for the 21st century: Disciplinary progress, transdisciplinary relevance, and the bi/multilingual turn: SLA for the 21st century. *Language Learning*, *63*, 1–24. https://doi.org/10.1111/j.1467-9922.2012.00735.x

Pennycook, A. (1994). Incommensurable discourses? *Applied Linguistics*, *15*(2), 115–138. https://doi.org/10.1093/applin/15.2.115

Pérez Andrade, G. (2019). *Language ideologies in English language teaching: A multiple case study of teacher education programmes in Chile*. PhD dissertation, University of Southampton.

Relaño-Pastor, A. M., & Fernández-Barrera, A. (2019). The "native speaker effects" in the construction of elite bilingual education in Castilla-La Mancha: Tensions and dilemmas.

Journal of Multilingual and Multicultural Development, *40*(5), 421–435. https://doi.org/10.1080/01434632.2018.1543696

Shepherd, E. (2005). *Eat Shandong: From personal experience to a pedagogy of a second culture*. Columbus, OH: National East Asian Languages Resource Center.

Stanley, P. (2012). *A critical ethnography of "Westerners" teaching English in China: Shanghaied in Shanghai*. London: Routledge. https://doi.org/10.4324/9780203078051

Steffensen, S. V., & Kramsch, C. (2017). The ecology of second language acquisition and socialization. In P. A. Duff & S. May (Eds.), *Language socialization* (pp. 17–32). New York: Springer International. https://doi.org/10.1007/978-3-319-02255-0_2

Tuchiya, S. (2016). *Perceptions of native and nonnative speakers and observational analysis of "divergent" Japanese language teachers in context*. PhD dissertation, The Ohio State University.

Walker, G. (2000). Performed culture: Learning to participate in another culture. In R. D. Lambert & E. Shohamy (Eds.), *Language policy and pedagogy* (pp. 221–236). Amsterdam: John Benjamins. https://doi.org/10.1075/z.96.14wal

Walker, G., & Noda, M. (2000). Remembering the future: Compiling knowledge of another culture. In D. Birckbichler & R. M. Terry (Eds.), *Reflecting on the past to shape the future*. Lincolnwood: National Textbook.

Weekly, R. (2018). Accepting and circumventing native speaker essentialism. In B. Yazan & N. Rudolph (Eds.), *Criticality, teacher identity, and (In)equity in English language teaching* (Vol. 35, pp. 141–162). New York: Springer International. https://doi.org/10.1007/978-3-319-72920-6_8

Wiley, T. (2001). On defining heritage languages and their speakers. In J. Peyton, D. Ranard, & S. McGinnis (Eds.), *Heritage languages in America: Preserving a national resource* (pp. 29–36). Washington, DC: Center for Applied Linguistics.

Young, L. W. L. (1994). *Crosstalk and culture in Sino-American communication*. Cambridge: Cambridge University Press.

Zhang, X. (2016). *Four-character idioms in advanced spoken Chinese: Perception and reaction of native speakers and a pedagogy of C2 expectations*. PhD dissertation, The Ohio State University. Retrieved from http://rave.ohiolink.edu/etdc/view?acc_num=osu1471797737

Zhang, X. (Forthcoming). "耳闻目睹'之体演文化:由实例观察入手的中美跨文化教学." In G. Liu & H. Wang (Eds.), *Tradition and transition: Teaching Chinese culture overseas 传统与现代:海外中文文化教学*. Beijing: Beijing University Press.

Zuengler, J., & Miller, E. R. (2006). Cognitive and sociocultural perspectives: Two parallel SLA worlds? *TESOL Quarterly*, *40*(1), 35. https://doi.org/10.2307/40264510

3 Negotiating intentions in intercultural conversational interactions

Excusing oneself from a family gathering

Bing Mu

Introduction

Understanding intention and the interpretation thereof is of critical significance for the study of human communication in both its verbal and non-verbal forms because understanding what another person intends is critical to how we make sense of their behaviors and their use of language (Gibbs, 2001). When it comes to intercultural communication, the notion of intention is of particular relevance because the failure to convey or interpret intentions is considered to be the most important contributing factor to intercultural communication breakdown (Gumperz, 1982). This chapter explores intention in intercultural conversational interactions by investigating how intentions are developed in the communication process between advanced-level Chinese as a Foreign Language (CFL) learners and Chinese native speakers.

Literature review

Defining intention

The discussion of intention has a long history across the disciplines of psychology, philosophy, anthropology and social cognition (Agar, 2013; Austin, 1962; Bratman, 1987; Duranti, 2015; Gibbs, 1999; Grice, 1957; Searle, 1983). As a result, the notion of intention has become a much disputed and debated topic among psychologists, philosophers, anthropologists and linguists (Sinha, 2017). The theorizing and conceptualization of intention broadly falls under two major approaches: The cognitive-philosophical approach and the sociocultural-interactional approach (Haugh, 2008a; Kecskes, 2014). The cognitive-philosophical approach views intention as the a priori mental state that instigates certain actions, while the sociocultural-interactional approach regards intention as "a post factum construct that is achieved jointly through the dynamic emergence of meaning in conversation" (Kecskes, 2014, p. 26).

This chapter adopts a socio-cognitive approach towards intention (Kecskes, 2014). Under this approach, both "the encoded and co-constructed sides of intention" (p. 26) will be considered, therefore intention is viewed as both "an a priori and a co-constructed phenomenon" (p. 25). To be specific, intention is the meaning that the speaker attributes to his/her own activity, which is "co-incidental with, or immediately precede[s], ongoing local action at the micro-level of analysis" (van Dijk, 2008, p. 81). Meanwhile, sometimes intention can be indeterminate enough to be shaped by social processes (Gibbs, 1999, 2001).

Conceptual background

The discussion of intention in this chapter is grounded in two conceptual frameworks. The first is Clark's (1996a, 1996b) conceptualization of communication as coordinated and cooperated; the second is Gibbs's (1999, 2001) conceptualization of intention as emergent from social interactions.

Clark (1996b) posits that in interpersonal communication, speaking and listening are not a sequence of two autonomous acts but rather participatory acts. Language use, as a result, is a joint action that requires the speaker and the hearer to coordinate their actions and constantly monitor the actions of their counterparts, just like people shaking hands, smiling at each other, or even walking past one another without colliding. He further argues that the coordination of actions happens in the speaker's and hearer's common ground, which is the sum of two people's mutual knowledge, beliefs and suppositions at the moment of their conversing. In the process of speaking and listening, common ground can serve as a coordination device to get the speaker's meaning and the hearer's construal of the meaning to match.

Based on the conceptualization of human communication as cooperative and coordinated, intention is conceptualized as emergent from social interactions; that is, the speaker and the hearer co-construct what the speaker means in a particular situation (Gibbs, 1999, 2001; Haugh, 2007, 2008b; Kecskes, 2010). According to Gibbs (1999), the recovery of what a speaker means is considered primary in human communication, however, successful communication demands that speakers do more than simply make their utterances and hope that hearers draw the right inferences about what they intend to convey. Instead, when speakers speak, they tailor their utterances for the hearers to understand, and the hearers also seek the most relevant interpretation of what the speakers mean among the possible interpretations based on what they have in their common ground. Therefore, "speakers and hearers must coordinate their common ground to increase the probability that what is intended will be recognized and thus understood" (p. 24). To capture this social dimension of human communication, Gibbs (1999, 2001) argues that sometimes a speaker's original intention can be indeterminate enough to be shaped by what others say and do. To elaborate on this point, Gibbs (2001) points out that many face-to-face situations do not come with pre-specified intentional meanings that originate in the minds of the speakers. Instead,

> speakers often deliberately offer their addressee a choice of construal, so when the addressee makes their choice, they help to determine what the speaker is

taken to mean (H. Clark, 1997). For instance, a speaker may present an utterance with one intention in mind, but where the addressee misconstrues it, the speaker then changes his or her mind and accepts the new construal.

(p. 109)

Gibbs's (1999, 2001) conceptualization of intention as emergent from social interactions presents a dynamic and interactive understanding of communication and intention. In particular, it provides a framework for the examination of intention in human communication on how one's intentions get taken up, developed, altered or even abandoned when the speaker and the hearer start to be engaged in the joint enterprise of communicative interactions.

Intention and intercultural communication

Intercultural communication, according to Bowe and Martin (2007), refers to "the shared communication between speakers from different language/cultural backgrounds" (p. 3). Specifically, it focuses on "the *symbolic exchange process whereby individuals from two (or more) different cultural communities negotiate shared meanings in an interactive situation*" (Ting-Toomey, 1999, pp. 16–17; author's emphasis).

To capture the unique features of intercultural communication and compare intercultural communication with intracultural communication, the following analogy of communicative interactions to ballroom dancing can be useful:

Chick (1990, p. 227) likens the coordination of intra-cultural interactions to the synchrony of "ballroom dancing partners of long standing, confident in the mutual knowledge of the basic sequence of dance steps and of the signals by which they inform one another of changes in direction or tempo, moving in smooth harmony." Intercultural encounters, in contrast, are more like ballroom dances between strangers who "misinterpret one another's signals, struggle to develop a sequence or theme, or establish a rhythm, quarrel over rights to lead, and metaphorically speaking, trample one another's toes."

(cf. Bailey, 2004, pp. 403–404)

To relate this analogy of intercultural communication to intention, we can say that the "signals" that are misinterpreted between ballroom dancing strangers can be considered as the intentions of the individuals in intercultural communicative interactions. According to Walker (2000), to successfully communicate across cultures, one's intention must be recognized and accepted by the people with whom he is interacting, and he must be able to perceive their intentions as well.

Intercultural communication has often been juxtaposed with intracultural communication. However, recent scholarship has increasingly focused on their compatibility. Kecskes (2014) points out that intercultural communication is comparable to intracultural communication, and they only differ in certain aspects such as features, emphases and strategies. Scollon and Scollon (1995) argue that "all communication is interpersonal communication and can never be intercultural communication" because "cultures do not talk to each other; individuals do" (p. 125). From this perspective, intercultural communication should be considered as a context for interpersonal interactions, therefore the premise to examine intention in intercultural communicative interactions is built upon the work laid out by Clark (1996a, 1996b, 1997) and Gibbs (1999, 2001) that communication, in nature, is the cooperative and coordinated work between the speaker and the hearer. However, the context of intercultural communication differs from interpersonal communication in that it significantly broadens the scope of and enriches the material for the research of interpersonal communication. Intention examined in intercultural communication, therefore, should demonstrate both the commonalities with and uniqueness from intention examined in interpersonal interactions.

Despite the centrality of intention in the studies of interpersonal communication, research that specifically addresses intention in intercultural encounters is scarce (Mu, 2018). To fill this gap, this study examines the interaction between advanced-level CFL learners and Chinese native speakers to investigate how the communication of intention unfolds in intercultural conversational interactions and what factors shape the negotiation of intention in the communication process.

Research questions

In light of the conceptualization of intention as shaped by social processes (Gibbs, 1999, 2001) and the significant role intention plays in intercultural communication (Gumperz, 1982), this chapter examines intention in intercultural conversational interactions. Specifically, this chapter aims to address two research questions:

1 What are the characteristics of intention in intercultural conversational interactions between L2 learners and native speakers?
2 How is the negotiation of intention in intercultural communication similar to or different from that examined in interpersonal interactions?

Data and research methodology

Data collection

The data for this chapter is drawn from a larger study that examines how intentions are communicated and interpreted in intercultural communicative interactions between advanced-level CFL learners and Chinese native speakers. Data collection was conducted over the course of three years when several classes on Chinese language and culture were observed and video-recorded (30 hours), individual interviews audio-recorded (seven hours) and observation and fieldnotes taken whenever necessary. The data analyzed in this chapter is part of the 30 hours of video recordings of classroom interactions.

Setting

The data for this chapter comes from the observation and video-recordings of a graduate-level class titled "Networking in China and America" in a large research university in the US Midwest. According to the syllabus, this course is performance oriented, where students come to class to perform in given contexts in both Chinese and American cultures. There are two groups of students in this class, advanced-level CFL learners and Chinese native speakers that consist of both graduate students and visiting scholars from China. The goal of this class is for the two groups of students to learn how to imitate and analyze observable behaviors in professional Chinese and American environments. To that end, these two groups of students serve as peer advisors for their classmates who are learning their base culture. The role of the instructor is to guide the two groups of students to interact with one another according to their respective native cultural norms. This class meets twice a week. Each week, the class focuses on one particular speech act; for example, in one week they focus on offering an invitation, and the next on performing a refusal. On the first day of the class, students focus on performing in American cultural contexts with Chinese students performing and American students evaluating and coaching their Chinese peers, and vice versa on the second day. This course is offered once every academic year, and three semesters of video-recordings were collected over the course of three years.

Classroom activities comprise two major components: Learners' performances and metapragmatic comments of both the instructor and the two groups of students. Performances, according to Walker (2000), are "conscious repetitions of 'situated events' that are defined by five specified elements: place of occurrence, time of occurrence, appropriate script/program/rules, roles of participants, and accepting and/or accepted audience" (p. 8). These five specified elements, Walker and Noda (2000) argue, are used to "situate behavior" and "create or interpret meanings" (p. 8). In this class, students situate their performances in contexts defined by these five specified elements. In addition to students' performances, this class also consists of a large amount of metapragmatic activities (Johnstone, Andrus, & Danielson, 2006; Kasper & Rose, 2002), that is, the discursive activities which explicitly talk about rules of use and about whether certain communicative functions, attitudes and ideas are considered proper in a given situation. In this class, after each performance, the instructor would ask the students to actively reflect upon what had happened, what had gone well and what could have been improved. Then the entire class would be engaged in a discussion on the execution and the authenticity of the performance. These kinds of metapragmatic activities can help students not only "mindfully abstract, reflect upon, and speculate upon patterns of use" (Hall, 1999, p. 140) but also develop cultural awareness and sensitivity by learning to analyze the cultural elements that are key to smooth communication in the target culture.

Due to the performing nature of this class, students sit in groups in the classroom, with one CFL learner paired with one or two Chinese native speakers. Before performing in groups in front of the entire class, students are usually given ten to 15 minutes to rehearse so that they can come up with a performance in a well-defined context that approximates the real-life situation to the best of their knowledge. After that, the whole class would be engaged in metapragmatic activities to discuss how the performance went. Each class session is 90 minutes in length.

This class was chosen as a site for data collection over naturally occurring conversations for three reasons. First, students' performances in well-defined contexts and the accompanying metapragmatic discussions provide an optimal mechanism for data triangulation. Second, compared with naturally occurring conversations, this class affords more voices, including first-person and third-person viewpoints, instructor's and peers' evaluations, and native and non-native perspectives on given contexts and the different cultural norms and expectations at play. Third, students' performances in this class can be compared to open role-plays, that is, role-plays that specify actors' roles without predetermining the course and outcome of the conversation. Félix-Brasdefer argues that open role-plays approximate natural data in terms of sequence organization and joint action by interlocutors (2018), and that when constructed with sufficient contextual information, open role-plays may offer some advantages over natural data for controlling for sociolinguistic variables (2007). Nevertheless, students' performances in the classroom do not carry the same social consequences as in real-life situations. Therefore, cautions should be taken to interpret students' performances and the resultant findings.

Data description

The data for this chapter was collected on September 14, 2017. In that day's class, the two groups of students were performing the speech act of excusing oneself from a social gathering. A two-minute and 40-second performance of how a CFL learner excused himself from a family dinner was selected for analysis. There was a 15-second introduction of context before the performance and a two-minute and 25-second metapragmatic section thereafter. Both the context introduction and the metapragmatic comments are included in the data analysis to situate the performance and interpret its meaning.

This particular performance was selected for two reasons. First, the performance is representative of the topic for the entire lesson: The speech act of excusing oneself from a social gathering. This particular class reflects the types of topics and typical class activities of the course. Second, this performance was selected due to its richness at multiple levels, including the context that the performers put forth at the beginning of the performance, the completeness of its structure, and the devoted actors and the engaged audience.

Participants

There are three types of participants in this performance: The actors, the audience and the instructor.

Actors

Kyle, a 27-year-old male American student, was a CFL learner and an MA student majoring in Chinese language pedagogy. It was his first semester of graduate studies when the data was collected. Before joining the program, he taught Chinese at an American university for two years.

Qi, a 26-year-old female, was a Chinese graduate student majoring in Chinese language pedagogy. She completed her master's degree in teaching Chinese as a foreign language at a Chinese university before coming to the US to pursue her PhD degree. This was her first year in her PhD studies and second year in this program. She was a native speaker of Chinese.

Chun, a 35-year-old female, was a visiting scholar from Hunan, China. She had over ten years of experience teaching Chinese as a Foreign Language in a Chinese university. She was also a native speaker of Chinese.

In this performance, both Kyle and Qi played the roles of themselves, and Chun played the role of Qi's mom. Kyle and Qi, in this performance and their daily lives, were classmates and friends. The performance was situated against the context where Qi invited Kyle to her house to have dinner with her and her mom.

Audience

There were six CFL learners and five Chinese native speakers as the audience in this performance. Among the six CFL learners, four were first-year MA students majoring in advanced Chinese language and culture, one first-year MA student majoring in Chinese linguistics, and one senior undergraduate student majoring in Chinese. Among the five Chinese native speakers, three were graduate students in Chinese language pedagogy and two were visiting scholars from China. The students' demographic information is given in Table 3.1.

Instructor

The instructor was a male professor in the Department of East Asian Languages and Literatures. Specializing in Chinese language and culture, he had extensive experience working with advanced-level CFL learners. He was a native speaker of Chinese.

Data analysis

Discourse analysis was adopted to analyze this piece of data. Contextualization cues were used to parse speakers' utterances into message units, the minimal unit of conversational meaning (Bloome, Carter, Christian, Otto, & Shuart-Faris, 2005; Bloome & Egan-Robertson, 1993; Green & Wallat, 1981). An adapted version of the transcription conventions established by Du Bois, Schuetze-Coburn, Cumming, and Paolino (1993) was adopted to transcribe the data (see Appendix 3.1 for the transcription symbols).

Table 3.1 Students' demographic information

Student	Major and year	Chinese proficiency	Ethnicity
Kyle	First-year MA student, Chinese language pedagogy	Advanced High	American
Annie	First-year MA student, Chinese linguistics	Advanced Mid	American
Nick	First-year MA student, advanced Chinese language and culture	Advanced Low	American
Justin	First-year MA student, advanced Chinese language and culture	Advanced Mid	American
David	First-year MA student, advanced Chinese language and culture	Advanced Mid	American
Todd	First-year MA student, advanced Chinese language and culture	Advanced Mid	American
Zoey	Senior, Chinese major	Advanced Low	American
Qi	First-year PhD student, Chinese language pedagogy	Native speaker of Chinese	Chinese
Tong	First-year PhD student, Chinese language pedagogy	Native speaker of Chinese	Chinese
Wen	Second-year MA student, Chinese language pedagogy	Native speaker of Chinese	Chinese
Min	First-year MA student, Chinese language pedagogy	Native speaker of Chinese	Chinese
Chun	Visiting scholar	Native speaker of Chinese	Chinese
Mei	Visiting scholar	Native speaker of Chinese	Chinese
Ling	Visiting Scholar	Native speaker of Chinese	Chinese

Results

In this section, results are presented following the actual flow of the class: First an introduction of the context and then the performance followed by the metapragmatic comments.

Context

Before the performance began, Qi and Chun spent 15 seconds to quickly set up the context (see Appendix 3.2 for transcript). The contextual information is given below as the five specified elements used to define a performance:

> Place of occurrence: Qi's home
> Time of occurrence: Dinnertime
> Appropriate script/program/rules: Chinese social protocol of guesting 客随主便 ('a guest conforms to the host's wishes')

Roles of participants: Hosts (Qi and her mom) and guest (Kyle, Qi's male friend and classmate)
Accepting and/or accepted audience: Not specified in the performance. By default, classmates as the audience in the classroom setting.

Performance

The performance is presented in Transcript 3.1.

Transcript 3.1 Excusing oneself from a family gathering

1 妈妈: 哎, 那个, 来, 这, <u>才出锅的</u>, <u>虾</u> 2 快吃吧 (所有人笑) 3 琦: 我妈做饭特别好吃 4 快尝尝 5 Kyle: 你妈做的菜都=真好吃 (所有人笑) 6 谢谢 7 妈妈: 你慢慢吃啊 8 我在厨房里还有菜 (所有人大笑) 9 琦: <A我再给你盛碗饭吧A> 10 Kyle: 不用 11 已经, 已经, 呃 (翻看笔记) 丰盛了 (中国人笑) 12 妈妈: 很丰盛 13 Kyle: 很丰盛 14 琦: 我再给你盛碗饭吧 15 敏 (先笑再看Kyle): <LO不用不用LO> 16 Kyle (看笔记, 无所适从, 笑): 哦我吃饱了 (伸手并摸肚子) 17 已经 (伸手), 太多了 (笑) (所有人笑) 18 (伸手) 我吃饱了 (Kyle手势示意继续) (所有人笑) 19 琦: 那我那我给你洗点水果去 20 Kyle: (伸手) 不用不用 21 我真的吃饱了 22 呃 <LO还有我LO> (看琦, 点头) 23 不好意思 24 我得<L走了L> (双手握在一起) 25 明天有考试 26 我得==回去 27 妈妈: △△<u>这么早</u>↑	1 Mom: aye, well, this, <u>just out of pot</u>, <u>shrimp</u> 2 dig in (everyone laughs) 3 Qi: my mom's cooking is especially good 4 try quickly 5 Kyle: the dishes your mom cooked are all=very delicious (everyone laughs) 6 thanks 7 Mom: take your time to eat 8 I still have dishes in the kitchen (Everyone laughs hard) 9 Qi: <A let me get you another bowl of rice A> 10 Kyle: no need 11 already, already, eh, (flip to check notes) sumptuous (Chinese people laugh) 12 Mom: very sumptuous 13 Kyle: very sumptuous 14 Qi: let me get you another bowl of rice 15 Min (first laughs then looks at Kyle): <LO no need no need LO> 16 Kyle (checking notes, looking overwhelmed, laughing): oh I am full (hand reaching out and touching belly) 17 already (hand reaching out), too much (laugh) (everyone laughs) 18 (hands reaching out) I am full (Kyle gestures to keep going) (everyone laughs) 19 Qi: then I then I will wash some fruits for you 20 Kyle: (hands reaching out) no need no need 21 I am really full 22 um <LO besides I LO> (looks at Qi and nods) 23 sorry 24 I need <L to go L> (hands together) 25 there is a test tomorrow 26 I need to==go back 27 Mom: △△<u>this early</u>↑

(*Continued*)

Transcript 3.1 (Continued)

28	这么早就回去	28	go back this early
29	这才<HI 几HI>点呀	29	<HI what HI> time is it
30	这才几点	30	what time is it
31	<A你等一下啊	31	<A wait a second
32	我马上去洗那个水果	32	I will immediately wash that fruit
33	还是从美国进口的	33	imported from America
34	等下等下	34	wait wait
35	(示意琦) 你把他留住A> (所有人笑)	35	(signaling Qi) you keep him here A> (everyone laughs)
36	Kyle: 好 (所有人笑)	36	Kyle: Ok (everyone laughs)
37	Kyle: XXX	37	Kyle: XXX
38	妈妈: 吃点吃点	38	Mom: have some, have some
39	这个..你成绩那么好	39	well..your grades are so good
40	学霸还用复习啊	40	scholar-<u>tyrant</u> needs to study
41	琦: 明天考试很简单别担心	41	Qi: tomorrow's test is very easy don't worry
42	妈妈: 对 [你看]	42	Mom: right [look]
43	琦: [多吃点水果]	43	Qi: [have more fruit]
44	我妈那超市还买了新的, 那=个然后	44	my mom also bought new things that=then
45	我妈还自己酿了红酒	45	my mom herself also brewed some wine
46	等会还可以喝点酒 (所有人轻声笑)	46	later we can have some wine (everyone laughs lightly)
47	Kyle: 可是留学生宿舍十== (看表) 点半关门	47	Kyle: but the overseas students' dorm 10== (checking his watch) 30 closes
48	妈妈: 十点半[关门, 现在↑]	48	Mom: 10:30 [closes, now↑]
49	琦 (看表): [哦, 宿舍要关门啦]	49	Qi (checking her watch): [oh, the dorm is going to close]
50	现在已经快十点了	50	now it is almost 10
51	妈妈: 哦, 那是有点, 有点, 那个有点晚了 (Kyle咧嘴再叹气)	51	Mom: oh that's a little a little late (Kyle draws back his lips and sighs)
52	不过<u>没关系的</u>	52	but it <u>doesn't matter</u>
53	开车嘛	53	driving
54	那个过去 (敏边笑边用手指妈妈, 所有人笑)	54	well there (Min laughs while pointing at mom, everyone laughs)
55	Kyle: (伸手) △△<A 不不 A>	55	Kyle: (hands reaching out) △△<A no no A>
56	我不要麻烦你了	56	I will not trouble you
57	我先去打车回去吧	57	I will go get a taxi back
58	没关系	58	It doesn't matter
59	(看笔记) 实在很 . . . (皱眉头, 摊手)	59	(checking notes) really very . . . (frowns and throws up his hands)
60	妈妈: 今天实在是招呼不<u>周</u>啊	60	Mom: Today we really are not treating you <u>completely</u>
61	梅: <P招呼不周P> (Kyle抿嘴, 笑, 再抿嘴) (所有人人笑, 敏鼓掌)	61	Mei: <P not treating you completely P> (Kyle purses his lips, laughs, and purses his lips again) (everyone laughs hard. Mın claps her hands)
62	Min: [XXX]	62	Min: [XXX]
63	Kyle: [XXX]	63	Kyle: [XXX]
64	我== (做起身状)	64	I== (about to stand up)
65	老师: Kyle (Kyle 回头看老师)	65	Instructor: Kyle (Kyle turns around to face the instructor)
66	见妈妈这么紧张 (中国同学大笑)	66	meeting mom so nervous (Chinese people laugh hard)

67 敏: 对==丈母娘见女婿 68 走不了了 　(Kyle先笑再托腮) 　(中国人拍手笑) 69 老师: 本来不该这么紧张啊 70 Kyle: XXX 71 老师: 主要是见了妈妈了 　(中国人大笑) 72 敏: 对 73 这 (指着妈妈) 丈母娘 　(中国人大笑) 74 所以就会紧张, 就会XXX 75 老师: 妈妈 嗯 76 Kyle: XXX 77 我先走了 (起身走) 　(所有人笑)	67 Min: yes== mother-in-law meeting son-in-law 68 can't leave 　(Kyle laughs then holds his chin in one hand) 　(Chinese people clap and laugh) 69 Instructor: not supposed to be this nervous 70 Kyle: XXX 71 Instructor: mainly because of meeting mom 　(Chinese people laugh hard) 72 Min: right 73 this (pointing to mom) mother-in-law 　(Chinese people laugh hard) 74 so he will be nervous, will be XXX 75 Instructor: mom um 76 Kyle: XXX 77 I'll leave first (stands up and leaves) 　(everyone laughs)

In this performance, the social protocol followed is embedded in a formulaic Chinese expression, 客随主便 ('a guest conforms to the host's wishes') (Walker, 2000, p. 10). The overarching goal of the Chinese hosts was to adhere to their social roles and display the competence of being good hosts. The means to achieve this goal was to "intuit a guest's unspoken needs" (Ames et al., 2001, p. 324) by making choices for the guest and insisting on these choices. In the context setup, Chun described the script of the hosts' performance as 非常非常热情的 ('very very hospitable'). The overarching goal of the guest, on the other hand, was to adhere to his social role and display the equally important social competence of being a good guest. This goal was achieved through politely declining the offer a couple of times followed by an acceptance of the offer made by the host to display his conformity to the host's wishes.

The choices that the hosts made for the guest include the offering of the shrimp (1), another bowl of rice (9 and 14), fruits (19, 32 and 43), wine (45–46), and a ride (53). In the face of such an overwhelmingly large array of offerings, Kyle also conformed to his social role by recognizing the cooking skill of Qi's mom (5), commenting on the quantity of the food (11 and 17), and providing evidence for the host's thoughtfulness, such as he was full (16 and 18). Through these multiple turns of interactive exchanges, they affirmed and reaffirmed their distinct social roles as the host and the guest so as to maintain positive social dynamics.

After these multiple rounds of social exchanges, the guest indicated to the host his intention to excuse himself (24 and 26). In order to do so without breaking the social harmony, Kyle issued an apology "不好意思" ('sorry') in the preceding line (23), and provided supportive evidence "明天有考试" ('there is a test tomorrow') in the following line (25). The intention of the hosts, on the other hand, was to convince the guest to stay longer. What the mom did to keep him longer was to first challenge the guest's intention to leave by questioning the timing (27–30), offer some fruits (32–33), and give Qi an imperative to keep him from leaving (35).

The whole series of different moves with the intention to keep him stay directly caused Kyle to temporarily abandon his intention to leave (36). Seeing the strategies to make Kyle stay work, the hosts gave reassurance to Kyle by complimenting the guest's good grades (39), downplaying the difficulty level of the exam (41), offering more fruits (43), and bringing up a trajectory to future action of having some wine later (46). At this point, Kyle adopted an indirect strategy of hinting his intention to leave by bringing up the reality that inhibited him from staying longer, that the oversea students' dorm would close at 10:30 p.m. (47). The reality brought up by Kyle was first questioned by the mom (48), then confirmed by Qi (49–50) and by the mom herself acknowledging that it was already late (51). To compensate for this adversity, the mom first reassured the guest that it was okay (52) and then offered to give the guest a ride (53–54). On seeing that this offering was declined by the guest (55–59), the mom initiated another compensation by apologizing to the guest for their oversight of the guest's needs (60) through the use of a formulaic expression, 招呼不周 ('not treating the guest completely'), despite the fact that they had gone all-out to entertain the guest well. To apologize for being unable to treat the guests completely is a common strategy employed by Chinese hosts to demonstrate their hospitality. Apparently, the employment of this formulaic expression to highlight the incompetence of the host as a means to build the image of a competent and considerate host was neither expected nor internalized by the guest, and this led to a moment of social awkwardness.

Kyle's struggle to come up with a coping mechanism to effectively handle the host's overwhelming hospitality subsequently triggered a small section of metacommunication within the performance, where the instructor stepped into the performance to comment on the learner's lack of "situational adeptness" (Cohen, 1996) that caused such social awkwardness; the reason he stumbled was because he was unfamiliar with the situation of meeting with a female friend's mom (66, 69, 71, and 75) in a Chinese context. Min, a classmate and friend of Kyle, also teased him by saying that the reason he was nervous was because he was meeting with his future mother-in-law. The entanglement of the performance and the classroom setting helped Kyle, the guest in the performance and the student in the classroom, to successfully discharge his intention to leave (77).

Metapragmatic comments

The two-minute and 25-second metapragmatic section (see Appendix 3.3 for transcript) mainly focused on helping Kyle to successfully discharge his intention to leave while avoiding the social awkwardness. First, the instructor commented that "妈妈做得很好，就是这样" ('Mom did great. It's just like this'). Although someone who is not familiar with Chinese culture may find Qi and her mom's hospitality a little over the top, what they did in this conversation, as a matter of fact, demonstrates the kind of normality that a foreigner can expect to encounter in a similar situation. In face of the level of hospitality that Qi and her mom demonstrated in this conversation, Kyle seemed overwhelmed. Not only did his linguistic ability start to shatter with lots of repetition, hesitance and utterances

Negotiating intentions 57

that were incomplete and incoherent, his frustration was especially salient in his non-verbal behaviors, which included various facial configurations, body gestures and nervous laughter. As Min commented, "他眼泪都快下来了" ('his tears were about to fall'). To help Kyle cope with the overwhelming hospitality and successfully excuse himself, the instructor encouraged the students to think about what they would do if they were in Kyle's position. The Chinese students offered their advice that in this situation, Kyle should have emphasized more the reason why he needed to leave instead of simply apologizing for the fact that he needed to go. This piece of advice was accepted immediately by Kyle with a verbal confirmation accompanied by a nod, and by the instructor himself, who subsequently elaborated on how to operationalize this suggestion. In this section, Kyle also laid out his rationale of how his intention to leave was developed over time, which will be taken into consideration when interpreting this performance.

The guest's intention to leave as negotiated

To map the course of the interaction in the performance, Figure 3.1 shows the social moves that the hosts and the guest adopted, respectively.

As shown in Figure 3.1, we can clearly see that the whole performance can be divided into two distinct yet complementary sections. The first section is from lines 1 to 21 and the second section is from lines 22 to 77. The first section focuses on the ritualistic exchanges of the hosts providing offerings to the guest, and the second section deals with how the guest excused himself from the social gathering. To understand how the guest's intention to leave has developed over time, we will focus on the second section.

In the second section, the guest's intention to excuse himself undergoes several distinct stages. He first brought up the intention to leave directly, and this intention was challenged by the hosts with exaggerated emotions and aggressive compensation moves, which included greatly increased volume, stress in utterances, expedition in the offering of the fruits, and an imperative to make the guest stay. All of these moves led directly to the stage where the guest temporarily abandoned this intention. Such an abandonment was also confirmed in the metapragmatic section, where Kyle explained that the host's compensation moves left him with no choice but to temporarily abandon his original intention to leave. Later, after the conflicts arose from the reality that the oversea students' dorm would close soon and the future action of having wine, the intention was reactivated in an indirect manner. The indirect hint of this intention was confronted with the host's mitigated moves acknowledging that it was already late and offering the guest a ride. The guest's refusal of the host's offer gave him a chance to specify the means to achieve his intention: He would take a taxi to go back. This direct refusal triggered the hosts to apologize for their failure to treat the guest completely, leaving the guest speechless for the lack of appropriate response due to the missing cultural knowledge. On seeing the guest's frustration, the instructor entered the conversation to provide some feedback, which eventually gave the guest a chance to implement

58 *Bing Mu*

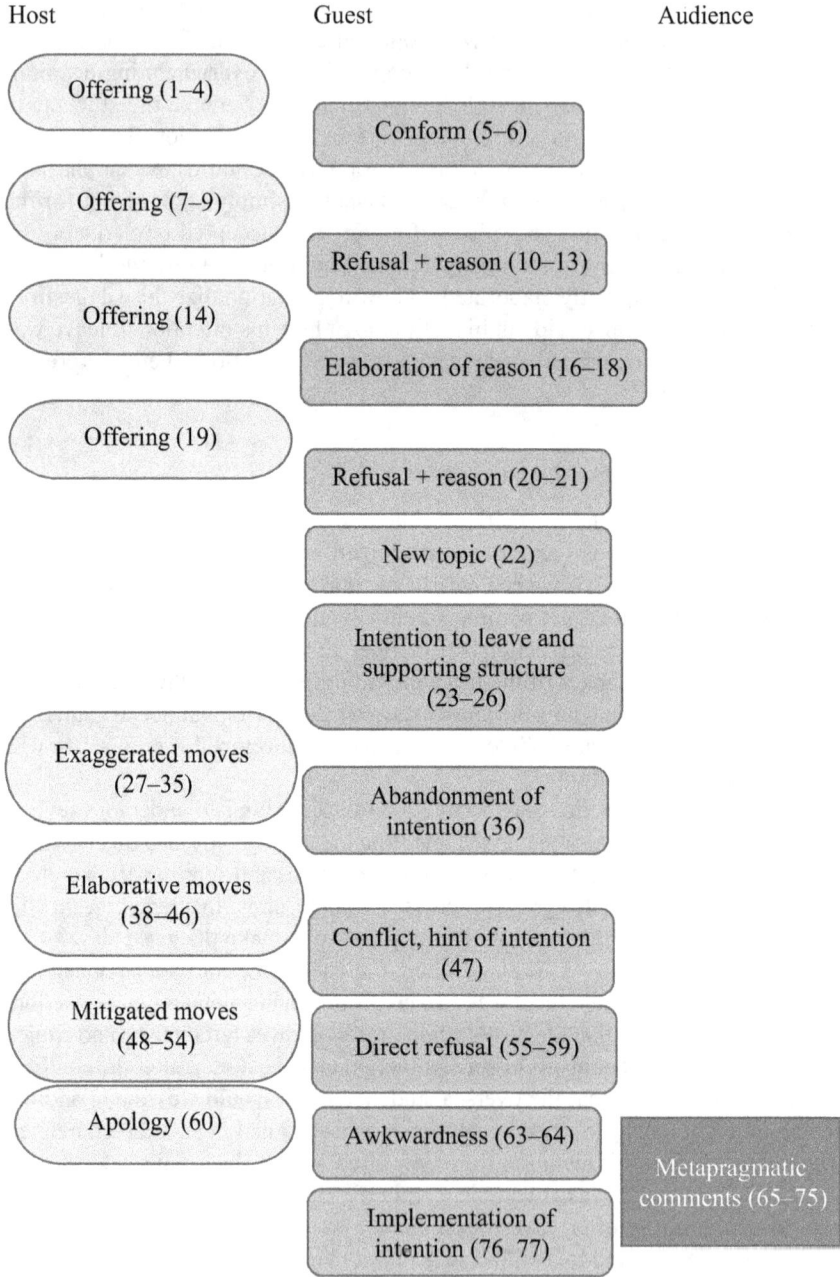

Figure 3.1 Social moves that the host and the guest adopt in a family gathering

Negotiating intentions 59

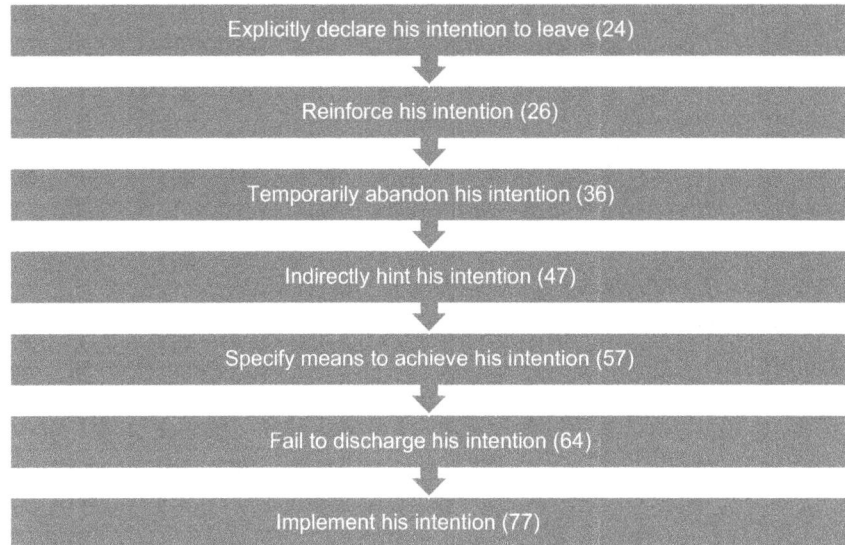

Figure 3.2 The development of the guest's intention to leave

his intention to leave. Figure 3.2 demonstrates the various stages of the guest's development of the intention to leave.

Figures 3.1 and 3.2 show that the development of the guest's intention to excuse himself is a negotiated process. The guest first explicitly declared and reinforced his intention to leave, but this intention could not be successfully discharged due to the hosts' challenge. In face of the host's challenge, all he could do was to temporarily abandon this intention. In other words, without the hosts' challenge, the guest's intention to leave would have been successfully discharged and the next stage of temporary abandonment of his intention would be non-existent. Similarly, the host's introduction of a new trajectory to future action created a conflict between the reality and the future, which enabled the guest to reignite his intention. As in the previous stage, without the hosts' mentioning of the future plan that was in conflict with the reality, the guest wouldn't have had the opportunity to bring up his intention to leave for the second time. The specification of the means to achieve his intention was only made possible after the host attempted to compensate for the fact that it was already late and offered to give the guest a ride. Without this step, the guest would be unlikely to spell out the means to achieve this intention. The failure to discharge his intention to leave was caused by the host's employment of a formulaic expression to demonstrate their hospitality by highlighting their incompetence, to which the guest lacked the linguistic and cultural knowledge to respond. Without this step, the guest would have successfully discharged his intention by resorting to the means previously mentioned. The final implementation of his intention was the product of the metacommunication part, when the instructor directly stepped into the performance and relieved the guest of the social awkwardness due to his lack of strategies to reply to the host's articulation of incompetence.

Discussion

This section discusses the results in light of the research questions and relates them to the conceptualization of intention.

The negotiation of intention and the factors that condition the negotiation

With regard to the first research question about the characteristics of intention in intercultural conversational interactions, the results illustrate that the development of one's intention is a negotiated process. To be specific, although Kyle's intention to leave originated in his mind, this intention was indeterminate enough to be shaped by what his interlocutors said and did (Gibbs, 1999, 2001). In Kyle's own words, "然后我就没办法, 我真的, 我真的需要再留一会, 所以我留了一会" ('then I have no way. I really, I really need to stay a while, so I stayed a while'). This said, the path from the articulation of his intention to leave to its final discharge was a negotiated result. Without the explicit negotiation from the both sides, intention can neither be discharged nor further developed. This finding is congruent with the conceptualization of intention in previous research: The speaker and the hearer co-construct what the speaker means in a particular situation (Gibbs, 1999, 2001; Haugh, 2007, 2008b; Kecskes, 2010).

Several factors have been identified to condition the negotiation process in this performance. First, the negotiation of the guest's intention to leave was shaped by the multiple social roles that Kyle assumed in the performance. Kyle, the CFL learner, was not only the guest in the performance but also a student to the instructor and a classmate to the others, including Qi and Chun, who were both the actors in the performance and the students in the classroom. To successfully discharge his intention to leave, Kyle coordinated his actions not only in relation to the conversation participants but also to the audience, including the instructor and his fellow classmates. The implementation of his intention to leave in the end was only made possible after he moved through time and space and opted in and out of his social roles as being both the guest in the performance and a student in the classroom. To be specific, the final utterance "我先走了" ('I'll leave first') can be considered as both a response to his role as a guest to excuse himself from the family dinner, and to his role as a student in the classroom after being coached by his instructor and his peers. The negotiation of the intention to leave, as a result, was the product of the coordination of actions between Kyle and his fellow classmates, as well as the instructor.

Another factor that shaped the negotiation of intention was the audience. After the host issued an apology for their oversight of the guest's needs to demonstrate their hospitality, Mei, an audience, repeated this utterance. The repetition here was the reaction to the societal knowledge—an apology for failing to attend to the guest's

Negotiating intentions 61

needs as a means to establish the host's hospitality—a piece of knowledge that the native speakers shared but to which the CFL learner lacked access. Kyle's lack of coping strategies was demonstrated in his facial configuration of pursing his lips and laughing awkwardly, which triggered the subsequent laughter and the clapping from the audience. This reaction from the audience directly dictated how the negotiation of the intention unfolded in the following lines and directly gave rise to the metapragmatic comments in the performance. The instructor's comments on and the audience's tease of Kyle's lack of strategies gave Kyle an opportunity to finally implement his intention to leave. From this perspective, we can say that not only are the audience's reactions an organic component of the performance, but sometimes they can also shape how intentions are developed and discharged in the communication process.

Intention in intercultural communication versus intention in interpersonal communication

The second research question asked how the negotiation of intention in intercultural communication is similar to or different from that in interpersonal interactions. As discussed earlier, intention examined in intercultural communication does demonstrate similarities with intention in interpersonal communication, in that a speaker's intention can be indeterminate enough to be shaped by what his interlocutors say and do and that the development of the speaker's intention should be viewed as a negotiated process. However, the negotiation of the intention in intercultural communication takes on a different character, such that it can turn into a lopsided process with the CFL learners and the Chinese native speakers shouldering different weight while negotiating. A salient example is the host's employment of the formulaic expression 招呼不周 ('not treating the guest completely') to apologize for their failure to attend to the guest's needs as a leverage to negotiate their competency as a host. Due to the uneven linguistic and cultural knowledge between the L2 learners and the native speakers, the seemingly balanced negotiation process came to a sudden halt at this point as a result of the lack of appropriate coping mechanism. Another example is where the Chinese audience teased Kyle's relationship with Qi by calling Qi's mom Kyle's future mother-in-law (67 and 73). Audience reaction was sharply differentiated: Chinese L1 speakers laughed and clapped while the CFL learners showed no response. Both instances directly shaped the course of the negotiation of the guest's intention, with the former causing the guest's failure to successfully discharge his intention and the latter facilitating the implementation of his intention to leave. Both examples, whether it is to highlight one's incompetence to demonstrate the host's hospitality or to poke fun at the relationship between the two friends of the opposite sex, point to the different weight that the CFL learners and the Chinese native speakers shoulder in the negotiation process due to their uneven linguistic and cultural abilities. For this reason, the negotiation process in intercultural communication sometimes becomes lopsided. Previous research highlighted the uneven linguistic ability of the conversation participants in steering the course of the interaction (Al-Gahtani & Roever, 2012; Hassall, 2019). This chapter illuminated that the uneven cultural knowledge and ability can also play a part in shaping how the negotiation of the speaker's intention unfolds.

Limitations, future research and pedagogical implications

There are two major limitations of using learners' performances and classroom data. First, although students' performances, or open role-plays, are arguably the closest to what we might expect to reflect naturally occurring events (Houck & Gass, 1996), the extent to which they can actually mirror real-life encounters is still uncertain. In the metacommunication section, the Chinese native speakers revealed that they viewed the class as an opportunity for the CFL learners to practice Chinese and to taste the "authentic" Chinese flavor. Therefore, they went all-out to make sure that they would provide "authentic" performances in such situations, when in real life they wouldn't have pushed the learner that hard. In other words, performing in an instructional context doesn't involve the same stakes that real-world communication usually involves (Bardovi-Harlig, 2010). Second, while it can be helpful to have audience in the classroom to offer feedback and comments from a pedagogical perspective, audience can be a confound in the performance because actors can recipient-design their behaviors to a third party (Hassall, 2019; Taguchi & Roever, 2017). Taguchi and Roever (2017) stated that "participants orient to two situations: the situation stimulated in the role-play, and the role-play as a situation itself" and that "being aware of being viewed, analyzed, and assessed leads role-play participants to recipient-design their behavior to the extraneous third party as well as to the interlocutor" (p. 90). In this performance, we can clearly see the interplay between the situation stimulated in the performance (guesting in someone's house) and the students' performance as a situation (a classroom segment involving different groups of students playing multiple roles). Therefore, recipient-design of the actors' behaviors to the third party as well as to one another is salient. Admittedly, while such recipient-design of one's behaviors to a third party is inevitable in naturally occurring events, it is necessary to recognize the different roles the audience plays in a classroom performance versus in real-life situations as well as the varied stakes at hand.

Due to these two limitations, caution needs to be taken to interpret the results and generalize the findings. For future research, it is recommended that natural data in similar situations be collected to examine to what extent students' performance approximates naturally occurring events. It would also be interesting to investigate the role of the audience in the negotiation of intention in both interpersonal and intercultural communicative situations.

This chapter detailed how intention was negotiated in an enactment of intercultural performance in the classroom setting and what factors could potentially condition this negotiation process. Attention was drawn to the cultural knowledge that learners should possess in order to facilitate the negotiation of intention. In light of this finding, it is suggested that learners be instructed on how to build a common ground with native speakers—linguistically, personally and culturally—to facilitate the negotiation of intention in intercultural communicative situations.

References

Agar, M. (2013). *The lively science: Remodeling human social research*. Minneapolis, MN: Mill City Press.

Al-Gahtani, S., & Roever, C. (2012). Role-playing L2 requests: Head acts and sequential organization. *Applied Linguistics, 33*(1), 42–65.

Ames, D. R., Knowles, E. D., Morris, M. W., Kalish, C. W., Rosati, A. D., & Gopnik, A. (2001). The social folk theorist: Insights from social and cultural psychology on the content and contexts of folk theorizing. In B. F. Malle, L. J. Moses, & D. A. Baldwin (Eds.), *Intentions and intentionality: Foundations of social cognition* (pp. 307–329). Cambridge, MA: MIT Press.

Austin, J. L. (1962). *How to do things with words*. Oxford: Oxford University Press.

Bailey, B. (2004). Misunderstanding. In A. Duranti (Ed.), *A companion to linguistic anthropology* (pp. 395–413). Oxford: Blackwell.

Bardovi-Harlig, K. (2010). Exploring the pragmatics of interlanguage pragmatics: Definition by design. In A. Trosborg (Ed.), *Pragmatics across language and cultures* (pp. 219–259). Berlin: De Gruyter Mouton.

Bloome, D., Carter, S. P., Christian, B. M., Otto, S., & Shuart-Faris, N. (2005). *Discourse analysis & the study of classroom language & literacy events: A microethnographic perspective*. Mahwah, NJ: Erlbaum Associates.

Bloome, D., & Egan-Robertson, A. (1993). The social construction of intertextuality in classroom reading and writing lessons. *Reading Research Quarterly*, 305–333.

Bowe, H., & Martin, K. (2007). *Communication across cultures: Mutual understanding in a global world*. Cambridge: Cambridge University Press.

Bratman, M. (1987). *Intention, plans, and practical reason*. Cambridge, MA: Harvard University Press.

Chick, J. K. (1990). The interactional accomplishment of discrimination in South Africa. In D. Carbaugh (Ed.), *Cultural communication and intercultural contact* (pp. 225–252). Hillsdale, NJ: Lawrence Erlbaum.

Clark, H. H. (1996a). Communities, commonalities, and communication. In J. J. Gumperz & S. C. Levinson (Eds.), *Studies in the social and cultural foundations of language, No. 17. Rethinking linguistic relativity* (pp. 324–355). Cambridge: Cambridge University Press.

Clark, H. H. (1996b). *Using language*. Cambridge: Cambridge University Press.

Clark, H. H. (1997). Dogmas of understanding. *Discourse Processes, 23*(3), 567–598.

Cohen, A. (1996). Investigating the production of speech act sets. In S. Gass & J. Neu (Eds.), *Speech acts across cultures: Challenges to communication in a second language* (pp. 21–43). Berlin: Mouton de Gruyter.

Du Bois, J. W., Schuetze-Coburn, S., Cumming, S., & Paolino, D. (1993). Outline of discourse transcription. In J. A. Edwards & M. D. Lampert (Eds.), *Talking data: Transcription and coding in discourse research* (pp. 45–87). Hillsdale, NY: Lawrence Erlbaum.

Duranti, A. (2015). *The anthropology of intentions*. Cambridge: Cambridge University Press.

Félix-Brasdefer, J. C. (2007). Natural speech vs. elicited data: A comparison of natural and role play requests in Mexican Spanish. *Spanish in Context, 4*(2), 159–185.

Félix-Brasdefer, J. C. (2018). Roleplay. In A. Jucker, K. Schneider, & W. Bublitz (Eds.), *Methods in pragmatics, series: Handbooks of pragmatics* (Vol. 10, pp. 305–334). Berlin: De Gruyter Mouton.

Gibbs, R. W. (1999). *Intentions in the experience of meaning*. Cambridge: Cambridge University Press.

Gibbs, R. W. (2001). Intentions as emergent products of social interactions. In B. F. Malle, L. J. Moses, & D. A. Baldwin (Eds.), *Intentions and intentionality: Foundations of social cognition* (pp. 105–122). Cambridge, MA: MIT Press.

Green, J. L., & Wallat, C. (1981). Mapping instructional conversations: A sociolinguistic ethnography. In J. L. Green & C. Wallat (Eds.), *Ethnography and language in educational settings* (pp. 161–205). Norwood, NJ: Ablex.

Grice, H. P. (1957). Meaning. *Philosophical Review*, 377–388.

Gumperz, J. J. (1982). *Discourse strategies*. Cambridge: Cambridge University Press.

Hall, J. K. (1999). A prosaics of interaction: The development of interactional competence in another language. In E. Hinkel (Ed.), *Culture in second language teaching and learning* (pp. 137–151). Cambridge: Cambridge University Press.

Hassall, T. (2019). Preference structure in request sequences: What about role-play? *Journal of Pragmatics*, *155*, 321–333.

Haugh, M. (2007). The co-constitution of politeness implicature in conversation. *Journal of Pragmatics*, *39*(1), 84–110.

Haugh, M. (2008a). Intention in pragmatics. *Intercultural Pragmatics*, *5*(2), 99–110.

Haugh, M. (2008b). The place of intention in the interactional achievement of implicature. In I. Kecskes & J. Mey (Eds.), *Intention, common ground and the egocentric speaker-hearer* (pp. 45–86). Berlin: Mouton de Gruyter.

Houck, N., & Gass, S. (1996). Non-native refusals: A methodological perspective. In S. Gass & J. Neu (Eds.), *Speech acts across cultures: Challenges to communication in a second language* (pp. 45–63). Berlin: Mouton de Gruyter.

Johnstone, B., Andrus, J., & Danielson, A. E. (2006). Mobility, indexicality, and the enregisterment of "Pittsburghese." *Journal of English Linguistics*, *34*(2), 77–104.

Kasper, G., & Rose, K. R. (2002). *Pragmatic development in a second language*. Oxford: Blackwell.

Kecskes, I. (2010). The paradox of communication: Socio-cognitive approach to pragmatics. *Pragmatics and Society*, *1*(1), 50–73.

Kecskes, I. (2014). *Intercultural pragmatics*. Oxford: Oxford University Press.

Mu, B. (2018). *Co-constructing intentions across cultures: Reframing CFL learners' communication in Chinese*. Doctoral dissertation, The Ohio State University, Columbus. Retrieved from https://etd.ohiolink.edu/

Scollon, R., & Scollon, S. W. (1995). *Intercultural communication: A discourse approach*. Cambridge, MA: Basil Blackwell.

Searle, J. R. (1983). *Intentionality: An essay in the philosophy of mind*. Cambridge: Cambridge University Press.

Sinha, C. (2017). From signal to symbol to system: The emergence of language. In *Ten lectures on language, culture and mind* (pp. 48–71). Leiden: Brill.

Taguchi, N., & Roever, C. (2017). *Second language pragmatics*. Oxford: Oxford University Press.

Ting-Toomey, S. (1999). *Communicating across cultures*. New York: Guilford Press.

van Dijk, T. A. (2008). *Discourse and context: A sociocognitive approach*. Cambridge: Cambridge University Press.

Walker, G. (2000). Performed culture: Learning to participate in another culture. In R. D. Lambert & E. Shohamy (Eds.), *Language policy and pedagogy: Essays in honor of A. Ronald Walton* (pp. 221–236). Philadelphia, PA: J. Benjamins.

Walker, G., & Noda, M. (2000). Remembering the future: Compiling knowledge of another culture. *Reflecting on the Past to Shape the Future*, 187–212.

APPENDICES

Appendix 3.1 Transcription symbols

Symbol	Representation
——	stress
=	elongation
↑	rising intonation
XXX	undecipherable
[	simultaneous talk
<HI HI>	higher pitch
<LO LO>	lowered pitch
<L L>	slow speech
<A A>	rapid speed
<P P>	soft
..	short pause
...	long pause
△△	greatly increased volume
(non-verbal behaviors)	extralinguistic features
1, 2, 3	line number

Appendix 3.2 Context setup

1 春: 我们的场景设置	1 Chun: our context setup
2 琦: (手伸向Kyle) 他是我同学	2 Qi: (hands extending to Kyle) he is my classmate
3 (手伸向春) 她是我妈妈	3 (hands extending to Chun) she is my mom
4 中国同学: 哦	4 Chinese classmates: oh
5 春: (点头) 非常非常热情的 (大家笑)	5 Chun (nodding): very very hospitable (everyone laughs)
6 琦: 做菜做得很好的妈妈 (Kyle深吸一口气)	6 Qi: mom who cooks very well (Kyle takes a deep breath)
7 琦: 然后他来我家做客	7 Qi: then he comes to my house as a guest

Appendix 3.3 Metapragmatic comments

1 老师: 妈妈做得很好	1 Instructor: mom did great
2 以后 ... 以后去家里吃饭之前先小心点, 打听一下妈妈是什么样的人	2 in the future ... in the future before going home for dinner, be careful, find out what kind of person mom is
3 妈妈做得很好, 就是就是这样	3 mom did great, just just like this
4 那如果说..你处于Kyle这种情况怎么办?	4 then if .. you are in Kyle's position, what do you do?
5 敏: <u>真</u>的不用客气 [我就要拎东西走]	5 Min: <u>really</u> no need to be polite [I just take the stuff to go]

(Continued)

(Continued)

6 春: [我觉得我觉得你一定要]强调原因，而不是说"实在对不起, 实在不好意思"	6 Chun: [I think I think you must] emphasize the reason rather than saying "really sorry, really sorry"
7 "实在不好意思我要走" 我觉得这个话一一次两次就可以了	7 "really sorry I need to go" I think this sentence is enough once or twice
8 一定要强调原因=	8 you must emphasize the reason=
9 因为对中国人来讲	9 because to a Chinese
10 他其实[更看重你为什么要走]	10 he actually [cares more about why you need to go]
11 Kyle (点头): [Oh yeah]	11 Kyle (nodding): [oh yeah]
12 春: 把原因说出来	12 Chun: say out the reason
13 老师: 是的	13 Instructor: yes
14 所以刚才说了你要走想好一个借口, 这个借口这个事情要说	14 So just now said you need to *go*, think of an excuse, this excuse this thing you need to say
15 她妈妈不会跟到学校, 明天到学校看看你是不是真的考试	15 her mom won't follow you to school, tomorrow to school to see if you really have a test
16 她不会的	16 she wouldn't
17 但是你说不说一个事, 让她感觉不一样	17 but whether you say a thing or not makes her feel differently
18 因为你光说"我就是要走就是要走"那不行	18 because you can't just say "I need to go I need to go"
19 要说一个事, 要考试要准备	19 you need to say a thing, you have a test you need to prepare
20 就把这个事情说就是了	20 just say this thing
21 你可以反复要说	21 you can say it repeatedly
22 梅: 态度上要诚恳坚决	22 Mei: be sincere and resolute in attitude
23 像Nick刚才就说得很好	23 like Nick just said it very well
24 敏: 他眼泪都快下来了	24 Min: his tears were about to fall
25 老师: 他是足够的诚恳, 不够坚决	25 Instructor: he is sincere enough, not resolute enough
26 春: 他有点吃了再吃点就可以再吃点	26 Chun: he is a little like eat a little more after eating, then he can eat a little more
27 Kyle: 我们练习的时候	27 Kyle: when we practiced
28 我先说了我的借口	28 I first said my excuse
29 说我明天要考试得走了	29 saying I have a test tomorrow and I need to go
30 然后她说"我还在厨房里还有点水果, 还有一个菜"	30 then she said "I still have fruit in the kitchen and a dish"
31 然后我就没办法, 我真的, 我真的需要再留一会	31 then I have no way, I really, I really need to stay a while
32 所以我留了一会	32 so I stayed a while
33 过了半个小时好我再试一试	33 after half an hour, good, I will try again

34 然后我们想的办法是说这个留学生宿舍快要关门	34 then we thought of a way to say that this overseas students' dorm will close soon
35 几点说话你..你可以改	35 which o'clock you..you can change
36 琦: 对, 可以改	36 Qi: yes, you can change
37 春: 我们只是就是希望他能够提供一个更多的锻炼口语的机会	37 Chun: we just hope he can be provided with more opportunity to practice speaking
38 但实际上在现实生活中你说你要考试的话, 作为家长她不会是这样的	38 but in reality in real life if you say you have a test, as a parent she wouldn't be like this
39 老师: 考考考试是个好借口, 关门更好借口	39 Instructor: test is a good excuse, dorm close an even better excuse
40 现在还关不关门就是?	40 now does the dorm close or?
41 Kyle: 不会	41 Kyle: no
42 都有卡	42 there is card
43 老师: 以前关门的, 现在不关门了	43 Instructor: before the dorm would close, now not any more
44 梅: 以前可以翻围墙 (中国人笑)	44 Mei: before you can climb the fence (Chinese people laugh)

4 Striving for the Third Space

An American professional's experiences in Chinese workplaces

Zhini Zeng

Introduction

Given the fast-growing global economy, there is an increasing demand for linguistically and interculturally competent professionals across a range of governmental and non-governmental enterprises. This need is reflected in the *World-Readiness Standards for Learning Languages* (2015), which confirm that foreign language education must prepare students to use the language "to function in academic and career-related situations" that require them to use language proficiently to address content across a range of disciplines. However, Kramsch (2014) pointed out that the disciplinary connections that are envisioned by the standards "did not get realized at the college level." Moreover, while the growing efforts to prepare future members of the international work force have been described and documented (Brecht et al., 2013; Damari et al., 2017; de Sam, Dougan, Gordon, Puaschunder, & St. Clair, 2008; Malone & Rivers, 2013; Mansilla & Jackson, 2011; Rivers & Brecht, 2018), relatively little is known about learners' post-program professional experiences.

This case study investigated one American student's post-graduation experiences working in China through the theoretical lens of the "Third Space" to conceptualize the observed cross-cultural interactions in Chinese workplaces. The findings revealed distinct yet consistently emerging instances in which the subject used the Chinese language in unconventional ways to negotiate meaning. By examining the rich detail of this meaning-negotiation process, the case study demonstrates how the subject appropriated the target language for his own use and constructed through discourse a cultural reality that differed from that of native speakers. On the one hand, the findings echo Kramsch (2009)'s description of a multilingual subject, who is "defined by the linguistic and discursive boundaries it abides by in order to, now and then, transgress them" (p. 185). On the other hand, the inclusion of evaluations of the foreign professional's performances by his native Chinese counterparts also brought to light the nuances in expectations regarding global talent within the evolving international business landscape. Native speakers' criticisms of the American professional's unconventional use of Chinese challenged the idealistic expectation that multilingual subjects can pass as "native speakers" or use "native-like" language to communicate idiosyncratic meanings. Instead, this study provides insights into an effective and desirable "Third-Space" persona which will better prepare multilingual professionals for the complexities of an unpredictable global world.

Literature review

In recent years, a paradigm shift has challenged the traditional view of languages as composed of phonetics, grammar and vocabulary; this shift has led to a greater understanding about the processes and patterns of diversification (Blommaert & Rampton, 2011) and has generated a new understanding of "what it means to mean" across languages and cultures. This view of language in society has yielded new conceptualizations, such as "Third Space" and "symbolic competence."

The concept of Third Space—explored under various names in various social science disciplines including cultural studies (Bhabha, 1994), literacy education (Gutierrez, Baquedano-Lopez, & Tejeda, 1999; Kostogriz, 2002), philosophy and literary criticism (Bakhtin, 1981) and foreign language education (Kramsch, 1993)—refers to a space that is located between dualities, an arena of dialogue, hybridity, exploration and invention. Based on the semiotic theory (Barthes, 1977; Peirce, 1898/1955), the concept of Third Space has an important antecedent known as "thirdness." According to semiologists, including Peirce, a sign not only has an object to which it is related but can also evoke in the mind of its interpreter another sign, which Peirce called "the interpretant." This triad of sign, object and interpretant, captured under the term "thirdness," provides useful insights into how meaning emerges from forms. Despite being conventional in nature, language can trigger quite specific interpretants for both the users and the receivers. This becomes more obvious in a heterogeneous environment bolstered by globalization, where language is used as a system of symbolic forms not only to represent the shared social reality of a speech community but also to evoke subjective resonances in the minds of its recipients.

Similar to Peirce's focus on the relationality of sign and meaning, literary theorist Bakhtin's (1981) "thirdness" stressed the relationality of Self and Other, capturing the triadic relationship among a Self, an Other, and a remembered/anticipated Self and Other. He defined this triadic interaction as a "dialogue." According to Bakhtin, language is never neutral or impersonal; rather, it always exists between oneself and the other. Bakhtin's theory has become a critical incentive allowing foreign language learners to free themselves from the very limited ways in which words are traditionally used to signify intention. It also has inspired educational linguists, such as Kramsch (2009), to propose an ecological view of language education as a tool to analyze how language users construct through discourse the social and cultural reality that in turn constructs them.

Post-structuralist scholars, such as Bhabha and Kramsch, focused on the rights of the learners whose base language and culture are less symbolically powerful, such as immigrants in the United States. Chinese pedagogy scholars Walker (2015) and Walker and Jian (2016) conceptualized the Third Space as the optimal social milieu in which Chinese language learners can achieve their professional goals through negotiating meanings and intentions with native speakers of the target culture. However, they approached this concept with a different emphasis than the post-structuralists. Instead of perceiving it as a place "of tactical subversion" where the learners "construct our space within and against their place," Walker and Jian emphasized that a Third Space must be co-constructed by people from the base culture (C1) and the target culture (C2) by recognizing their shared goals, which will benefit both groups. Therefore, negotiating a Third Space means negotiating what the language learner chooses to be in the specified context while meeting the expectations of the Chinese organization(s) for which they work. It is important to examine this role reversal because Chinese language learners who are studying and working in China are placed in a position in which their base language and culture either actually are, or are assumed to be, more powerful than the target language and culture (McAloon, 2008; Jian, 2018). Although the current study owes a great deal to the post-structuralists' desire to eschew dichotomizing and essentializing tendencies regarding language education, the subversive potential of the Third Space cannot be smoothly transplanted to the field of Chinese pedagogy.

Multilingual subjects and symbolic competence

The concept of Third Space has been theorized and applied to foreign language education, leading to a critical re-examination of the traditional native speaker (NS)/non-native speaker (NNS) dichotomy that used to greatly influence perceptions of program and learner goals and outcomes (Kramsch, 2014). By eschewing the ideal embodied in the traditional conceptualization of the NS, Kramsch (2009) exhorted teachers and learners not to abandon their unique multilingual perspectives on the foreign language and forcefully defended the right of non-native speakers to "appropriate" the target language for themselves and give it meanings that might be very different from those of native speakers. These inclinations have provided both background and incentive for the current discussion, particularly because the communicative situations in which global professionals currently engage are not necessarily amenable to straightforward exchange of information and opinions in a concise and sincere manner. Instead, these exchanges have become inordinately more sophisticated, always requiring the participants to persistently and subtly negotiate intended meanings not only through verbal expressions but also non-verbal forms of communication and even silence (Kramsch, 2009; Blommaert, 2005). In order to produce speech that is not only to be understood but also to be listened to and recognized as acceptable, as Pierre Bourdieu (1991, p. 55) has warned us, "Social acceptability is not reducible to mere grammaticality."

Therefore, social actors in today's global business landscape must have more than just communicative competence; they must have knowledge of various linguistic codes and the subjective resonances of these codes. Kramsch (2006) and Kramsch and Whiteside (2008) defined such ability as "symbolic competence," which involves the ability to "play with various linguistic codes and with the various spatial and temporal resonances of these codes" (Kramsch & Whiteside, 2008, p. 664) to "create alternative realities and reframe the balance of symbolic power" (p. 666). Due to its acceptance by scholars such as Kramsch, "symbolic competence" has been adopted as a framework in several studies to illuminate how multilingual and multicultural subjects use languages. A handful of these researchers have utilized the ethnographic method and discourse analysis, which have also greatly inspired the current study and will be reviewed in detail in this chapter. In addition, a number of scholars who had been attracted by this concept proposed by Kramsch also started looking for various ways to put the concept in practice in the classroom. Included among these endeavors have been efforts to expand language instructors' understanding of language learning and attitudes toward language, culture and learning (Scarino, 2014), to assess instructional approaches that include a film-based pedagogical activity "semiotic gap" to help students explore their cultural imagination and subjectivities (Étienne & Vanbaelen, 2017), and to train students to embrace the ambiguity and to become aware of boundaries between languages, contexts and speakers (Richardson, 2017).

Intercultural performances in globalized working spaces and other global settings

The paradigm shift brought up by the early work of sociolinguistic scholars such as Rampton (1990, 1995) and Blommaert (2005, 2010) has created avenues for conducting research on culturally diverse subjects in naturalistic settings outside the classroom. Kramsch and Whiteside's (2008) study of multilingual interactions among immigrants in San Francisco vividly illustrated the significance of "symbolic competence" by demonstrating how the use of different codes can evoke various cultural memories and with them, social symbolic power.

Following Kramsch and Whiteside, Back (2013) also utilized the case study method and discourse analysis to explore a Spanish speaker's attempt to claim and practice his second language (Quichua) by "performing a series of contextual symbolic competences" (p. 393). However, the target community to which he attempted to become a part was resistant to his efforts, which "eventually led to his marginalization" (p. 393). Both works have provided methods for coping with the difficulties of analyzing abstract concepts such as competence by demonstrating how an effective analysis of symbolic performances can reveal the complications of embracing or resisting certain types of symbolic competence. The definition of *performance,* which is discussed in this study and aligns with these previous studies, is perceived to be beyond Chomsky's original conception. According to Walker (2010), performances are enactments of scripts or behaviors that are situated at a specified time and place with particular roles and audiences. As Turner (1991) explained,

> Performance does not necessarily have the structuralist implication of manifesting form, but rather the procedural sense of "bringing to completion" or "accomplishing." To perform is thus to complete a more or less involved process rather than to do a single deed or act.
>
> (p. 101)

Therefore, the professional performances observed in the current study, although not artistic in nature, also convey an aesthetic aspect not unlike a performance on stage. Similar to a dramatic actor "who earns admiration by braving the boundaries of his art," the foreign student who dares to perform in a foreign language and embrace a new culture is engaging in "no less a risky business, no less a matter of flirting with failure" (Walker, 2010, p. 8).

Despite the burgeoning role of foreign professionals in globalized industry, very little is known about their adventures abroad, dancing on the boundary between the two cultures. Not surprisingly, there are many obstacles to obtaining empirical data from real professional settings, such as the concerns about the confidentiality of sensitive business matters and interference with work productivity (Zeng, 2015). However, a careful review of the very limited body of available research offers a glimpse into rarely accessed globalized working spaces.

First, despite the paucity of empirical data, there still exists a concerted effort to document the experiences of foreign professionals' practices in the target professional community to discover the challenges they have encountered. He and Qin (2017) and Wu (2017) explored Chinese language learners' internship experiences in Chinese workplaces and revealed insightful findings about the challenges these students encountered. These included language and cultural barriers (Wu, 2017; He & Qin, 2017), a lack of knowledge and experience of a specific domain, such as sales (Wu, 2017), and a mismatch between the American students' expectations about the internship and the host organization's expectation about them (He & Qin, 2017). These preliminary findings have highlighted the importance of going beyond classroom practices to conduct further studies into different types of authentic settings, especially in the workplace. Moreover, both studies proposed incorporating learners' critical reflections, either through written or oral journals, into the program to enhance their internship experiences. For this reason, the current study adopted the stimulated recall (SR) approach to elicit the subject's opinions regarding his linguistic performances at work. However, these two studies differ significantly from the current study. These scholars utilized controlled tests, self-assessment and mentor assessment to determine students' gains rather than focusing on their practical language use at work.

In many ways, Moody's (2017) study filled the research gap in bringing in empirical data about workplace interactions of American interns in Japanese companies, for example, and uncovered the complex conflict between the interns' effort to establish a sense of belonging and the reality of being positioned as outsiders in terms of the institution's actual needs. Their attempts to act in ideologically native-like ways, demonstrated in their use of Japanese honorifics, was constantly denied by the members of the target culture, as their Japanese co-workers expected them to hold on to their "foreign features" rather than seek to assimilate. In addition to using honorifics in a conventional way to demonstrate conformity and knowledge of the culture, the American interns were also able to utilize addressee honorifics in a creative way to index "aggressive, ironic, and playful" stances (Moody, 2017, p. 21).

While Moody narrowly focused on addressee honorifics, McAloon (2008, 2015) sought to describe what advanced-level, non-native speakers of Chinese were able to accomplish in Chinese within a professional setting by shadowing five English speakers (four American and one English) and also interviewing their Chinese colleagues about their work performances. McAloon found that the NNS demonstrated domain knowledge, understanding of Chinese culture and the ability to avoid conflict in a culturally appropriate way. However, findings from the native speakers' quantitative evaluations also showed that the non-native speakers' performances were perceived and evaluated quite differently on the students' self-evaluations and by their domain peers.

In addition to these two studies focusing on professional experiences in a natural setting, Leaver and Atwell's (2002) retrospective interview-based report of the Interagency Language Roundtable (ILR) scale level 4 learners' personal and professional lives also provided valuable side notes to what may occur in the Third Space. They argued that the ability to express one's own personality and emotional states in culturally appropriate ways is a vital new component of communicative competence. It was at ILR level 4 that they observed the occurrence of the elision of the learner' personality in C1 and in C2. Beyond negotiation of meaning, advanced learners were able to use words, gestures and behaviors in telic ways.

Collectively, these studies offer valuable insights into the type of interactions that take place within the Third Space. In particular, the post-modernist view, which is endorsed by such scholars as Kramsch (2009, 2014), Kramsch and Whiteside (2008) and Back (2013), has kindled interest in further exploring the analytical richness inherent in the theory of the Third Space. At the same time, an alternative perception of this concept, which has been proposed by pioneering scholars of Chinese pedagogy, also suggested that current study cautiously accept the Third-Space framework and obtain more in-depth observation of Chinese learners. Finally, a handful of scholars, reviewed earlier (Wu, 2017; Moody, 2017; Back, 2013; McAloon, 2008; Kramsch & Whiteside, 2008), have adopted ethnographic methods and discourse analysis to study the real-world language used in naturalistic settings, which has informed the research methods utilized in this study. Drawing on these previous studies and motivated by the goal of making more well-informed decisions about the most fruitful ways to prepare our learners for participation in such complex interactions—in particular, to take advantage of the analytical richness inherent in the theory of Third Space—first-person data about the strategies a foreign professional should deploy and what native expectations he/she will need to deal with are required.

To that end, this case study focused on one foreigner's experiences in a globalized workplace and sought to demonstrate the ways in which foreign professionals challenge, reappropriate and resignify the conventional use of language in the process of communication to achieve their own communicative goals. The study addressed the following questions: (1) How does the foreign professional discursively carve out an in-between Third Space in which the same signs are "appropriated, translated, rehistoricized and read anew"? (Bhabha, 1994, p. 37).

(2) How do the foreign professional's Chinese counterparts perceive or evaluate the professional's discursive behavior in the Third Space?

Methods

Study design

Similar to the previous studies of intercultural interactions in natural settings reviewed earlier, this study utilized ethnographic and case study approaches to facilitate its revelatory nature (Yin, 2014). Given the difficulty of finding suitable participants, as revealed in previous studies (McAloon, 2008; Zeng, 2015), the single-case research design was chosen to illustrate the complexities of real-life situations that are beyond the scope of controlled methods. Despite the fact that such a design may reduce the generalizability of the findings, focusing on one participant in a case study approach allowed the researcher to include rich construct, deep descriptions, and personal accounts. This in-depth examination of the workplace of one professional who was highly proficient in Chinese thus allows a glimpse into the nuances and complexities of meaning-making within unscripted interactions.

Participant

The subject, Alan (a pseudonym), began his Chinese learning experience with a two-month immersive independent study at the end of his sophomore year, in the summer of 2009. His Chinese martial arts teacher in the United States invited him to spend two months with a friend's family in the small town of Xiaoyi, in Shanxi, China, where he taught English and martial arts to the local students. With no formal Chinese language training and only an introductory textbook he had purchased from the university bookstore, he taught himself to communicate with the locals. After returning to college in the United States, Alan began officially taking Chinese classes and was placed directly into Chinese 103. Also, at this time, he was admitted to the Chinese language flagship cohort program at his college, a nationwide intensive program with the goal of developing professional-level proficiency. In the summer of 2010, Alan was admitted to a study-abroad program in Qingdao for two months, which included attending four hours of advanced Chinese classes every day and engaging in cultural activities and community service. He went back to the United States to finish his senior year and completed an independent study in Chinese classical and modern literatures. In the winter of 2011, he went to Nanjing University in China, where he completed a semester-long study-abroad program as a last requirement for graduating with a BA in Chinese.

Alan did not discover the world of visual arts until after graduating from college and moving to Beijing. In Alan's own words, his obsession with this field came about as a result of "a kind of fatigue with writing and language." He was so taken with art that he soon changed his original plan to become a novelist. According to Alan, pursuing Chinese language and culture while becoming an artist in China was "an intellectual, emotional and philosophical decision." After graduation, Alan did an two-month internship at the Ullens Center for Contemporary Art (UCCA), a well-known gallery in Beijing, after which he worked as a freelance English tutor and Chinese-to-English translator and periodically wrote a column for a fashion magazine. In the meantime, he studied for the graduate school entrance examination and applied to the MA program at the Central Academy of Fine Arts (CAFA), which launched an MA program for international students in 2008. After spending seven months in Beijing being tutored by a local art teacher to acquire basic painting skills and independently reading about the mainstream theories of art that were prevalent in the Chinese academic world, Alan was accepted to the CAFA in May 2012. During the same month, he received "Superior" on an official Oral Proficiency Interview (OPI) through the American Council on the Teaching of Foreign Languages (ACTFL)—three years after being thrown into Xiaoyi, Shanxi, with an introductory textbook.

His previous martial arts training sparked his interest in studying Chinese culture as a comprehensive system that included everything from food to physical culture, from medicine to visual arts. Moreover, born into a multicultural family, Alan said he experienced "the constant tension" between the American culture from his Italian American mother and the Middle Eastern culture from his Iranian father, which cultivated his strong desire to explore an alternative to the worldview into which he was born. He strenuously resisted a superficial fascination with Eastern culture, which he described as "Orientalism, whether in the form of Indian yoga, Chinese Zen or Japanese tea ceremonies," all of which were very common on the West Coast, where he grew up and went to college. Chinese art, especially calligraphy and ink painting, instead provided him with a rigorous and scholarly way to approach Chinese culture. Alan also attributed his fascination with Chinese art to his view of Chinese traditional culture as "his religion of life," which was again an alternative to his father's Muslim culture and his mother's Christian religion. He said he wished to "apply traditional Chinese culture to the contemporary realities of life as a scholar and artist."

After being admitted into the three-year MA program in Chinese painting at CAFA, Alan actively engaged in various types of domain-related practices including attending exhibitions as a student artist, routinely engaging in discussions of his art with peers and professors, writing art critiques for news outlets and providing professionally commissioned translation work. During the data collection period of this study, Alan also accepted a one-year part-time teaching position at the only secondary fine arts school affiliated with CAFA, where all interactions with students and fellow teachers, preparations of pedagogical materials and lectures on Chinese art and culture were conducted exclusively in Chinese. At the time of this study, Alan was in the last year of graduate school and had built a strong interpersonal network with well-known Chinese artists and scholars in his field.

Research context

Alan's profession-related activities operated in three major contexts, constituting multiple research sites for the current study. They included CAFA, the affiliated high school of CAFA and Today Art Museum, in which he set up his work for an exhibition.

CAFA

CAFA is the most prestigious and renowned art academy in China and is under the direct charge of the Ministry of Education of China. According to Alan's mentor, CAFA is one of the most selective schools in China and turns away more than 90% of its applicants each year. However, the requirements for international student applicants are much lower than for Chinese students due to the institution's strong desire to attract more foreign students. Alan's interaction with his peers and professors within CAFA was exclusively in Chinese.

CAFA high school

Closely tied to CAFA, the CAFA high school plays a unique role in preparing young artists at the secondary level. Being similarly selective, the majority of students in CAFA high school hope to continue their study in CAFA after four years. However, the group of students Alan taught was different. These students were recruited through a system that operated in the international section of the school, and, according to Alan, this sub-group of students was "far less competent" than the average student in the high school in both arts and other school subjects, and had lower learning motivation. None of the students planned to apply to CAFA after four years but rather planned to continue their study abroad, most likely in the United States or other European countries. Alan had 60 students in class. Except for one American-Chinese student who had just come back to China for high school, the rest of his students did not have any experience studying or living abroad. His classes, therefore, were taught completely in Chinese.

Today Art Museum

Alan's interaction at Today Art Museum was limited to one museum staff member, several student volunteers from CAFA and a few Chinese workers who worked there hanging paintings. As a private, non-governmental entity, the museum aims to promote Chinese contemporary art, which has also attracted many international artists and art exchanges. The museum staff member with whom Alan constantly interacted had two years' study-abroad experience in the United Kingdom. Their interactions were again exclusively in Chinese, occasionally involving some code-switching practices.

Procedures

By using data and method triangulation, this study aimed to enhance the credibility and validity of the findings from a single case study and to fully explain the richness and complexity of the observed behavior. The study made use of ethnographic observation at Chinese workplaces, stimulated recall (SR) tasks to explore the subject's concurrent thinking and open-ended interviews with both the subject and his Chinese counterparts. The ethnographic observation of the subject allowed a glimpse into the American professional's discursive practices in a natural working setting, in which the researcher shadowed the subject for four weeks, watching and documenting him at work in everyday settings. The shadowing consisted of formal observations involving video or audio recordings. The majority were non-participant observations with only one exception, which occurred at a post-exhibition banquet at which the presence of a non-participant at the event would have been socially inappropriate. However, participation in this particular event did not appear to affect the setting for language use in any significant way. The recording began whenever the subject entered a situation using Chinese to communicate and was stopped when the conversation ended or switched permanently to English. A professional performance portfolio was created, containing 11 performance samples. A detailed description of the content of these samples can be seen in Appendix 4.1.

SR was chosen rather than the think-aloud technique to elicit verbal accounts of the subject's thought processes during the recorded performances for three reasons. First, the latter is not suitable for use in situations in which the subject is expected to participate in many verbal interactions. Second, many scholars have verified their concerns about verbalizing one's "inner speech" during the concurrent performances as these verbalizations are often subject to judgment bias (Nisbett & Wilson, 1977). Third, choosing SR for this study may significantly benefit education/training as the recorded introspection portfolio can be used as an effective training method to help lower-level students learn by utilizing the strategies and comments of a more proficient learner. Following each recorded event, the researcher played back the video to the subject and asked him to recall what he had been thinking during the interaction. A list of SR interview questions can be found in Appendix 4.2. The SR data in this study complements the recorded interactions from the ethnographic observation and the interplay between the two data sources allowed topics and themes to be illuminated.

In addition, the researcher conducted open-ended interviews with both the American subject and six Chinese counterparts so as to contextualize the captured performances and to gain a holistic understanding of what the subject was able to achieve beyond the finite number of recorded samples. The six Chinese interviewees included two of Alan's classmates at CAFA, his art project collaborator and mentor, and three domain experts who were all experienced practitioners in both Chinese painting and art education. Although Alan's classmates in CAFA and his mentor had known him for approximately two and half years at the time of the interview, the other three domain experts were not acquainted with Alan in any way.

Among these six interviewees, Alan's mentor, Shao, was the only one who had any experience as an expatriate. He had studied and lived in New York for almost ten years while extensively traveling in Europe and South America. However, Alan's communication with Shao was exclusively in Chinese as he claimed that

Shao's English was not good enough to sustain in-depth conversation. None of the three domain experts demonstrated any level of proficiency in English and their only contact with foreigners had taken place when they traveled abroad. The other two CAFA graduate students, despite having scored high in the standardized English test on the Postgraduate Admission Test, admitted that they rarely conversed in English, although they had every opportunity to chat with the 200 international students who attend CAFA every year. Interviews were conducted individually, and each interviewee was asked to evaluate each one of Alan's performance samples. The general background of each Chinese evaluator can be seen in Appendix 4.3. A list of interview questions for the Chinese evaluators and Alan can be found in Appendices 4.4 and 4.5, respectively.

Data analysis

By examining the strategies which the subject used to negotiate his own meaning during work-related intercultural communication and how Chinese people who share a common domain expertise perceived his linguistic and behavioral practices, this study sought to provide "thick description and grounded interpretation" (Prior, 1995, p. 321) of interactions that took place in the Third Space within the workplace. For data analysis, the commonly used constant-comparative method was employed to develop categories and thematic patterns (Glaser, 1978; Strauss & Corbin, 1998). Recorded videos from the natural ethnographic observations, SR protocols and audio-recorded interviews were all transcribed, and each document was read in its entirety numerous times. The researcher then wrote down key words, phrases and notes on each section of each document, which became the groundwork for open coding. These tentatively coded units of data were then compared with subsequent units to identify recurring regularities. During the open-coding process, any unit of the data was compared across all data sources. For example, the recorded performances from the ethnographic observation served as the main set of data from which the subject's discourse features were first identified. The units of data in these recorded performances were then compared with those in the subject's SR narrative on that particular performance and the transcribed interview results to see if they corresponded to the identified characteristics.

After open coding, axial coding was applied until "categories are related to their subcategories to form more precise and complete explanations about phenomenon" (Strauss & Corbin, 1998, p. 124). For instance, while multiple examples supported the category "engage the subjective resonance with the linguistic code," in which Alan inflected certain conventional form in Chinese with personal or even idiosyncratic meaning, another category called "creatively index alternative symbolic meaning to exert subjectivity," in which Alan appropriated a commonly used expression in Chinese to index a different socio-cultural situation, was also established through open coding. These two categories were identified as mutually contributing to the overarching theme of "a foreign professional's unconventional use of language," as both involve Alan's attempt to creatively play with the language and appropriate the language for his own use.

Any emerging theme, with its categories, was then applied to the data again in an iterative, spiraling analysis so that further details could be identified and an overall theoretical understanding of the data could be achieved. Although the data were mainly coded by the researcher, a peer-debriefing process (Creswell, 2003) was used so as to enable a fellow researcher who had been skillfully using the constant-comparative method in her own studies to cross-check the coding and resulting data set.

Results

Alan's creativity in using Chinese

Alan's workplace interactions typically involved discussions and debates over various art-related topics with his co-workers. Excerpt 4.1 illustrates a representative encounter which occurred when Alan was setting up his ink-wash painting exhibition at the Today Art Museum. During this encounter, Alan creatively invented a phrase, *yingzao yige chang* (營造一個場, 'to create a field'), to communicate his idea of how to display a sculpture. He suggested removing the pedestal and allowing the artwork to naturally fit into the surroundings. Alan considered it outdated to have a sculpture sit on a pedestal in isolation from its surroundings. Alan was able to effectively communicate his perception of an ideal interaction between the sculpture and the other artwork, which should, in his thinking, work together to "create a field."

According to the lexical frequency patterns, the phrase "create a field" appeared three times (Excerpt 4.1, lines 1, 8 and 10) within this 40-second interaction. Such repetition and a rising intonation at the end of the last character indicated Alan's delight in creating and using this phrase. This satisfaction is also reflected in the SR interview, shown in Excerpt 4.2, in which Alan commented that this phrase, although unusual, "seems very appropriate." Alan's explanation of this collocation further revealed a metaphoric mapping onto the lexical item he used based on a blend of two types of analogies: The iconic analogy between the perceived shape of the traditional Chinese character *ying* (營, 'camp') and an imagined human community and the indexical analogy between the lexical item *chang* (場, 'field') as the translation of Foucault's term and the Western influence on Chinese contemporary art. Both analogies inspired Alan's unique linguistic choice, which signified rich personal and even idiosyncratic meanings, even though it might not be sanctioned by the dictionary or accepted by most Chinese native speakers.

Moreover, Alan understood the word *chang* (場, 'field') as both "Western," a part of Foucault's philosophy, and "Chinese," based on the two ideologically laden Chinese vocabularies with which he is familiar. Alan attempted to make a connection between these two words by cultivating an in-between cultural space where he was able to imbue the foreign sign with a new, blended meaning. He seemed especially satisfied about being able to explain this idea in Chinese to native speakers without relying on translation of English terms or jargon. This sentiment was also echoed in his criticism of a "very unquestioning and superficial appropriation

Excerpt 4.1 Offering suggestion to a colleague (40 seconds)

Setting: Alan participated in a discussion with a museum staff (Yu) and a student artist (Ko) on how to display Ko's sculpture work at the exhibition.

1 → Alan: 這個可以擺在地上，對不對？這個，也可以就是，把最小的掛在牆上。他的那個就是說，就是<u>形成一個場</u>。This can be put on the floor, right or not? This, can also just be, hang the smallest one on the wall. His (work), what I meant is, just <u>to form a field</u>.

2 Yu: 可能就是擺在地上就行，不用，不用展台。Perhaps just put them on the floor, don't use, don't use a pedestal.

3 Alan: 我覺得不用，最好不用展台。I think don't use, you'd better not use a pedestal.

4 Yu: 因為展台對你的作品是一個介入。Because the pedestal is an interference with your work.

5 Alan: 對，是一個介入。Yes, it is an interference.

6 Yu: 你的作品就不完整了。Your work will be incomplete.

7 Ko: 我們把它打開，把它打開。Let's open it, open it.

8 → Alan: 就是我覺得它，最好是能夠<u>營造一個場</u>。I just think, it, you had better find a way <u>to create a field</u>.

9 Yu: 對對對，他說的就是，對對對 . . . Yes, yes, yes, what he meant was, right, right, right . . .

10 → Alan: 就是<u>營造一個場</u>，因為這些雕塑都是非常傳統的，都是擺在那兒，擺在那兒。Just <u>to create a field</u>, because these sculptures are very traditionally (displayed), (they) were just left there, be left there.

11 Yu: 對，而且一個白色的展台也不好看啊……Yes, also, a white pedestal is not pretty either.

Excerpt 4.2 Alan's explanation for the phrase he created

SR Protocol 1, 7 minutes and 20 seconds

I was kind of 營造一個場 ('create a field'), you know, I was influenced by that idea. 營造 ('to create, to build') is my favorite word. It's so Chinese. I like the word 經營 ('to manage') and 營造. If you think about the Chinese character for "camp" (營), you know you are laying something down in your arrangement to build something you know. It's like the character for 營 ('camp'), with two "fires" (火) on the top and below is a 宮 ('palace'). I think it's a very beautiful symbol for human community. . . . The word 場 ('field'), I think I have encountered in Chinese before, especially when people have used translation. When people talk about Foucault, I think one of the word the translator uses is 在場 ('at the field, presence') or 不在場 ('not at the scene, absence'). It is kind of becoming popular in contemporary art in Beijing, like to describe the word presence. But also people say 場 like you know, 飯局啊 ('banquet'), 官場啊 ('official circle'), like it's a very Chinese idea. This field of people, this environment. But I love the word 營造 because it's also so important in Chinese painting and architecture. On one level, this idea of 在場 is translation of Western philosophy. But then by taking a native a word that is so native to the Chinese tradition of art, 營造, and putting the two together, for some reason, seems very appropriate. I think it really communicates one of the very important ideas that is inherited in the ritual of exhibition. And I think the exhibition is a very interesting modern ritual. I'd like to see how artists build that ritual to his audience.

of Western terms in translation without the foundation of Western philosophy and western tradition" in an earlier interview.

In addition to creating new phrases, Alan's unconventional use of language was also reflected in his repurposing a linguistic form to index a different sociocultural dimension that may be unfamiliar to Chinese native speakers. Excerpt 4.3 contains a conversation between Alan and a museum staff member about the design of the exhibition tags. Alan tried to persuade the staff member to adopt a particular layout suggested by administrative officials from CAFA, which did not meet the museum's requirements. Within the 90-second conversation, Alan used the unusual term of address *lingdao* ('leader') three times, which contrasted with the term *laoshi* ('teacher'), which is more commonly used in the context of a university. Among the variety of synonyms for "head of an institution," the particular expression *lingdao* is more often used in a political context, connoting the Chinese Communist ideology. The particular *lingdao* to which Alan referred, which he later confirmed during the SR interview, is indeed to reference the Party Committee Secretary of CAFA. However, according to the native speakers interviewed in this study, in order to downplay the hierarchical differences within the university context, *laoshi* is more widely used to address a professor, an administrative official or a staff member. Moreover, a Chinese colleague pointed out a mismatch between Alan's use of *lingdao*, indicating an in-group member within the university official system,[1] and his bold comment about the university official's unprofessional behavior (Excerpt 4.3, line 16).

Excerpt 4.3 Complaining about an order (90 seconds)

Setting: At Today Art Museum, Alan and his classmate Yu, are talking to an art museum staff Ko concerning the design of the exhibition tag.

1 Alan: 你覺得哪方面不行？顯得奇怪嗎？ What aspect do you think will not work? Does it appear strange to you?

2 Yu: 就是我會覺得……另外就是那個美術館是有這個規定。 Well, I would think.... Also because it is the rule of our museum.

3 Alan: 這個規定特別沒有餘地是麼？ So this rule does not have space (for negotiation)?

(Alan and Yu walk closer to the artwork on the wall and the museum staff Ko joins the discussion)

4 → Alan: 因為我們主要是個什麼考慮呢，就是說，要是太寬的話，太寬的話，就是這種寬度的話，作品之間顯得特別擠，但是我們這個<u>學校的領導(lingdao)</u>又要求我們一定要照片。 所以我們本來就像乾脆就這麼一個標簽，但是呢，那個展簽呢，<u>就領導(lingdao)說非得有照片了</u>，所以呢，我們只能就是說折中一下，就是這麼一個…… Well, you know, what we mainly are concerned about is whether it is too wide. I mean, if this is too wide, if it's too wide, I mean if we keep the current width, the artwork will appear too close to each other. But <u>our school official</u> required us to keep the photo (of the artist) there. So our original thought was also just having a tag like this, but, that tag, <u>our school official</u> said, must have a photo on it. So, we have to compromise, like this . . .

(*Continued*)

Excerpt 4.3 (Continued)

5 Ko:	相當於兩個展簽了？	Then this means two tags?
6 Alan:	對，就這樣。	Yes, just like this.
7 Ko:	放得下嗎，那麼多字？	Is there enough space for so many words?
8 Alan:	不，這個說明不要了。	No, so we will delete this part of introduction.
9 Ko:	說明不要了?	Delete it?
10 Alan:	不要了。	Delete it.
11 Ko:	這樣很怪的。你這上面放照片，下面放……這樣很怪的。要不然就把照片去掉，為什麼非要放照片呢？	This looks very odd. You put a photo on the top, and below it, you put . . . this is really weird. What about just getting rid of the photo. Why do you have to include a photo?
12 Alan:	我也不知道為什麼要放照片	I also do not know why we have to include a photo.
13 Ko:	為什麼要放照片呢？	Why include a photo?
14 → Alan:	我們也不懂，真的，<u>我們領導(lingdao)</u>說的。	We also don't understand, really, <u>our official said that</u>.
15 Ko:	我們做了那麼多展覽，沒有放照片的。	We had done many exhibitions but none of them had a photo on the tag.
16 → Alan:	<u>我也覺得很業餘搞的</u>，我告訴你。	Let me tell you this, <u>I also think it's very unprofessional</u>.

However, as Alan recalled, he intentionally chose the expression *lingdao* to emphasize the fact that he was forced to choose that particular design in deference to the school official. In response to the challenge raised by his Chinese colleague, he further defended his linguistic choice:

> (Interviewer: Do you think it is inappropriate for you to say your *lingdao* is unprofessional?) No, because we students all dislike *lingdao*. The *lingdao* refers to the Party Committee Secretary of CAFA. We students always think he knows nothing so students can always complain about him. When I mentioned *lingdao*, everyone understood what I was implying.[2]

Alan's comment revealed that he deliberately used the expression *lingdao* to reinforce his social identity as a student outsider instead of an in-group member of the official system, as the critic had assumed. In the SR interview, Alan's use of a newly coined Internet expression *tucao* ('to complain') to indicate that every student likes complaining about their *lingdao*, again reinforced his identity as a student. Although *lingdao* may index an inferior social stance with a strongly reverent tone in many other contexts, in this student exhibition, Alan repurposed the word *lingdao* to distance himself from the administration and show his allegiance to the students.

Native speakers' expectations of a global professional

However, even though Alan demonstrated quite advanced proficiency and followed all the linguistic and cultural conventions, his creative language play was challenged by the authority coming with the native speakership. However, this seemingly demanding expectation for linguistic conformity goes far beyond simply being "native-like," because Alan was also expected to retain some "foreign flavor," or to put it in a nicer way, to possess some "global qualities" that could benefit the organization for which he worked. Some representative cases illustrate the complexity of this situation.

On one hand, Alan's Chinese counterparts expected him to conform to the conventions of communication that reflect a deep adherence to Chinese cultural values, attitudes and traditions. For this reason, they interpreted the inventive form he used as a mistake made by a non-native speaker and were always ready to provide corrective feedback. They became significantly less tolerant when they recognized this creative language play as an attempt to challenge or to re-appropriate conventional expressions, such as *chengyu*,[3] "a unique composition of four characters that was frequently found in ancient Chinese historical records and literary works" (Zhang, 2016, p. 29). Such an observation is deeply rooted in the native speaker's perception of who is a legitimate user (or even a legitimate adapter) of these communicative conventions.

In fact, interviews with all six native speakers revealed an enthusiastically positive evaluation of Alan's Chinese proficiency in general, such as "He sounds no different than a native Chinese" ("聽上去和中國人沒什麼差別"), "I have nothing to say, just one word, wonderful" ("沒什麼可說的，一個字，棒") or "clear pronunciation, natural and appropriate speech" ("吐字清晰，自然得體"). However, the positive evaluations did not extend to the creative deviations they encountered in Alan's speech. For example, while half of the evaluators (three out of six) did not notice the creatively coined phrase *yingzao yige chang* ('to create a field'), the other three perceived it as "awkward" ("生造的"), "very raw and bitter (i.e., being awkward in Chinese)" ("很生涩") or "a somewhat problematic" ("有點問題的") expression. Two of them slightly changed their attitudes after hearing Alan's justification of his linguistic choice, admitting that the idea was "refreshing" ("新鮮"). However, the other evaluator continued to insist that Alan misunderstood the interplay between shape and meaning in the Chinese characters and claimed that his justification was merely "unilateral willingness" ("一廂情愿"). He even identified such behavior as a mistake that is typical among *laowai* ('the old outsider'), a common term to refer to foreigners in China.

In fact, such strict analysis of non-native speakers' use of conventional expressions in Chinese is sometimes manifested in an extreme way. One example can be seen in the criticism of Alan's use of the four-character idiom *gancuilisuo* ('crisp and straightforward'), a slightly different version of the more commonly used idioms *ganjinglisuo* ('neat and straightforward') or *gancuililuo* ('crisp and brisk'), for praising the design of an exhibition label. In fact, all the three collocations appear in Chinese dictionaries with very similar meanings, although the last two are more common than the one Alan used. However, three out of six Chinese evaluators explicitly marked this as "incorrect" as it "cannot be used to describe a design" ("不能形容设计") and "was mixed up" ("搞混了"). Ironically, one evaluator actually misheard the idiom Adam used as the more common version *gancuiliuo* ('crisp and brisk'), but she still marked it wrong and changed it to the other common version *ganjinglisuo* ('neat and straightforward').

However, despite this demand for conformity, there were occasions when native Chinese speakers appeared to be more lenient toward some special usage of Chinese when it was associated with features of foreignness. For instance, when Alan described the cold but clear weather in Beijing as *jīngshen* ('energetic'), no Chinese evaluators attempted to correct him despite the fact that this adjective is conventionally only used to in reference to a person. One of Alan's classmates was complimentary about his creativity by attributing this special linguistic usage to a typical "Westernized personality" ("西方人的性格") that is "liberal" ("自由") and "lively" ("活潑"). This simple example provides a glimpse into how a foreign identity can sometimes be used to one's advantage by emancipating the speaker from the shackles of linguistic convention.

In fact, such generosity was manifested more in the evaluation of the foreigner's unconventional behavior than in the assessment of his or her creative use of language, ranging from overlooking Alan's Americanized dining habits, such as eating a huge Subway sandwich in one sitting, to tolerating his bold challenge to the authority of university officials. For example, Alan's graduate school classmate commented in the interview that Alan's blunt manner when engaging in academic debate with a professor was a manifestation of his "American liberalism." Although this type of rebellious behavior was always considered to be culturally inappropriate, especially in the context of the devout master-disciple relationship at a university, his classmates still admired it.

It is also interesting that some of the native Chinese seemed to develop an antipathy towards Alan's exhaustive use of Chinese conventional expressions because they lacked the "foreign flavor" desired by his Chinese counterparts. The comment "He appears too Chinese" was no longer a compliment on the authenticity of his Chinese use but a lament over his losing an asset—his globalness. Criticism of this type further uncovered two layers of expectation regarding how a global professional should speak and how he or she should engage in his or her work.

First, the native Chinese interpreted Alan's excessive use of conventional expressions as incongruent with his foreign identity. In one interview, Alan's graduate school classmate frankly recalled the embarrassment of a group of Chinese students when Alan insisted on translating to modern Chinese an ancient hexagram text based on *Yijing*/*I-Ching* (or *Classic of Changes*), which was written in classical Chinese. Even though this Chinese interviewee admitted that Alan's ability to read and interpret classical Chinese was impressive and might be better than most ordinary Chinese citizens, such a performance still made the Chinese audience members uncomfortable as they felt they were "losing face" ("顏面掃地"). A more serious criticism emerged from a review that Alan wrote for an exhibition catalogue, in which he referred to himself as "a man grinding Chinese ink" ("研墨的人") and modestly admitted that he was "too young to understand the Confucian rituals" ("我年少不知禮") before he boldly evaluated the works of some senior artists. However, his attempt at modesty was not recognized by the Chinese evaluators. One domain insider considered such attempt as "pretentious"

("比較虛"), even though he repeatedly stressed that this was only his subjective and personal opinion. He continued to point out that the phrase "a man grinding Chinese ink" did not match his identity as a foreigner. In addition, the other evaluator questioned Alan's use of written literary expressions because his writing style was similar to the discourse of the Chinese literati, a group to which Alan obviously did not belong.

Moreover, as previously stated, the expectation for a global professional to be "not too Chinese" even goes beyond his or her linguistic performance. Based on the interviewees' evaluation of Alan's work-related video samples, it is clear that as a global professional, he was expected to act in a somewhat Westernized fashion which could be distinguished from that of his Chinese counterparts. Among the three domain fields in which he frequently performed, Alan received the lowest evaluations for his teaching at the CAFA high school. After watching Alan's teaching video, one domain-insider evaluator who also taught Chinese painting and calligraphy at a private middle school boldly questioned whether Alan was just hired as "window dressing" to make that department appear more "international," as its name *guojibu* (international section) indicates. When asked to elaborate on his reasons, this evaluator harshly commented that Alan's performance reminded him of a mundane Chinese grade school art teacher. He criticized Alan's demanding, and sometimes even discouraging, style of providing feedback to his young students. Although this method is common within the Chinese pedagogical paradigm, it contradicts the stereotype of a Western teacher, who is expected to be personable and encouraging. In fact, while Alan agreed with this assessment in his SR interview,[4] he expressed his disappointment over his teaching style and attributed the ineffectiveness to his attempt at reproducing a Chinese pedagogical paradigm. Although he chose to comply with the traditional Confucian paradigm—authoritarian master and devout disciple—to which he was exclusively exposed throughout his years learning Chinese, this form of imitation made him lose his "outsider status," which was seen as an asset in a globalized workspace.

Discussion

Drawing on data from multiple sources, this study explored the experiences of a foreign professional and focused specifically on his discursive performance in negotiating a Third Space at work with people from the target culture. Interviews with his Chinese counterparts revealed both their acceptance of and their resistance to his performance.

Alan's discursive performance in negotiating a Third Space at work

As discussed earlier, it is obvious that Alan had surpassed the stage of simply striving to approximate native speakers. On the contrary, it is clear that what he strived for was room for play, and using creativity, with the new language.

The abundant ingenuity in Alan's discursive performance seems to have originated from two sources. First, as an expert user of Chinese, Alan possessed a highly developed and flexible communicative repertoire. This not only consisted of a wide range of informal vocabulary and phrasing that was appropriate to his identity as a student, but it also included very formal expressions such as occupational jargon, literary allusions and formulaic expressions. Beyond the lexical level, he was also familiar with a variety of discourse genres and a wide range of conversational strategies, and he possessed a well-developed awareness of potential registers. Such a broad communicative repertoire allowed him to utilize these discourse features skillfully in various contexts to signify personal involvement, including individual identity and group membership, as well as to convey attitudes and emotions. Second, as a recognized professional in his particular field, Alan's creative exploration of meaning was also inspired by his expertise in art, or more specifically, in Chinese painting. His ability to creatively communicate his ideas about how to ideally display works in an art exhibition came from not only his extensive linguistic repertoire but also from a wide array of knowledge about his field, such as the conventions and trends of exhibition in both Chinese and American cultures and Foucault's philosophy of art. These two aspects went hand in hand to highlight Alan's flexibility to creatively use new linguistic forms to communicate his knowledge of art and his expertise as a user of Chinese.

Another salient motif that emerged from the data was Alan's ability to appropriate a linguistic term to creatively convey his own intentions. To theorize such discursive practices demonstrated by Alan, one might consider again Bakhtin's proposal that every utterance is a repurposing or resignification of other people's words:

> As a living, socio-ideological concrete thing, as heteroglot opinion, language, for the individual consciousness, lies on the borderline between oneself and the other. The word in language is half someone else's. It becomes "one's own" only when the speaker populates it with his own intention, his own accent, when he appropriates the word, adapting it to his own semantic and expressive intention.
> (Bakhtin, 1981, pp. 293–294)

It is clear that Alan had mastered the strategy of appropriating "the other's" language to signify his own intentions. The rich indexical knowledge displayed in his speech was at the core of his linguistic and cultural competence, which allowed him to take an active part in the ongoing process of constructing meaning within specific domain activities. Moreover, Alan's adept use of the term *lingdao* to emphasize his allegiance to his fellow graduate students and to distance himself from the official circle also indicated a certain amount of culturally appropriate irony and humor, which again accentuated his expertise in communicating in Chinese.

Chinese counterparts' perceptions of Alan's discursive and professional performance

In general, interviews with Alan's Chinese counterparts revealed a twofold high expectation for the discursive and professional behavior of a foreign professional. On the one hand, their challenge or sometimes outright rejection of Alan's discursive efforts at creativity and appropriation echoed Prodromou's (2003) comment:

> Non-native speakers, even if they have reached a very advanced level, are still considered incapable of playing with the language; if they attempt to do so, they will be regarded with suspicion and, consequently, they will fail to communicate their meaning.
>
> (p. 46)

The pride most citizens feel regarding China's 5,000-year history and culture (Walker, 2000; Zeng, 2015; Zhang, 2016) can explain their strong resistance to Alan's unconventional use of *chengyu*. Such overcritical evaluation, again, echoes Zhang's suggestion, (2016, p. 175) "A foreign language learner would want to retain native Chinese judges' expectations slightly above the minimum tolerable performance that admit the learner into the game." In fact, the Chinese counterparts interviewed in this study appeared to react to Alan's mistakes in a very lenient fashion when they believed them to be unintended. However, they were less tolerant if they recognized some of Alan's creative language play as intentional, which they interpreted as adopting a certain "affective stance" (Ochs, 1996, p. 410) indicating arrogance or glibness.

However, there is an intricate exception to the expectation of adherence to linguistic conformity described earlier. We can observe an overwhelming use of communicative conventions that closely adhere to Chinese values and traditions in Alan's speech that may have aroused suspicion and made him appear "pretentious." Such a phenomenon raises the important question of how far should one go to emulate native-like discourse. Twenty years ago, Kubler (1997) warned foreign language learners about the risk of being "too target-culture like," which he described below:

> Pretending to be a member of another culture, when one is obviously not, can be seen by members of that culture as presumptuous or even intrusive. This perception of "invasion" by members of a culture is not so much linguistically based as it is communicatively based. A foreigner's excellent control of pronunciation, grammar, vocabulary, and the like is seen as a positive factor. However, if foreigners use communicative conventions that reflect an adherence to Chinese cultural values, attitudes, and traditions, there is a natural suspicion that they are pretending to be Chinese when they are not.
>
> (Kubler, NFLC Guide, 1997)

On the surface, Alan's experience may echo Moody's (2017) finding that even a successful emulation of native-like use of honorific terms can cause a foreign worker to stand out. This is illustrated by his comment, "If foreign workers are not expected to conform to local norms, then attempts to do so can trigger 'othering' responses" (p. 15). However, an in-depth look into Alan's specific situation reveals that the rejection seemed to come more from the foreign subject's lack of authority to say certain things than from different expectations regarding linguistic conformity for non-native speakers. According to Bourdieu, "A performative utterance is destined to fail each time that it is not pronounced by a person who has the 'power' to pronounce it." In other words, it was agreed that Alan did not have the right to say those words. No matter how grammatically correct or sophisticated they may be, he was destined to fail.

Despite the intricate evaluation of Alan's discursive behavior discussed earlier, his Chinese counterparts' expectations for his professional behavior is more straightforward yet demanding as well. Alan was expected to retain his "outsider status" to sustain the symbolic power of the host institution, which wished to appear more globalized. Alan's attempt to reproduce the Chinese pedagogical paradigm of the strict, authoritarian teacher in the classroom disappointed his colleagues because they had expected the stereotypical Western pedagogical paradigm of an equal teacher-student relationship that would inspire critical thinking, imagination and creativity within the students. Therefore, although Alan could be forgiven for being blunt with his professor, when he was perceived as not having his own *tese* (literally 'special color,' which can be understood as one's unique feature), he was no longer an asset to his group when he attempted this behavior in the classroom.

Implications for Chinese pedagogy at the advanced level

From a pedagogical standpoint, the results point to a number of implications for the curriculum design, in Chinese as well as in other languages, at the advanced level. These implications place an emphasis on developing learners' expertise in both using the language in general and in their own disciplinary domain. First, it is imperative that instructors help students to develop multilingual capability so that they may effectively function within multiple languages and cultures. In order to be true assets in the global community, L2 learners must be encouraged to reject the traditional role of foreigners who are anxious to abide by the rules and approximate the idealized NS image. Alan, who displayed a high level of awareness of semiotic, linguistic and cultural diversity, was able to assume full responsibility for his creative linguistic choices. In terms of teaching practices, this requires instructors to bring to life rich cultural details and create contexts in which symbolic competence may emerge. Moreover, instructors must also be able to demonstrate the types of variation within the language that are necessary to function effectively within an unfamiliar culture. To achieve this goal, the instructors are encouraged to demonstrate the myriad ways in which the language can be used to communicate, even by discussing unorthodox approaches that challenge mainstream society. Instructors must thus be able to distance themselves in order to explain cultural nuances objectively and to step out of their comfort zones to explicitly discuss hidden assumptions. As reviewed previously, a number of pioneering scholars have explored various techniques for developing this awareness (Scarino, 2014; Étienne & Vanbaelen, 2017; Vinall, 2016; Richardson, 2017). The current study verified the necessity of experimenting with these teaching approaches and further examining the effectiveness of these techniques for helping students to develop semiotic awareness and symbolic competence.

In addition, analysis of the evaluations by Alan's Chinese counterparts can be used to help students recognize the boundaries of creative play with the new language. For example, students should realize the potentially negative consequences of an attempt to play with the Chinese four-character idiom *chengyu*. Recognition of the boundary, however, is not contradictory to encouraging students to develop their symbolic competence. Instead, recognizing the boundaries of creatively using a language, in this case Chinese, means being able to identify the contexts in which such creativity would be more (or less) appreciated than in others. Learners may still practice creative appropriation in their blogs or with close friends. However, in some formal, professional situations, they may wish to use terms like *chengyu* only in their most conventional form to demonstrate their abundant knowledge of Chinese culture and their respect for the rich cultural references that are hidden in these phrases.

As previously stated, considering that Chinese learners are placed in very different situations than immigrants in the United States, it would be both useless and unrealistic for instructors to overemphasize the subversive potential of the Third Space. While it carries the possibility of opening up areas for alternative language use in advanced-level classrooms, it is essential that learners become aware of the expectations that exist within the target culture, as this space should be co-constructed and beneficial to both foreigners and local citizens.

Lastly, the goal of pedagogy at the advanced level, in Chinese and in all other languages as well, should be to help students to develop expertise as global professionals rather than simply promoting language proficiency. One aspect of such expertise is the ability to convey one's domain expertise to counterparts from the target community. Alan's success in introducing the Western philosophy of art exhibitions to his Chinese peers and his failure in reproducing a traditional Chinese pedagogical paradigm in his art class shows this importance. Recalling Kramsch (2014)'s criticism that few college students are able to "imagine they might gain any disciplinary knowledge taught in a FL that they might not get when taught in English," it is especially important to develop and extend an awareness of the relativity of language and thought to students' domain knowledge and train them to articulate their domain expertise using the target language. Conducting more qualitative studies into the professional world of various domains in the target society will help both instructors and students to construct a clearer idea about the expectations of the end users.

Limitations of the current study

One may argue that the case discussed in this chapter does not reflect common experiences. However, such imaginative language use and subjective interpretation have been prevalently shown in many foreign language learners' testimonies (Kramsch, 2009). Alan's performance exemplifies Kramsch's description of a competent multilingual individual who is willing to "engage with differences" as they "imbue the conventional expressions with personal, sometimes highly idiosyncratic meaning" (Kramsch, 2009, p. 42). Moreover, even if some comments made by the native Chinese might be perceived as their personal opinions, they are part of the workday life in which both students and educators will take part. After all, as long as our learners will be expected to interact with people other than their language teachers, these subjective evaluations, and even the biases, will become assets.

Of course, as a single case study, the current research has its own limitations in terms of its generalizability. However, by offering additional methodological possibilities for studies of advanced L2 learners' professional experiences, it will help researchers to identify areas which require further study and refine the design of future studies. First, the limited number of subjects and performance samples in this study points out the necessity for keeping track of advanced Chinese learners at the college level after they graduate. Since art is not a common professional domain in which most language learners participate after graduation (McAloon, 2008), it will be of great value to investigate learners' professional experience across a range of other fields. Second, the Chinese counterparts interviewed in this study were not those who had directly interacted with Alan in the performance samples. Therefore, their evaluations of his performance might change if they had been able to interact with Alan directly. In future studies, it would be useful to analyze the attitudes of those Chinese interlocutors who were directly involved in the conversation using multiple data collection methods to compare the findings with the current study.

Conclusions

Utilizing the theoretical lens of the Third Space to conceptualize the observed cross-cultural interactions, this study revealed distinct yet consistently emerging themes concerning an L2 Chinese learner's professional experiences in China. Alan demonstrated a strong desire to go beyond the limits of linguistic conventions and social acceptability to creatively appropriate the target language for his own use. His attempt to engage in the subjective resonances that were triggered by the use of symbols united with his advanced language skills and cultural knowledge and allowed him to assume full responsibility for his own linguistic choices.

In addition, the inclusion of evaluations of this American professional's performances by his Chinese counterparts revealed a twofold set of high expectations for his performances. While objecting to some of his innovative attempts at language play, Alan's Chinese colleagues also expected and overtly looked for some "global qualities" in his performances in order to highlight the symbolic power of their globalized organization.

Based on these empirical findings, the study illuminates the participant's ability to negotiate a Third Space with people from different cultures as an advanced-level strategy that could reduce the possible fatigue and conflicts that advanced-level learners may gradually develop. The study proposes that instructors of advanced-level learners focus on developing learners' multilingual capacities, that is, their ability to operate successfully between languages, as well as their strategies for demonstrating to, and negotiating their domain expertise with, members of the target community. At the same time, pedagogues should help students to recognize the boundaries of transgression and the expectations that are held by the target community so as to co-construct a desirable Third Space for both parties.

Acknowledgement

This chapter was originally published in the journal *Foreign Language Annals* (Vol. 51, p. 658–684). I want to thank editor Dr. Anne Nerenz and four anonymous reviewers for their constructive feedback to my original paper. I also thank the managing editor Luke Polonsky for his patient guidance during the preparation for final publication.

Notes

1 The original comment was made in Chinese "好像是官場上, 那種體制內的人。" ("Just like people within the circle of officials. People belonging to the system.")
2 This was the only SR interview comment that Alan made in Chinese as he naturally chose during the very first interview he did. After this first interview, he switched to English upon the researcher's request. The original Chinese comment is "沒有, 因為我們學生都討厭領導嘛。領導就是黨委書記, 我們學生都覺得他什麼都不懂的, 學生都可以吐槽吐槽他嘛。我一說領導, 他們就懂了。" ("No, since we students all hate school officials. *Lingdao* is the party secretary. We all think he doesn't know anything. Students can *tucao* (complain about) him. As soon as I said *lingdao*, they understood what I meant.")
3 *Chengyu* is a unique type of conventional expression in Mandarin Chinese, usually composed of four characters, commonly used in formal speeches and conversations as well as casual conversations. According to Zhang (2016), the ability to properly use *chengyu* in modern Chinese indicates "authority derived from the wisdom of the tradition" (p. 50), "a well-educated individual" (p. 51) and "shared knowledge and respect of the tradition" that consequently signifies "one's legitimate membership in Chinese culture" (p. 53).
4 During the SR interview, Alan said, "so my issue with this video is not about language, but that I am so Chinese. It's a problem. In this situation, this pedagogical paradigm is so Chinese. I think that's why the class is not so successful. My point is that this pedagogical paradigm of master and disciple is especially easy, because that's what I think they are used to, because all Chinese education is based on that idea. Learning is the process someone who has skill and knows the standard response imparting it to someone who does not. And the responsibility in the students is to achieve standard responses. But in our education, this is completely abandoned. The mainstream idea behind our education is not craft-based. . . . I sound just like a CAFA professor. It's so CAFA. It's so ridiculous. That's so CAFA. Oh my god. *wangxiayanjiu* (continue to research) I sound like Xu Bing. So CAFA, oh my god. The entire language is like everything is in this school. *Niyao wangxia yanjiu; zhegexian yao yadeyun.* (You should continue to study it. This stroke should be balanced.) It sounds like *Guohuaxi* (Department of Chinese Painting). . . . But the entire narrative of being authoritative, wise master and deferent disciple is something I found very depressing. I do not think it is effective for participating in Western global society."

References

Back, M. (2013). "La Orquesta": Symbolic performance in a multilingual community of practice. *Modern Language Journal, 97*(2), 383–396.

Bakhtin, M. (1981). *The dialogic imagination* (M. Holquist, Ed., C. Emerson & M. Holquist, Trans.). Austin: University of Texas Press.

Barthes, R. (1977). *The third meaning: Image-music-text* (pp. 52–68, S. Heath, Trans.). New York: Noonday Press.

Bhabha, H. K. (1994). *The location of culture.* London: Routledge.

Blommaert, J. (2005). *Discourse.* Cambridge: Cambridge University Press.

Blommaert, J. (2010). *The sociolinguistics of globalization.* Cambridge: Cambridge University Press.

Blommaert, J., & Rampton, B. (2011). Language and superdiversity. *Diversities, 13*(2), 1–21.

Bourdieu, P. (1991). *Language and symbolic power* (J. B. Thompson, Ed., G. Raymond & M. Adamson, Trans.). Cambridge: Polity Press.

Brecht, R., Abbott, M., Davidson, D. E., Rivers, W. P., Weinberg, A., & Yoganathan, A. (2013, September 10). *Languages for all white paper (draft).* Retrieved March 10, 2014, from http://languagesforall2013.blogspot.com/

Creswell, J. W. (2003). *Research design: Qualitative, quantitative, and mixed methods approach* (2nd ed.). Thousand Oaks, CA: Sage.

Damari, R., Rivers, W. P., Brecht, R. D., Gardner, P., Pulupa, C., & Robinson, J. (2017). The demand for multilingual human capital in the U.S. labor market. *Foreign Language Annals, 50*(1), 13–37.

de Sam, M., Dougan, B., Gordon, J., Puaschunder, J., & St. Clair, C. (2008). *Building a globally competent citizenry in the United States.* Washington, DC: US Department of Education.

Étienne, C., & Vanbaelen, S. (2017). Exploring symbolic competence: Constructing meaning(s) and stretching cultural imagination in an intermediate college-level French class. *L2 Journal, 9*(2), 63–83.

Glaser, B. (1978). *Theoretical sensitivity: Advances in the methodology of grounded theory.* Mill Valley, CA: Sociology Press.

Gutierrez, K. D., Baquedano-Lopez, P., & Tejeda, C. (1999). Rethinking diversity: Hybridity and hybrid language practices in the third space. *Mind, Culture, and Activity, 6*(4), 286–303.

He, Y., & Qin, X. (2017). Students' perceptions of an internship experience in China: A pilot study. *Foreign Language Annals, 50*, 57–70.

Jian, X. (2018, February). *The pedagogy of co-constructing a multilingual and cross-cultural third space.* Paper presented at the Symposium on interdisciplinary approaches to East Asian Languages Pedagogy, Columbus, OH.

Kostogriz, A. (2002). *Teaching literacy in multicultural classrooms: Towards a pedagogy of "Thirdspace."* Paper presented at the Annual conference of the Australian Association for Research in Education, Brisbane. Retrieved September 5, 2016, from www.aare.edu.au/data/publications/2002/kos02346.pdf

Kramsch, C. (1993). *Context and culture in language teaching.* Oxford. Oxford University Press.

Kramsch, C. (2006). From communicative competence to symbolic competence. *The Modern Language Journal, 90*(2), 249–252.

Kramsch, C. (2009). Third culture and language education. In L. Wei & V. Cook (Eds.), *Contemporary applied linguistics: Vol.1. Language teaching and learning* (pp. 233–254). London: Continuum.

Kramsch, C. (2014). Teaching foreign languages in an era of globalization: Introduction. *Modern Language Journal*, 98(1), 296–311.

Kramsch, C., & Whiteside, A. (2008). Language ecology in multilingual settings: Towards a theory of symbolic competence. *Applied Linguistics*, 29(4), 645–671.

Kubler, C. (1997). *NFLC guide for basic Chinese language programs*. Washington, DC: National Foreign Language Center and The Ohio State University Foreign Language Publications.

Leaver, L., & Atwell, S. (2002). Preliminary qualitative findings from a study of the processes leading to advanced professional proficiency level (ILR 4). In B. Leaver & V. Shekhtman (Eds.), *Developing professional-level language proficiency* (pp. 260–279). Cambridge: Cambridge University Press.

Malone, M. E., & Rivers, W. (2013, November). *Global education and educational cooperation: Exemplary practices from the United States*. Retrieved March 10, 2014, from www.languagepolicy.org/wp-content/uploads/2013/11/Global-Education-and-Educational-Cooperation.pdf

Mansilla, V. B., & Jackson, A. (2011). *Educating for global competence: Preparing our youth to engage the world*. New York: Asia Society.

McAloon, P. (2008). *Chinese at work: Evaluating advanced language use in China-related careers*. Doctoral dissertation. Retrieved from https://etd.ohiolink.edu/

McAloon, P. (2015). From proficiency to expertise: Using HR evaluation methods to assess advanced foreign language and culture ability. In T. Brown & J. Brown (Eds.), *To advanced proficiency and beyond: Theory and methods for developing superior second language ability* (pp. 153–170). Washington, DC: Georgetown University Press.

Moody, S. J. (2017). Fitting in or standing out? A conflict of belonging and identity in intercultural polite talk at work. *Applied Linguistics*, 2017, 1–25.

The National Standards Collaborative Board. (2015). *World-Readiness standards for learning languages* (4th ed.). Alexandria, VA: Author.

Nisbett, R. E., & Wilson, D. (1977). Telling more than we can know: Verbal reports on mental processes. *Psychological Review*, 84, 231–259.

Ochs, E. (1996). Linguistic resources for socializing humanity. In J. Gumperz & S. Levinson (Eds.), *Rethinking linguistic relativity* (pp. 407–437). Cambridge: Cambridge University Press.

Peirce, C. S. (1898/1955). *Philosophical writings of Peirce* (J. Buchler, Ed.). New York: Dover.

Prior, P. (1995). Tracing authoritative and internally persuasive discourses: A case study of response, revision and disciplinary enculturation. *Research in the Teaching of English*, 29(3), 288–325.

Prodromou, L. (2003). Idiomaticity and the non-native speaker. *English Today*, 2, 42–48.

Rampton, M. B. H. (1990). Displacing the native speaker: Expertise, affiliation, and inheritance. *ELT Journal*, 44, 97–101.

Rampton, M. B. H. (1995). *Crossing: Language and ethnicity among adolescents*. London: Longman.

Richardson, D. (2017). Beyond a tolerance of ambiguity: Symbolic competence as creative uncertainty and doubt. *L2 Journal*, 9(2), 12–34.

Rivers, W., & Brecht, R. D. (2018). America's languages: The future of language advocacy. *Foreign Language Annals*, 51(1), 24–34.

Scarino, A. (2014). Learning as reciprocal, interpretive meaning-making: A view from collaborative research into the professional learning of teachers of languages. *Modern Language Journal, 98*, 386–401.

Strauss, A., & Corbin, J. (1998). *Basics of qualitative research: Techniques and procedures for developing grounded theory*. Thousand Oaks, CA: Sage.

Turner, V. (1991). Dramatic ritual/ritual drama: Performative and reflexive anthropology. In B. Marranca & G. Dasgupta (Eds.), *Interculturalism and performance* (pp. 99–113). New York: PAJ Publications.

Vinall, K. (2016). "Got Llorona?": Teaching for the development of symbolic competence. *L2 Journal, 8*(1), 1–16.

Walker, G. (2010). Performed culture: Learning to participate in another culture. Language policy and pedagogy. In G. Walker (Ed.), *The pedagogy of performing another culture* (pp. 1–20). Columbus, OH: National East Asian Languages Resource Center at The Ohio State.

Walker, G. (2015). 美國對外漢語教學：轉變期的教學法、語言文化學習及研究生培養 (Teaching Chinese as a foreign language in the United States: Pedagogy, language and culture studies and graduate program under a paradigm shift). *Newsletter of the International Society for Chinese Language Teaching, 4*, 72–80.

Walker, G., & Jian, X. (2016). *A Chinese language pedagogy for the 21st century: Basic assumptions* (Lecture Video). Retrieved from www.youtube.com/watch?v=ApNFVYHKIeU

Wu, S.-L. (2017). The planning, implementation, and assessment of an international internship program: An exploratory case study. *Foreign Language Annals, 50*, 567–583.

Yin, R. K. (2014). *Case study research design and methods* (5th ed.). Thousand Oaks, CA: Sage.

Zeng, Z. (2015). *Demonstrating and evaluating expertise in communicating in Chinese as a foreign language*. Doctoral dissertation. Retrieved from https://etd.ohiolink.edu/

Zhang, X. (2016). *Four-character idioms in advanced spoken Chinese: Perception and reaction of native speakers and a pedagogy of C2 expectations*. Doctoral dissertation. Retrieved from https://etd.ohiolink.edu/

APPENDICES

Appendix 4.1 Descriptions of performance samples in Alan's portfolio

Samples	Format	Length	Description	Domain/Role
1	Text	/	An art exhibition review written for the exhibition catalog.	Art/Artist
2	Video	8'32"	A conversation with exhibition staff about the design of the exhibition tag during a pre-exhibition setup.	Art/Artist
3	Video	2'11"	A conversation with exhibition staff and the other artist about the display of a piece of artwork during a pre-exhibition setup.	Art/Artist

Samples	Format	Length	Description	Domain/Role
4	Video	4'2"	Teaching practice of giving instructions at the beginning of a class on some "housekeeping" issues.	Pedagogy/Teacher
5	Video	5'54"	Teaching practice of giving instructions to three students regarding their respective pieces of art.	Art Pedagogy/Teacher
6	Video	1'33"	A conversation with a student who refused to participate in class activities.	Art Pedagogy/Teacher
7	Video	4'18"	Teaching practice of demonstrating calligraphy to a group of students.	Art Pedagogy/Teacher
8	Audio	3'53"	A WeChat voice message on a few art/culture-related topics including idioms and Chinese and Western painting.	Academic/Graduate Student
9	Video	8'28"	A discussion with a friend about his graduate art project.	Academic/Graduate Student
10	Video	4'16"	A conversation with a student committee leader to recommend someone's artwork.	Academic/Graduate Student
11	Video	10'54"	Discussing a scholarship on Chinese history at a reading group meeting.	Academic/Graduate Student

Appendix 4.2 Stimulated recall interview questions for Alan

1. Please comment on the frequency of the recorded event; how often does it happen in your work?
2. (By pausing the video) What did you say here?
3. Why did you say that?
4. What were you thinking when you were doing that?
5. What do you think of that person's response?
6. How will you evaluate your performance in this video? Was your communication effective? Why do you think so?
7. If there's a chance for you to redo it, will you do it differently? How? Why?
8. Do you think the recorded event reflect your average level of performance?
9. In addition to the recorded events, is there any other work-related activity you used to do? What's the frequency?

Appendix 4.3 Chinese evaluators' background information

Domain insider who does not know Alan		Alan's colleagues and classmates	
1. Yang	An artist and part-time instructor for 30 years	4. Shi	Alan's graduate school classmate in CAFA

(*Continued*)

(Continued)

Domain insider who does not know Alan		Alan's colleagues and classmates	
2. Yu	A calligraphy artist and instructor for 18 years	5. Shu	Alan's colleague working on the same student committee at CAFA
3. Yi	A college art lecturer and a watercolor artist for 15 years	6. Shao	Alan's supervisor/mentor, working together on an art project

Appendix 4.4 Interview questions to the Chinese evaluators

C1. Interview questions to Alan's colleagues and classmates (Shi, Shu and Shao)

1 請您簡述您和XX (name of the subject) 是怎麼認識的。
2 請您形容一下您與 XX的關係
3 您如何評價XX中文水平？請給出一些具體的例子說明。
4 您如何評價XX在工作中的表現？請給出一些具體的例子說明。
5 XX在說話、行事等各個方面有沒有讓你覺得特別的地方？(比如和你特別不一樣的地方, 或者和中國人很相似的地方？)
6 在您的生活、工作中，還接觸過這樣會說中文的外國人嗎？他們的表現和視頻裡的外國人有什麼不同？
7 在對這個視頻的評價中，您覺得他表現如何？哪些地方做得好？哪些地方做得不好？為什麼？
8 您覺得他的這句話/這個詞用得這麼樣？他的意思是什麼？

Translation in English:

1 Please tell me briefly about how did you come to know XX (name of the subject).
2 How would you comment on your relationship with XX? (Colleagues? Friends? Very close friends?)
3 How would you evaluate XX's Chinese level? Please give some concrete examples.
4 How would you evaluate XX's performance at work? Please give some concrete examples.
5 What do you think of the way XX speaks or acts? Is there anything special, such as something that is very different from you, or vice versa?
6 Do you know any other foreigners who speak Chinese? Please mention a few and compare their communications in Chinese to XX's.
7 In your evaluation of this performance sample, what do you think of his performance in general? Specifically, which part is good and which is not?
8 How would you interpret this sentence/word? What did he mean?

Striving for the Third Space 97

C2. Interview questions to domain-insider evaluators
(Yang, Yu and Yi) who do not know Alan

1 請簡單地介紹您自己 (年齡/職業/教育背景/工作經歷/是否會方言? 是否會外語?)
2 在對這個視頻的評價中，您覺得他表現如何？哪些地方做得好？哪些地方做得不好？為什麼？
3 看了這個人的一些表現後，您對他有什麼印象？ 您是否願意與他繼續交流？
4 您覺得他的這句話/這個詞用得這麼樣？他的意思是什麼？
5 在您的生活、工作中，還接觸過這樣會說中文的外國人嗎？他們的表現和視頻裡的外國人有什麼不同？

Translation in English:

1 Please briefly introduce yourself, including age, occupation, educational background and any foreign language or dialect you speak.
2 In your evaluation of this performance sample, what do you think of his performance in general? Specifically, which part is good and which is not?
3 After watching a few videos of him, what is your general impression of him? If you are the interlocutor, are you willing to further communicate with him?
4 How would you interpret this sentence/word? What did he mean?
5 Have you ever communicated with foreigners speaking Chinese in your life? Can you compare the subject in the video with other Chinese-speaking foreigners you know?

Appendix 4.5 Interview questions to Alan

1 Please talk about your Chinese learning experiences, including language program(s) you attended, classes you took, study-abroad experience and your experiences in taking OPI test experiences and scores.
2 Why did you choose to learn Chinese at the beginning?
3 Do you consider yourself still studying Chinese now? If yes, what is the frequency? How much time do you spend? Can you identify all kinds of practices you usually engage to improve your Chinese? Is there any resources you used?
4 Please describe your Chinese-related working experience.
5 How did you make the choice to work in China?
6 Do you think you have close Chinese friends? Can you mention three people and comment your friendship with them?
7 How do Chinese people around you (your teachers, classmates, friends, colleagues, employers and business partners) evaluate your Chinese?

8 Recall a few situations described as follow, if they once happened in your life:

   a   Your misuse of Chinese caused misunderstanding or embarrassment that harmed your business.
   b   Your misuse of Chinese caused misunderstanding or embarrassment that harmed your relationship with Chinese colleagues or friends.
   c   Your successful use of Chinese that benefited your business.
   d   Your successful use of Chinese that enhanced your interpersonal relationship with Chinese people.
   e   Your demonstration of your identity as a foreigner or any foreignism in communication with Chinese people brought advantages to you.

9 In what aspect of your Chinese do you think you need to improve most?
10 There is one observation of advanced-level foreign language learners: It seems that the higher proficiency level in the target language they reach and the more in-target culture experience they have, the less likely they are willing to perform to meet the prescribed "native expectations" and the more strongly they desire to assert their "self" in communicating in the target language. Does this observation apply to you? Does this observation apply to any foreigners in China you know? What is your comment on this phenomenon?

5 Establishing domain expertise in the Third Space

Constructing language learning motivation to perform beyond proficiency

Junqing (Jessie) Jia

Introduction

Language learning motivation as a key factor in the process of second language acquisition (SLA) has been widely studied by scholars of various fields. However, few works have explored the learning motivation of advanced-level Chinese language learners, and even fewer address *how* their learning motivation sustains through pedagogical designs. To fill this gap, the chapter[1] explores the construction of advanced-level Chinese learners' motivation, in particular how the process of negotiating a Third Space and establishing domain expertise with Chinese associates contributes to learner motivation at an advanced level. The following questions are investigated: First, how do we define expertise in learning Chinese as a foreign language? Second, what is the importance of establishing domain-specific knowledge and vision? Third, which experiences are considered as crucial and motivational by advanced-level Chinese learners? Lastly, how does co-constructing a Third Space with Chinese associates correlate with learner motivation?

The chapter divides the discussion into three sections: First and foremost, concepts such as learner motivation, domain expertise and Third Space are theoretically discussed in the context of learning Chinese as a foreign language. Second, an advanced-level Chinese language curriculum focusing on training students to perform professionally in a specific domain is introduced as a case for analysis. Third, empirical data collected with 33 advanced-level Chinese learners who extended their language skills into their careers is included to discuss motivating factors from learners' perspectives. Pedagogical implications are drawn on in the discussion in these three sections.

The major argument of this chapter is that establishing domain expertise and achieving common goals with the Chinese counterparts through negotiating a Third Space helps advanced-level learners sustain their learning motivation. The findings of the study echo with this proposal indicating advanced-level Chinese language learners highly recognized the motivating influence of socialization with native speakers.

Learning motivation, domain expertise and Third Space

Given that mastering any subject is a long-term journey, researchers and educators in the learning motivation domain have recognized variation in motivation as one's expertise develops (Hallam et al., 2016; Hüffmeier, Kanthak, & Hertel, 2013). Learning a foreign language to an advanced level of language and cultural competence is no exception. While language learners at different levels could be motivated by similar factors, such as successfully interacting with native speakers of the target languages, it is worth discussing the specific challenging issue of learner motivation at an advanced level. For instance, beginning-level foreign language students gain a strong sense of progression through receiving instant feedback from their instructors and peers. However, an advanced-level Chinese language learner does not always have access to that learning environment. Instead, successful language learners ideally develop a crucial skill of negotiating meanings with native speakers and gaining a sense of achievement through those challenging experiences.

In the following section, the author's understanding of Chinese learner motivation, domain expertise, and Third Space is presented. Most importantly, along with scholars whose understanding of learning motivation has broken the divide between socio-psychological approaches (Gardner, 2001, 2010) and cognitive-situated perspectives (Dörnyei, 2005, 2009; Muir & Dörnyei, 2013), this chapter understands Chinese learners' sustainable motivation as a cyclic construction of their vision, socialization within the target community and a continued sense of progression (Jia, 2019). The correlation of vision, socialization and a Third Space is also discussed in this section.

Establishing a vision of domain-specific self through socialization

Scholars of learning motivation have long been exploring the process of achieving expertise. One example is Hallam et al. (2016), who studied 3,325 young musicians (aged 6–19) and their motivation development as their level of expertise increased. The findings suggested that the strongest predictors for one's level of expertise were "music constituting an element of social life and enjoyment of performance" (p. 545). It is not surprising that there is a linear relationship between musicians' aspirations and their level of expertise, but it is an inspiring statement that one's musical expertise is closely related to one's social life and the value of playing an instrument, for instance, having many friends who also play instruments, playing an instrument as an important part of their social life, and brothers and sisters liking them playing a musical instrument (p. 534). The authors further argued that it is important for the players to establish a positive musical identity over time, for instance, having self-belief in musical ability, setting high standards, achieving successful task performance and demonstrating resilience.

Jia (2019) also argues that socialization should be considered as "both the content and outcome of a successful vision system" (p. 48). More specifically, interacting with people from the target culture effectively to achieve personal or professional goals should play a central role in advanced-level Chinese learners' vision construction. In this chapter, a "domain-specific self" refers to one's visualized image of performing specified tasks in a specified field, for example, a joint venture manager introducing the historical background of the company or an American college student applying to an intern position at a language school in Shanghai. In most cases, these performances are socially constructed with the involvement of native speakers. By orientating a domain, students are able to identify the specific learning strategies, procedures and outcomes. They are also able to bring together their existing individual memories of exploring domain knowledge with language learning. This indication of a domain-specific identity corresponds with Dörnyei's (2009) L2 motivational self system, where he proposed three main sources of L2 motivation: The ideal L2 self that a language learner hopes to be, the ought-to L2 self that a learner is expected to be, and the perceived L2 learning experiences.

Although Dörnyei's (2009) discussion of L2 motivation mainly focuses on the cognitive and psychological constructs of the process, the third component of the construct, the L2 learning experience, clearly suggested that one's long-term motivation is usually socially constructed over time. In his recently published article (Dörnyei, 2019), he defined the L2 learning experiences as "the perceived quality of the learners' engagement with various aspects of the language learning process," which includes but is not limited to school context, syllabus and teaching materials, learning tasks and one's peers and teacher (p. 25). When discussing the learning motivation of advanced-level learners who can live and work successfully in Chinese, their engagement with the target community needs to be extended beyond the classroom. More specifically, learners are often introduced to meaningful social and learning experiences that have a correlation with their domain-specific interests. Learners who create meaningful relationships with domain experts are much more likely to dramatically improve their language abilities, cultural competencies and learning motivation. Moreover, the marginal benefit from establishing these types of relationships for an advanced-level learner greatly exceeds that of simply learning new vocabulary or grammar.

Thompson's (2017) investigation of two L1-English-speaking advanced language learners of Chinese and Arabic also revealed the strong impact of socialization on one's development of selfness. The author argued that it is through pleasant or discomforting socializing experiences that language learners develop an "anti-ought-to self" (reactions against external expectations). Furthermore, the study suggests that learners could sometimes intentionally adjust their learning behaviors and strategies due to the vision of an anti-ought-to self. For example, one of the participants in the study developed an anti-ought-to self along his journey of learning Chinese and interacting with native speakers of Chinese. He claimed to be motivated by a language teaching assistant from China who told him that he was not very good at the end of his first semester of learning Chinese (p. 43). He also stated that "the other related thing that drove me for many years was the absence of positive/ideal NNS (non-native speaker) role models who could speak Chinese in a way that drew praise from Chinese people" (p. 44). In fact, this complex system of anti-ought-to self is particularly well observed among advanced-level Chinese language learners who aim at achieving an unexpected level of language and cultural competence in a specific domain. There is no doubt that they are introduced to a highly challenging task. However, as Thompson suggests, the more challenging the goal becomes, the more motivated some learners could become through establishing an anti-ought-to self.

In other words, advanced-level Chinese language learners should be encouraged to visualize themselves responding to challenges and difficulties in a field that they are familiar with, namely, establishing a vision of successful domain-specific self.

Expertise in communicating in Chinese

Within the fields of L2 acquisition and foreign language education, the definition and description of language proficiency have been a favored topic. However, relatively few studies have touched on the nonlinguistic variables of successful Chinese language learners (McAloon, 2015; Zeng, 2018). This chapter suggests that when considering language learning as an extended journey to achieve expertise, we are not only focusing on students' language proficiency or how they adapt to the target culture. Rather, one's expertise should at least include learners' cultural competence to negotiate in the target culture and their well-developed learning mechanism on the whole.

The notion of language proficiency has long been widely embraced by federal agencies and some college-level institutions in the United States, where students' capability in the foreign language is highly correlated with their scores in a standardized test such as the American Council on the Teaching of Foreign Languages (ACTFL)'s Oral Proficiency Interview (OPI). Thus, in a language program that focuses on students' OPI performance, factors such as test results and teacher's feedback could play an important role in motivating students to practice. However, taking achieving intercultural capacity into account, advanced-level language learners must seek opportunities to use and improve their foreign language skills outside a classroom setting (Ryan, 2006). They are also expected to constantly modify their worldview to understand and deal with unexpected foreign cultural differences, which can also be described as interacting and negotiating with the target community.

Zeng (2018) introduced one superior-level Chinese language learner's (Alan) work experiences in China. The case study reveals that, instead of expecting a young foreign professional to behave as a local person, those Chinese people who interacted with Alan actually indicated an expectation for a global professional to be "not too Chinese." Moreover, this expectation even goes beyond the linguistic performance (p. 673). It is clear that a high level of language proficiency contributes to foreigners' career development in China. However, they will not be able to establish long-term meaningful relationships with their Chinese counterparts without developing their multicultural capacities and identities.

In fact, Leon Festinger's (1962) cognitive dissonance theory may have shed some light on the Chinese counterparts' reaction in Zeng's (2018) study. Festinger suggested that people experience some degree of discomfort when encountering an inconsistency between the reality they are facing and their own personal understanding and feelings and have a motivational drive to reduce that dissonance. Based on this theory, when Chinese people encounter a foreigner with expert-level Chinese language skills, it is natural for them to seek the "foreignness" in the person. By the same token, when Chinese language learners intentionally adopt Chinese conventions and are still considered "foreign," they may tend to reduce their cognitive and conative gap by forming a new hypothesis of the culture. In other words, it is in fact beneficial to both ends of the communication if cross-cultural expertise can be clearly distinguished from "being Chinese." More importantly, the higher skill level a language learner reaches, the more essential cultural dissonance one potentially needs to confront. Therefore, to achieve an ideal communicative result between participants from two different cultures, it is important for them to negotiate a mutually recognized domain-specific purpose. In addition, advanced-level language learners must gradually develop a third-space persona (Zhang, Chapter 2 of this volume) and sustain their motivation to achieve this goal.

As mentioned earlier, another important feature of language learners' expertise is their overall learning mechanism, including their capacity of monitoring and evaluating their current levels of mastery and understanding, also referred as metacognition in some studies (e.g., Brown & Smiley, 1977). In contrast to novices who need clear and detailed instructions, advanced-level language learners with a goal of achieving expertise do not benefit greatly from redundant domain-general information (Rey & Buchwald, 2011). Through interacting with native speakers of Chinese in social and professional contexts, the advanced-level learners increase their ability to identify their specific role and assess their own performance in domain-specific situations. In fact, as their expertise in communicating in a foreign culture increases, they also demonstrate a higher level of resilience and self-assurance in acquiring effective practice strategies. It is also noteworthy that different negotiation and communication skills are involved in various fields; for instance, being able to interact successfully with a Chinese entrepreneur requires a very different skill set than does navigating an academic environment. In other words, in order to achieve a dynamic learning mechanism, one should take both learners' general transferable skills (monitoring one's own progress, ability to tolerate ambiguity, ability to convey information to a non-expert audience, etc.) and domain-specific knowledge (business banquet etiquette, using jargon appropriately, ability to impress a domain-specific audience, etc.) into consideration.

Sustaining learner motivation through negotiating a Third Space

As discussed, meaningful socialization between language learners and the target community plays an important role in sustaining one's long-term language learning motivation (Jia, 2019). From a practical standpoint, working on a domain-specific project in Chinese propels students into a community where they have the chance to exchange opinions and seek feedback from native speakers who share common interests. It is also expected that advanced-level language learners are only able to gain a constant sense of achievement when they focus on improving their performance in a specific area. Indeed, the more specific one's short-term objectives are, the easier it becomes to monitor the progress (Stratton, 2005).

Taking into consideration that one's domain-specific vision not only helps to select the content of learning, it is also through the vision of a successful L2 self that advanced-level learners build the connection between their language knowledge and professional objectives. It is widely observed that advanced-level learners who are able to associate language learning with their career aspirations are more likely to sustain their motivation than those who are not. Furthermore, the effectiveness of vision construction largely depends on the details of the learning tasks. In a program that focuses on domain training, students are encouraged to establish knowledge and accomplish contextualized tasks in the target language. This approach emphasizes learners' integrative multicultural abilities, which directly influences learners' behaviors in terms of how they approach the materials and evaluate themselves. Both language fluency and accuracy are important predictors of learners' achievement in a different culture. However, an advanced-level curriculum that merely focuses on learners' fluency is considered not ideal or inapplicable in terms of vision construction. By the same token, students who are able to read and write thousands of Chinese characters may not realize what they can achieve in a Chinese workplace with those skills. In creating the vision of successful L2 selves, it is crucial to provide learners clear and recognizable domain-specific details, for instance, a digital genre such as an email, so that they can quickly build the correlation between the current learning tasks and future career orientations. Therefore, this chapter suggests that to sustain advanced-level learners' motivation, the focus of the curriculum needs to shift from one's linguistic abilities to their overall multicultural capacities, including cognitive mechanisms such as goal setting and self-assessment.

This proposed view of advanced-level curriculum also indicates that students should establish ideal future selves through co-constructing a meaningful relationship with people from the second culture (C2), namely, a Third Space where various levels of communication and negotiation is involved. In other words, being able to negotiate and co-construct a Third Space is a cultural and cognitive competence that motivated language learners must acquire. Discussing Third Space in the context of motivation construction, three features of this concept are further explored: First, as Jia (2019) stated, a Third Space is co-constructed by people from one's native culture (C1) and counterparts from a second culture (C2), and should benefit both groups (p. 47). More importantly, a beneficial third-space relationship not only leads to tangible positive outcomes, but on the other hand, in many cases both groups seek and obtain emotional achievements such as a strong sense of progress or *mianzi*. That is to say, this level of negotiation and communication is highly related to an individual's emotional and psychological needs. It is also understandable that not each individual is equally interested in or driven by the same kind of socialization.

Second, constructing a Third Space requires both groups to have developed a third-space persona, which has not been taken into serious consideration in the field of foreign language education. One common misconception of training language learners is, to put it simply, "When in Rome, do as the Romans do." In other words, even when culture becomes part of the conversation, the emphasis has been laid on the agreement that learning Chinese well equals being culturally adapted to what Chinese people do. It may be helpful advice for someone who visits a foreign country for a short period of time. On the contrary, we hardly observe advanced-level Chinese learners successfully achieve their professional goals and sustain their long-term motivation through "performing as a Chinese person." For example, Chinese people often comment on the unsatisfactory performance of their national men's soccer team; however, if a foreigner joins with complaints in fluent Chinese, the conversation may not continue smoothly. A motivational vision of one's L2 self must be an image who receives positive feedback from the target community, namely, a detailed successful Third-Space self.

Thirdly, examining the process of constructing a Third Space, one cannot overlook the importance of individual traits such as extraversion, curiosity, agreeableness, willingness to compromise, reciprocation and one's motivation to learn. It is clear that one's rich knowledge of a foreign language and culture does not make up for his cross-cultural abilities. It is also clear that an ideal "Third-Space self" still needs to be closely related to "oneself." As with the soccer example, an outgoing and humorous person may participate in the conversation by commenting on the US men's national soccer team. On the contrary, one can simply sustain the conversation by asking if the Chinese team has improved recently. Each individual needs to find and keep revising their own strategies in this process of negotiation. One feature that distinguishes a cultural expert from a novice is their ability to handle difficult and uncomfortable situations and their resilience to resume learning. This chapter suggests that on the one hand, advanced-level learners gain a sense of achievement and sustain their learning motivation through a third-space vision. On the other hand, the driving force to learn Chinese to a high level of proficiency and cultural expertise helps them overcome the challenges and continue developing their individualized recipe to navigate the cultural game.

An advanced-level curricular design focusing on L2 domain expertise

Considering that the Midwest US-China Flagship Program is one of the few Chinese programs in the United States that focuses on training American students to function professionally in Chinese culture, the curriculum of the program is introduced in this section to further contextualize the discussion of vision, domain expertise and negotiating a Third Space.

Long-term and short-term goals

The Midwest US-China Flagship Program is a two-year master's degree program. These students have various learning backgrounds, but generally speaking, they all have studied Chinese for years and have reached a decent level of language proficiency before joining the program. Students expect to further improve their language capacities, and many of them have the long-term goal of extending their Chinese learning into their future careers.

The program clearly states that one of its educational goals is to train advanced-level Chinese learners to work in China. Students spend their first year on a US campus taking Chinese language and content courses, such as Chinese linguistics, literature and intercultural communication. Most of these content courses are offered in Chinese. During their second year, they study at a Chinese university to further improve their Chinese and work as interns in a company or organization in China. They are also expected to write their theses in Chinese during the second year of the program. The program, in the long run, expects these Chinese learners to establish some domain knowledge and become Chinese *users* who can perform well in Chinese-speaking workplaces. Specifically, these students are not only expected to demonstrate high-level language skills, but they are also expected to negotiate meanings and construct meaningful relationships with their Chinese counterparts as young professionals. These long-term goals are supported by short-term curricular objectives, such as building domain knowledge of Chinese language (Chinese linguistic course), practicing adjusting cultural expectations and analyzing different cultural behaviors (Chinese interpersonal relationship course) and exploring domain-specific research and methodology development. In the process of taking these courses, students establish their memories of using Chinese and performing various cultural contexts. Meanwhile, they receive instant feedback on how much they have progressed through all different types of interactions with native speakers.

Domain-specific learning experiences

Students are encouraged to gradually develop an individual research domain and eventually write their thesis on a specific topic that they select. Starting with their first year in the program, they work closely with professors and domain tutors to determine a topic that they are interested in exploring. Students are trained to focus on using their Chinese language skills to explore the topic and convey their developing understanding of the topic in Chinese.

Both the domestic courses and study-abroad experiences of the program focus on expanding learners' language and C2 knowledge within a specific field. The approach is applied through these specific curricular decisions: First, the program provides students with a high level of autonomy to select the topic; they usually have some prior knowledge of what they choose to work on. Therefore, students have the motivation and propensity to transition from learning Chinese to learning the topic *in* Chinese within a relatively short period of time. Second, in contrast to a curriculum that focuses on one's ability to conduct linguistic tasks in a wide range of topics and scenarios, the Midwest US-China Flagship Program's domain-specific training helps students to clearly recognize how newly adopted language skills contribute to their improvement of a specific task. The learning activities such as weekly presentations on one's research project help learners to monitor their periodical progress and identify their particular areas for improvement, and thus gain a sense of achievement. Lastly, in the process of establishing domain expertise, the program creates opportunities for students to develop a variety of transferable skills, such as convincing an audience that does not share similar opinions, identifying research sources in Chinese, and communicating with non-expert audiences through a Chinese Q&A platform online. These skills are in fact widely recognized as attributes of advanced-level learners, and exercises to develop the skills have been often adopted in advanced-level courses.

Interaction with native speakers

In this chapter, students' social configuration with a C2 community has been regarded as one of the most important factors in motivation construction. In the program introduced in this section, students construct their vision of using their language skills through interacting with Chinese instructors, tutors and other native speakers.

For instance, during the first year of the Midwest US-China Flagship Program, each student has a domain tutor who helps them to build discourse around a specific topic. When the study was conducted (introduced in the next section), most of these domain tutors were visiting scholars from China. For some of the students, their interaction with the domain tutor was when they first experienced using Chinese to communicate domain knowledge with a native speaker who does not teach them Chinese. The program expects the students to invest a great amount of effort in practicing establishing professional Third-Space relationships with their domain tutors.

These students are also provided opportunities to present their domain knowledge to an audience that is from the target community but might not be familiar with the topic. Students are highly encouraged to spend a summer in China after their first year of learning. During the summer, these students present their domain topics on a weekly basis. When possible, the program invites both domain experts and native speakers with little knowledge about students' topics. After each presentation, students receive feedback and questions from their instructors, tutors, domain experts and native speakers who are not familiar with their topic. This process of interacting with different types of native speakers not only helps them extend their domain knowledge, but they also successfully establish memories to negotiate meanings with different groups.

Role model as vision construction

Muir and Dörnyei (2013) suggested that an ideal L2 vision should be an image that is sufficiently different from a learner's present self but also achievable through procedural strategies. Along the same lines, Jia (2019) argued that one of the most effective approaches to construct an ideal L2 self is to have learners interact with other learners whose level is slightly higher than their own.

In addition, it would be optimal if these role models share a lot of similarities with the learners, such as age, gender, ethnicity and training background. The Midwest US-China Flagship Program serves as a good example in this regard. It seeks opportunities to bring current students with these alumni together so that the students can learn more about their working experiences in a professional Chinese working environment. Students who graduated from the program and those who currently work in China are invited to the classroom on campus and talk to junior learners of Chinese about their career in China. In terms of learners' motivation construction, this type of interaction creates a good chance for students to establish a long-term vision, and therefore, their learning performance may increase.

In a program that focuses on learners' ability to perform well in Chinese culture, instructors play various roles when interacting with students, for instance, coaching, criticizing and commenting on each performance. It is likely that students are not able to adapt to this dynamic instructor-student relationship right away, especially if they have been told that obeying teachers' opinions is important in Chinese culture. However, students should be provided the opportunities to practice negotiating with instructors, such as determining a research topic, defending one's arguments and seeking a mutually benefiting learning environment. In an optimal situation, a domain-focused curriculum creates a sequential arrangement of learning opportunities throughout the years that helps learners to expand their social milieu, establish a domain-specific self and negotiate a Third Space with a variety of native speakers. Students should also constantly revise and further improve their performance of specified tasks.

Learners' perspectives on motivating factors

Methodology

An online questionnaire with 15 Likert-type questions was conducted with 33 advanced-level Chinese language learners who graduated from the Midwest US-China Flagship Program and had lived and worked in China (see Appendix 5.1 for the questionnaire). They were provided a link to access the online questionnaire, and their answers were recorded and submitted through an online platform. They were not allowed to rewrite or revise the responses after submission. The questionnaire was designed to understand which experiences are considered motivating learning experiences from the perspectives of these learners. Based on the understanding that Chinese learner motivation is a combination of socialization, vision and sense of progression, the questions included in the survey were designed around these three aspects. The findings in the following section were mostly drawn from the questionnaire results.

Seventeen of the 33 subjects participated in a follow-up interview to further discuss their experiences of learning Chinese. The follow-up interviews were conducted via Skype or by phone due to their distant physical locations. The interview, conducted in English, was designed around the online questionnaire, where learners were asked to describe their journal of learning Chinese and identify motivation-related experiences. Each interview lasted approximately 30–40 minutes.

Findings

First, the survey discovered that subjects indicated exceedingly strong agreement with the statement that interaction with native speakers motivates them to spend more effort on learning the language; 25 subjects out of 33 strongly agreed with this statement. This finding was also supplemented by Q5, where 28 subjects strongly agreed or agreed that their eagerness to improve their language abilities increased after their first study-abroad experiences. Some of the subjects who participated the follow-up interview suggested that they were highly motivated to study Chinese through study-abroad experiences because of their direct interaction with native speakers. They had all encountered difficulties and misunderstandings, but being able to use what they had learned in the classroom in an authentic context with Chinese people was a significant motivating experience. Interestingly, the interview findings suggest that more than half of the subjects indicated that they were no longer satisfied with the domestic learning environment after living in China for a few months. By returning to the United States, they were once again restricted to using Chinese in a limited number of places and with a limited amount of people. This interview finding, together with the questionnaire results, clearly demonstrated the heavy influence human interaction has on learner motivation. Their answers to Q3 in the questionnaire (whether their interaction with their language teacher motivated them) also confirms that those interactions with native speakers other than their instructors was indeed highly valued by this group of language learners, who reached high levels of proficiency and working capacity. Only 14 subjects strongly agreed that their interaction with their teachers motivated them.

Second, one finding of the survey that was also supported by the follow-up interview results is the importance of long-term goals in the context of foreign language learning. The survey showed that among this group of successful Chinese language learners, only a small percentage (6 out of 33 subjects) strongly agreed that they were motivated by short-term goals. This finding was further clarified through the interviews with selected subjects. It was mentioned by most interview subjects that competing with their classmates was a significant motivating factor during their first year of learning Chinese. But once they reached higher levels, they constantly compared their performance with Chinese learners who were one or two years ahead of them. In other words, they no longer focused on short-term goals that are usually closely related with curriculum requirements.

Nearly 85% of the subjects associate their language learning motivation with future career prospects (28 out of 33 subjects strongly agreed or agreed with the statement). Five of the subjects disagreed with the statement. Through more in-depth discussion of this statement with selected learners, it was clear that those who had established the connection between language learning and career development (indicating strong agreement in Q9) were the students who also strived for a higher level of working capacity compared to other members of the cohort. Some findings help us to further understand the role one's domain-specific vision could play in motivating students: 27 out of 33 subjects indicated strong agreement or agreement with the statement that their biggest drive toward improving their Chinese after they reached an advanced level was to apply it to what they did as a professional.

Third, the findings revealed a resilient journey of learning Chinese and motivation construction. To put it another way, each subject had experienced some kind of motivation challenge, such as not meeting their own expectations and failed experiences of fitting into a local community. Based on the questionnaire findings, students' past exposure to the foreign language and culture may have an impact on their decision of which language to study, but it is certainly not sufficient to sustain them on the long journey toward becoming an expert. As the numbers in Q7 indicated, only 9 out of 33 subjects considered their previous exposure to Chinese as significant motivating experiences.

The interview subjects also consistently reported that their initial inclusion into Chinese companies or institutions as employees was a critically low point of motivation. Being a semi-insider in the working environment, these language learners were no longer surrounded by people such as their Chinese teachers and language partners. Subjects reported that they were expected to work efficiently and achieve common goals with their colleagues. In some regions in China, Chinese is the primary working language, while in cities such as Hong Kong or Shanghai, some subjects reported that they needed to be extremely persistent to get their colleagues to consider using Chinese with them. Negotiation of a Third Space often involves this matter of what language to use. Not being able to express and defend one's needs could lead to unsatisfactory results for both groups. As the interview results suggested, the frustration sometimes is also caused by Chinese employers' expectations for a foreign employee, for example, when to be a Chinese culture expert and when to be a foreigner. A foreign employee who considers himself as an insider, a Chinese-like employee, would be highly demotivated when treated as a foreigner in some contexts.

Discussion

Subjects showed the highest agreement to the motivating influence of socialization. This group of Chinese language learners who have gained different levels of expertise in Chinese working culture explicitly indicated in follow-up interviews that interacting with Chinese people is not always pleasant. In fact, several of them stated that it was through a combination of pleasant and unpleasant experiences that they learned the skills necessary to achieve their personal and career goals in China. Another important notion in the understanding of socialization is that language learners' interaction with their peers and learners whose Chinese was one or two levels higher than theirs (role models) could be as crucial as their interaction with native speakers of Chinese. These interactions were described as one of the most motivating experiences by some subjects, as meeting real-life examples of people with similar backgrounds who have already achieved similar career goals was a unique experience. Those subjects who intend to work in China after graduation are likely more motivated and better able to picture their future selves when presented with living examples of people who have achieved similar goals. The Chinese language in and of itself hardly constructs an appealing and sustaining vision. The positive effects of bonding between previous and current students tightens when those experiences are intentionally designed into the program.

In addition, a student's social milieu ideally expands with his or her interaction with Chinese people. The findings suggested we should reconsider the possibility of motivating students through constructing a Third Space in the domestic learning environment. What should we focus on in an intermediate- to advanced-level Chinese classroom? Shall we focus on students' fluency, or do we prepare them to perform appropriately and negotiate well in the target culture? The latter task is much more complicated, but that is indeed where we should be focusing our efforts. When students return to the domestic learning environment from study abroad and experience a lack of motivation, the instructors could take advantage of this timing and train them to maintain the relationship with their Chinese associates in China. Consequently, students are able to develop their communicating and negotiating skills through social media to handle this authentic challenge.

Curriculum design and each instructor's pedagogical decisions play an important role in sustaining learners' motivation, including both pedagogical materials and learning activities. For example, the subjects in this study had the chance to present their ideas in front of a Chinese audience. This is a challenging task for most students. However, the sense of achievement, the attention and individualized feedback received from such training was recognized as having a positive effect by the subjects. It was also no surprise that students reported being able to discuss their professional interests with Chinese tutors as a meaningful experience that associated their language learning with their future career. Aside from incorporating socially meaningful activities, identifying the best type of learning materials to motivate learners is also crucial, which will be discussed in the following section.

Constructing learner motivation through negotiating a Third Space

Based on the discussion in the previous sections, some pedagogical implications are proposed in this section. On the practical side of selecting learning materials, the motivating dimension of said materials is usually not the primary concern. However, there are two common misunderstandings about what to include in the learning materials to motivate language learners. One is the introduction of Chinese culture through a separate section commonly titled "culture notes." It is claimed by those materials that introducing cultural facts about the target culture, such as Chinese festivals, the Great Wall, or modern city life in China, "motivates" students to learn the language. As suggested by this chapter, students' previous exposure to Chinese culture has minimal impact on their lifelong Chinese learning journey. A "reason" or an "interest" in the target language or culture does not necessarily increase learners' efforts or affect their long-term learning mechanism. Another commonly observed phenomenon of some popular Chinese learning materials is the attempt to "motivate" students by selecting the topics that are perceived to be interesting to young American adults, such as air pollution or contraception in China. It is believed that by increasing students' participation in the classroom, they are more motivated to learn and use Chinese. The author does not doubt that students show a high interest in discussing these topics in the Chinese-language classroom. What concerns people is that, how do the language students construct and sustain their learning motivation if they were fully interested in discussing contraception or air pollution with people they meet in China? In an advanced-level curriculum, what we train our students to perform is highly related to what they can achieve in the target culture and how they sustain their motivation to interact with the target community.

The curriculum of the Midwest US-China Flagship Program provided a good example of how to help learners construct a domain-specific vision and negotiate a Third Space with a large variety of native speakers. Being able to interact with Chinese peers and teachers in academic contexts is certainly an important genre to command. However, the subjects introduced in this chapter who intended to work in Chinese culture took full advantage of interacting with people outside the campus when they studied abroad. It is for the same reason we should encourage advanced-level students to establish a vision of using Chinese in a specific domain so that it becomes easier for them to monitor their own improvements. For instance, if a student hopes to start a career making movies and documentaries in China, they ideally should visualize how to interact with people from the film industry and master industry-specific language and norms. In addition to involving role models to support vision construction, it would also be helpful if learners could constantly imagine their future self performing in predictable contexts through reflecting on their current and past selves. In an ideal learning situation, one's developing performance will soon serve as one's "past self" that can be reflected on, and this revisiting and comparing process drives one to move forward to an even higher level of learning. Ideally, students should constantly visualize their near-future successful self by comparing their own performance with an existing recorded performance done by other students whose level is slightly higher than theirs.

Domain-specific training makes it more feasible for advanced-level students to monitor their progress and gain a sense of achievement. In addition, a learner who has never been trained to understand and adopt a working persona in a foreign culture has a much smaller chance of overcoming this motivation-challenging period than students who were required to perform the role of a Chinese employee from their first Chinese class. By the same token, a Chinese learner who does not know how to negotiate and sustain motivation for both groups would be in an even more challenging situation when trying to navigate the Chinese workplace. For example, knowing when and how to strategically use the most effective foreignism is a crucial skill in the process of constructing a Third Space; therefore, it should be introduced to the students from an early stage. Students with the goal of becoming language and culture experts should continually accumulate memories of failing, revising, improving and polishing their performance.

Conclusion

The Third Space is certainly not a prevalent cultural environment, nor is it a simple task to achieve. In reality, even advanced-level language learners will still need to exert themselves to keep practicing so that they are able to co-construct ideal relationships with their counterparts from the target community. However, as discussed, both groups (C1 and C2) should be able to realize their professional, cultural and cognitive goals through this process of negotiating meanings with each other. The chapter suggests that interpersonal relationships built through negotiating a Third Space could play an important role in motivating learners who aim at performing professionally in Chinese culture.

Both the survey and interview findings in this chapter suggest that the journey to make an appearance of a Third Space is long and complex. Students encounter several motivational crises, such as post-study-abroad and early career experiences. This also reminds us that learning motivation should not be simply understood as an anchored starting point; rather it develops closely with learners' comprehensive learning mechanism and changes promptly with different contexts. On the theoretical side, the conception of a Third Space shares similar features, namely, it is a highly interpersonal but highly pliable social co-construction. For instance, at an early stage, when students perform negotiating a Third Space with instructors, domain tutors, and language partners, they might only have one simple hypothesis of how the Third Space should function. However, when their social milieu expands through amplified professional tasks, the Third Space they co-construct with native speakers would also diversify.

The study included in this chapter was limited by the size of the data pool. Subsequent research is needed to further determine motivating experiences and factors from learners' perspectives. Furthermore, the interview was only conducted with subjects who had already reached an advanced level of language and cultural capacities. Their successful learning outcomes could influence how they recall and interpret their early learning experiences. Future studies should also compare novice or intermediate-level learners' perspectives on similar aspects in order to verify the generalizability of some of the findings.

In conclusion, the long-term journey of visualizing and establishing a mutually beneficial Third Space should be considered as one significant motivating factor in an advanced-level curriculum. On the practical side, the skills one needs to achieve a Third Space highly correspond with the motivating factors in an advanced-level curriculum. It is commonly accepted that curriculum design plays an important role in improving students' language capacities. This chapter suggests that it is also through curriculum design that students have the opportunities to construct and sustain their learning motivation. Specifically, achieving commonly recognized goals with C2 counterparts, developing domain knowledge in the target language and visualizing a successful professional self are the three major motivating strategies explored in this chapter.

Note

1 This book chapter derives contents and findings from the author's PhD dissertation (2017) titled *Motivating Experiences in an Extended Chinese as a Foreign Language Learning Career: Identifying What Sustains Learners to Advanced-Skill Levels*.

References

Brown, A., & Smiley, S. (1977). Rating the importance of structural units of prose passages: A problem of metacognitive development. *Child Development, 48*(1), 1–8. https://doi.org/10.2307/1128873

Dörnyei, Z. (2005). *The psychology of the language learner individual differences in second language acquisition*. Mahwah, NJ: Lawrence Erlbaum.

Dörnyei, Z. (2009). The L2 motivational self system. In Z. Dörnyei & E. Ushioda (Eds.), *Motivation, language identity and the L2 self* (pp. 9–42). Bristol: Multilingual Matters. https://b9f19ceb-f720-4252-a2beccde56c0821f.filesusr.com/ugd/ba734f_08e57fb08186 4ecd9b98274bf24e23c6.pdf?index=true

Dörnyei, Z. (2019). Towards a better understanding of the L2 learning experience, the Cinderella of the L2 motivational self system. *Studies in Second Language Learning and Teaching, 9*(1), 19–30. https://doi.org/10.14746/ssllt.2019.9.1.2

Festinger, L. (1962). Cognitive dissonance. *Scientific American, 207*(4), 93–107. https://doi.org/10.1038/scientificamerican1062-93

Gardner, R. C. (2001, February 17). *Integrative motivation: Past, present and future*. Japan Distinguished Lecturer Series. Philadelphia, PA: Temple University.

Gardner, R. C. (2010). *Motivation and second language acquisition: The socio-educational model*. New York: Peter Lang.

Hallam, S., Creech, A., Papageorgi, I., Gomes, T., Rinta, T., Varvarigou, M., & Lanipekun, J. (2016). Changes in motivation as expertise develops: Relationships with musical aspirations. *Musicae Scientiae, 20*(4), 528–550. https://doi.org/10.1177/1029864916634420

Hüffmeier, J., Kanthak, J., & Hertel, G. (2013). Specificity of partner feedback as moderator of group motivation gains in Olympic swimmers. *Group Processes & Intergroup Relations, 16*(4), 516–525. https://doi.org/10.1177/1368430212460894

Jia, J. (2017). *Motivating experiences in an extended Chinese as a foreign language learning career: Identifying what sustains learners to advanced-skill levels*. PhD dissertation, The Ohio State University. Retrieved from http://rave.ohiolink.edu/etdc/view?acc_num=osu1500339643646484

Jia, J. (2019). Chinese language learner motivation: Vision, socialization and progression. *Studies in Self-Access Learning Journal, 10*(1), 44–60. https://sisaljournal.org/archives/mar19/jia/

McAloon, P. (2015). From proficiency to expertise: Using HR evaluation methods to assess advanced foreign language and culture ability. In T. Brown & J. Brown (Eds.), *To advanced proficiency and beyond: Theory and methods for developing superior second language ability* (pp. 153–170). Washington, DC: Georgetown University Press.

Muir, C., & Dörnyei, Z. (2013). Directed motivational currents: Using vision to create effective motivational pathways. *Studies in Second Language Learning and Teaching, 3*(3), 357–375. https://doi.org/10.14746/ssllt.2013.3.3.3

Rey, G., & Buchwald, F. (2011). The expertise reversal effect: Cognitive load and motivational explanations. *Journal of Experimental Psychology: Applied*, *17*(1), 33–48. https://doi.org/10.1037/a0022243

Ryan, S. (2006) Language learning motivation within the context of globalization: An L2 self within an imagined global community. *Critical Inquiry in Language Studies*, *3*(1), 23–45. http://doi.org/10.1207/s15427595cils0301_2

Stratton, R. (2005). Motivation: Goals and goal setting. *Strategies: A Journal for Physical and Sport Educators*, *18*(3), 31–32. https://doi.org/10.1080/08924562.2005.10591138

Thompson, A. (2017). Don't tell me what to do! The anti-ought-to self and language learning motivation. *System*, *67*, 38–49. https://doi.org/10.1016/j.system.2017.04.004

Zeng, Z. (2018). Striving for the third space: A U.S. professional's experiences in Chinese workplaces. *Foreign Language Annals*, *51*(3), 658–684. https://doi.org/10.1111/flan.12352

APPENDIX

Appendix 5.1 Online questionnaire with 15 Likert-scale questions

1 Interacting with native speakers of Chinese encouraged me to improve my Chinese.

   Strongly agree   Agree   Neutral Disagree   Strongly disagree

2 My personal interest, such as music, sports or business, encouraged me to spend more time on improving my Chinese.

   Strongly agree   Agree   Neutral Disagree   Strongly disagree

3 At a certain stage of my Chinese learning journey, I was motivated to work hard by my language teacher.

   Strongly agree   Agree   Neutral Disagree   Strongly disagree

4 Some learning materials I used have influenced my willingness to engage and practice.

   Strongly agree   Agree   Neutral Disagree   Strongly disagree

5 I was eager to improve my Chinese after I visited China/Taiwan for the first time.

   Strongly agree   Agree   Neutral Disagree   Strongly disagree

6 I was once motivated to improve my Chinese for a scholarship or job opportunity.

   Strongly agree   Agree   Neutral Disagree   Strongly disagree

7 I had a clear reason to start learning Chinese (family roots, Chinese-related hobby, job, etc.).

   Strongly agree   Agree   Neutral Disagree   Strongly disagree

8 I was once motivated by Chinese language learners who can speak fluent Chinese, and wanted to reach their level someday in the future.

   Strongly agree   Agree   Neutral Disagree   Strongly disagree

9 When I realized that Chinese would be related to my future career and life, I was more willing to improve my language performance.

   Strongly agree   Agree   Neutral Disagree   Strongly disagree

10 I have experienced a tough time of learning Chinese, but I eventually pushed through because I knew Chinese will be related to my future life or career.

   Strongly agree   Agree   Neutral Disagree   Strongly disagree

11 I did not have a long-term goal for learning Chinese, but I had some short-term goals that kept me going.

   Strongly agree   Agree   Neutral Disagree   Strongly disagree

12 The Flagship Program I attended helped me to establish a foundation of using Chinese in my career.

   Strongly agree   Agree   Neutral Disagree   Strongly disagree

13 Being asked to give presentations on our own research project in a public setting encouraged me to practice a lot.

   Strongly agree   Agree   Neutral Disagree   Strongly disagree

14 My biggest drive to improve my Chinese after I reached advanced level is to actually apply it to what I do as a professional.

   Strongly agree   Agree   Neutral Disagree   Strongly disagree

15 I will work hard to improve my Chinese at this point if there is tangible reward involved, such as money, promotion or a new job opportunity.

   Strongly agree   Agree   Neutral Disagree   Strongly disagree

6 Online forum as Third Space?
CFL learners' experiences on an online knowledge-sharing community

Zhini Zeng

Introduction

Technology has the potential to bring together communities of learners. At the same time, the electronic medium presents new forms of subjectivity. Online space, brought about by the development of new communication technologies, has been optimistically touted as a liberating playground where the dominant, normative perceptions and behaviors of society can be challenged and set aside in favor of hybridity and ambiguity. It is, therefore, imagined to have the same potential as a "Third Space" which, according to Soja (2009), is "a space of extraordinary openness, a place of critical exchange" (p. 50) that can transcend geography and other types of boundaries and binaries.

This chapter explores the concept of Third Space in relation to the online knowledge-sharing communities through an empirical study. The Third Space in this study is conceptualized as both a location and a practice. As a location, it is a technology-mediated online space for knowledge sharing where meaning making and expertise are negotiable between old timers and new members, experts and non-experts. It is also an emergent intercultural space where members from different cultural backgrounds put their perspectives, experiences and expertise in play. As a practice, it is the deliberate act of recognizing the conflict between the dichotomous ideologies, perceptions and interests and engaging them strategically through a mutual path to eventually transcend the dichotomy.

The study focuses specifically on a group of upper-intermediate to advanced-level CFL learners' experiences of participating in discussions on *Zhihu*, the most widely used social question and answer (SQA) site in China, and how they utilize the online knowledge-sharing community as a learning space in which they negotiate their identities as legitimate knowledge contributors. In addition, it explores how the Third Space, as a practice, may or may not emerge from CFL learners' interactions with Chinese users in the Zhihu community. Through a careful application of data triangulation, this chapter identifies factors that potentially contribute to the success or failure of establishing a Third Space.

Literature review

Grounded in social learning theory, this chapter conceptualizes learning as a social activity that takes place within communities of practice and is mediated by cultural artifacts. In a virtually mediated world, online participants use language to search for connection and to negotiate membership within various communities. Useful frameworks of the Third Space and community of practice are employed to interpret American CFL learners' experiences of interacting with native speakers of Chinese in the online community of Zhihu.

Third Space

This chapter builds upon Homi Bhabha's (1994) conceptualization of Third Space and hybridity as a constructive model for understanding the interactions between American students learning Chinese and the Chinese netizens on Zhihu. For Bhabha, Third Space is an in-between place that brings together contradictory information, practices, and discourse in which signs can be "appropriated, translated, rehistoricized, and read anew" (p. 37). Bhabha's model focuses on the asymmetrical power relations between two oppositional parties and the dominating influence of one party over the other. These differences are "irresolvable," meaning that one party cannot be "persuaded or 'educated' out of" their principles by the other, which therefore makes the space productive.

Acknowledging that these characteristics of a Third Space, as Bhabha describes, can be found in the intercultural communication taking place within an online community, I take a more constructive view of what makes up a Third Space. Instead of perceiving the Third Space as a simple *encounter*, it is identified as a *deliberate engagement*, which involves a cooperative effort from both parties who are working toward mutually recognized common goals. As revealed in a study of American professionals in Chinese workplaces (Zeng, 2018), Third Space does not emerge automatically through the process of intercultural communication. Instead, its establishment requires constant investment of effort and strategies.

Currently, scholars in the field of foreign language education who have embraced this Bhabhaian conceptualization of Third Space exclusively focus on implementing students' non-mainstream linguistic practices in class through creative pedagogical approaches (Gutiérrez, Baquedano-López, & Tejeda, 1999; Kramsch, 2009; Flores & García, 2013). On the one hand, these researchers have collectively conceptualized the complexity of learning spaces as a Third Space where "alternative and competing discourses and positionings transform conflict and difference into rich zones of collaboration and learning" (Gutiérrez et al., 1999, pp. 286–287). On the other hand, as Zeng (2018) criticizes, these studies may have gone a bit too far to recognize the boundaries of creative play with the target language. After all, the Third Space is not about subversively establishing "our" space to take over "their" space; rather the goal is to create an opportunity for sincere consideration of the interests and objectives of both parties and to allow for a strategic negotiation between them.

As stated in earlier, this chapter conceptualizes the Third Space as both a location and a practice. To avoid the pitfall of seeing the Third Space as a static encounter between two stable entities, this chapter emphasizes that it is the deliberate and dynamic practices taking place within this space that make a Third Space productive. In addition, the contested struggle characteristic of the Third Space as defined in Kramsch's (2009) study does not transfer to the Third Space practice defined in the current study. As the phrase "western-dominated globalization" (Hogarth, 2013) suggests, English is always assumed to be the working language dominating the global community and "the western way" is always preferred. Therefore, unlike immigrants in the United States whose base language and culture are less symbolically powerful, for CFL learners examined in this study, their base language and culture are usually assumed to be more powerful than the target language and culture. Third Space, as a practice, refers to active negotiation of what one chooses to be in the specific context and, in the meanwhile, seeking the optimal way to meet the expectations from players from the other side.

Communities of practice in a virtual environment

An SQA site, like Zhihu, constitutes a type of community of practice (Lave & Wenger, 1991; Wenger, 1998) that people participate in for knowledge sharing and other social purposes, such as to interact with like-minded people or to build relationships with experts. Communities of practice have three defining characteristics: Mutual engagement among members, a joint enterprise and a shared repertoire (Wenger, 1998). A community is more than a group or a team. It instead requires concrete practices demonstrated in the form of mutual engagement among its participants. According to Wenger, what makes the engagement in practice possible and productive is not its homogeneity but its diversity. Therefore, a joint enterprise implies more than agreement among its members, but a communally negotiated enterprise. Given the entity of the SQA site, disagreement can be viewed as a productive part of the enterprise. However, in the meanwhile, over the time of jointly pursuing an enterprise, members in the community do share a repertoire as shared references for meaning negotiation. It reflects the history of mutual engagement, which can be further applied to innovative contexts. Particularly in the case of Zhihu, this shared repertoire includes words, ways of using the website, symbols and genres that this online community has created and adopted in the course of its existence. As Wenger (1998) pointed out, this shared repertoire is never fixed but is "inherently ambiguous" (p. 83).

Inspired by the tradition of apprenticeship, the concept of legitimate peripheral participation (LPP), proposed by Lave and Wenger (1991), refers to the process by which a newcomer becomes part of a community of practice. The word "legitimate" indicates the importance of participation as a means of belonging to a certain community. For a knowledge-sharing online community, activities such as becoming a registered member, receiving "likes" or "dislikes" from other users and gaining the right to edit one's own or others' posts all validate or invalidate the participant's "legitimacy." The word "peripheral" suggests that there are multiple varied levels of engagement and specific ways of becoming established in the fields of participation defined by a community (Lave & Wenger, 1991, p. 36). It must be noted that a great many registered users do not post regularly on this knowledge-sharing website but are content just to read the posts of other members. In Internet lingo, they are called "lurkers," which in this context has no negative implications such as "unrelatedness" or "irrelevance." It instead describes the dynamic process of gaining access to sources for greater understanding through growing involvement.

From this perspective, the construct of LPP, in one way, draws attention to "the richness of the periphery and the learning enabled (or not) by it" (Smith, Wenger, & White, 2009). However, in another way it also reminds us that, to some extent, power relations between old-timers and newcomers often restrict learners' access to these communities that provide opportunities for practicing their language skills, leaving learners to negotiate a different social identity deemed worthy of this access (Norton, 2000; Norton Pierce, 1995; Toohey, 1996).

Research questions

This study addresses two major questions:

1 What is the nature of students' interactions on Zhihu? Through the theoretical lens of communities of practice and a textual analysis of students' posts and the responses they received, this study examines whether American students have become legitimate members of the Zhihu community they identified.
2 What factors have facilitated or impeded students' endeavors to engage with the community? By identifying the potential factors that contributed to the success and/or failure of engaging with the Zhihu community, this study is particularly interested in the role that the Third Space practice played in this process. The hypothesis is that the emergence of Third-Space practice must contribute to students' successful engagement with the Zhihu community.

Methods

Research site: the Zhihu website

Viewed as the Chinese equivalent of Quora, Zhihu (知乎), meaning "Do you know?" in classical Chinese, is the largest SQA site in China. It encourages knowledge exchange and social collaboration among its users. Launched in 2011, Zhihu, as of this writing, has 220 million registered users who have posted 30 million questions and more than 130 million answers on the site. Before March 2013, for nearly two years, user registration on Zhihu was by invitation and referral only. This exclusive beginning has led to a belief among

Chinese Internet users that Zhihu users are highly educated, are accustomed to reading long articles and enjoy participating in serious debates. According to statistics, 80.1% of Zhihu users have a college degree or above, and 76% of them are at the middle or higher end of a salary range (Da Hua Yun Ying, August 2018). A recent survey also points out that Zhihu users now desire "to find new knowledge and self-improvement articles (71%), to follow topics that are of interest (68%), and to seek professional expertise (66%)." Relatively few (27%) members use Zhihu "as a pastime or for entertainment purposes" (iClick Zhihu Research, July 2017).

The linguistic repertoire adopted exclusively by members of the Zhihu community, known as *Zhihu ti* ('Zhihu style') is unique. For example, questions posted are mostly presented in a conversational style, such as "What is it like to be (e.g., a profession)?" (...是怎样的体验), and "How would you evaluate (e.g., a product)?" (如何评价...?). Other typical Zhihu discourses include "Thank you for inviting me to answer this question (谢邀)," "Let me share my own experiences (说说我的故事吧)," and "Please allow me to add a few points (我再补充几点)." In these samples, respondents politely acknowledge the interlocutors' authority as legitimate knowledge contributors as well as their epistemic stances.

Participants: the CFL learners

Forty-one participants were recruited for this study, American students learning Chinese in an intensive Chinese language program at a public university in the United States. Specifically, students are recruited from two classes, one upper-intermediate-level course and one advanced-level course, both of which required students to use Zhihu as part of their in-class activities and/or after-class assignments. Although a few students had previous experience with this forum, either formally through curricular activities in other classes or casually through recommendations from Chinese friends or teachers, their previous activities on Zhihu were not included in the current study.

The 41 students in the two different classes engaged with Zhihu through two different types of activities designed by their respective instructors.

1 *Curriculum-based Zhihu activities for the upper-intermediate-level Chinese class.* The upper-intermediate-level Chinese class is called "Media Chinese," which was to introduce students to heatedly debated topics on Chinese media and expose them to a variety of media discourses in Chinese. The class also utilized a textbook, *The Routledge Advanced Chinese Multimedia Course: Crossing Cultural Boundaries* (文化纵横观) (Lee, Liang, Jiao, & Wheatley, 2010), as the base and organized other authentic videos and readings from various Chinese media outlets as supporting materials. The Zhihu platform was therefore introduced to students in this context as supplementary reading resources and writing exercises. Each week, the teacher identified a few discussion threads on Zhihu related to the topic covered in that week's class, which was from the textbook, and asked students to read them before class,

to discuss their thoughts in class and sometimes, to respond to their selected topics on Zhihu as homework.

2 *Extracurricular Zhihu activities for the advanced-level Chinese class.* The advanced-level Chinese class is the last class that students need to complete before they go to China for one year doing both study abroad and internship, as required by the program. This class, titled "Networking in Chinese Workplace," is thus designed to prepare students professionally in their respective domains, which is their second major in addition to Chinese study. Zhihu in this context was utilized in a way that is much more independent of the course contents although it still contributed to the general course objectives of developing students' ability to demonstrate their domain expertise in Chinese. All work on Zhihu was, therefore, to be done outside of class as a routine weekly assignment. Each week, students were encouraged to browse extensively on Zhihu, select topics of interest to them and consistently participate in discussions within one specific domain chosen at the beginning of the semester. The students are encouraged to choose topics from the career field they want to pursue during their upcoming year in China, but they are also allowed to choose a domain outside their career field in which they still demonstrate rich experiences and expertise.

To make the corpus of data manageable, this study mainly focused on students whose posts on Zhihu received responses from other users. Although it might have been interesting to investigate why some students' posts received hundreds of responses while others were virtually ignored, this was not the focus of the current study. Lack of popularity can be attributed to many factors that are not necessarily linked to students' performances, such as the outdatedness of the original question thread. Based on this criterion of selection, 16 students were further identified from these 41 students participants as focal research subjects. Among them, ten were from the upper-intermediate-level course and six were from the advanced-level course. However, three of the advanced-level students also took the upper-intermediate-level course in the previous year, so some of their Zhihu works produced at that level were collected as data as well. A more detailed explanation about what types of data were collected and the rationale for data collection will be presented in the next section.

Data collection

The broader corpus of data used in this study consisted of texts collected from the response posts students wrote on Zhihu and the comments they received from other users, who were mostly assumed to be Chinese netizens. To make the corpus of data manageable, the study focused on the 632 pieces of writing collected from the 16 focal research subjects for textual analysis. Among them, 19 were original answer posts composed by the students and the rest are responses they received from other users. These posts, as mentioned earlier, represent the most

Table 6.1 Data collected from curriculum-based Zhihu activities at upper-intermediate level

Most Selected Zhihu Questions	Relevant Curricular Theme	Students (Pseudonyms)	Number of Responses
1. Why is Tumblr, instead of Facebook, the most widely used social media among American teenagers? 为什么美国青少年使用最多的社交网站是 Tumblr 而不是 Facebook？	Social media	Helena	15
		Tina	49
		Hanna	3
2. What is Chinese food culture like? 中国的饮食文化是什么样的？	Chinese food culture	Kate	15
		Jake	11
		Catherine	14
		Shaun	7
		Vivian	17
3. What are the existing disadvantages of American democracy? 美国现有的民主弊端在哪儿？	American democracy	Mike	108
		Cara	10
		Melisa	3
		Lynn	3
		John	8

popular topics selected for the two types of Zhihu activities consistently used in the Chinese program.

From upper-intermediate-level students, posts on three of the most chosen topics are collected for analysis in this study: Social media (社交网络), Chinese food culture (中国饮食文化) and American democracy (美国民主). A list of Zhihu questions related to these topics and the number of responses that students received are presented in Table 6.1.

As for advanced-level students, who have the freedom to determine the topic themselves, their selections of topics can be categorized into three major themes: Personal hobbies, career interests and general discussions on lives in America, which is labeled as "American Ambassador" in this study. Based the criterion of identifying focal participants as mentioned earlier, two students' posts in each category that had received the most comments from the Chinese netizens were chosen for analysis. A list of specific Zhihu questions answered by the students and the number of responses they received is presented in Table 6.2.

In order to better answer the second research question, five students are further identified as successful and/or unsuccessful cases who had semi-structured face-to-face interviews with the researcher. At the same time, writings collected from those non-focal student participants will be discussed when they correspond to the emerging themes. All of these were utilized as a broader context to facilitate interpretation of the selected data.

124 *Zhini Zeng*

Table 6.2 Data collected from extracurricular Zhihu activities at advanced level

Zhihu Questions	Extracurricular Zhihu Activity Types	Students	Number of Responses
1. How do you like the game Tooth and Trail? 如何评价尾牙 (tooth and trail)?	Hobby; Game	William	3
2. What is the experience of raising a cat like? 养猫是一种什么样的体验？	Hobby; Pets	Mary	53
3. What is the fundamental cause of the serious obesity in the United States? 美国人肥胖严重的根本原因是什么？	"Ambassador"; American life	Jane	19
4. To what extent are Americans prejudiced against China? 美国人对中国的偏见究竟到了什么样的程度？	"Ambassador"; American people	Helena*	255
5. How does a computer science professional get started with network intrusion? Are there any professional books to recommend? 计算机专业如何入门网络入侵？有哪些专业书单值得推荐？	Professional; Internet security	Mike*	13
6. What do you think of Democratic Senator Dianne Feinstein's being asked by a group of students to support the Green New Deal? 如何看待民主党参议院 Dianne Feinstein 被一群学生要求支持 Green New Deal?	Professional; Environment and public health policy	Tina*	7

* indicates that the student has participated in Zhihu tasks at both upper-intermediate and advanced levels.

Data analysis

For data analysis, qualitative data were categorized into major themes related to the two research questions. Specifically, in order to find out the nature of students' interactions on Zhihu, all the 613 responses they received from Chinese users were examined and further divided into three categories: Content focused, identity focused and language focused. Examples of these three types of responses can be found in Table 6.3.

The first type of responses centered on the information and/or opinion presented in the original posts, such as expressing agreement or disagreement and

Table 6.3 Examples of three types of responses received from Chinese Zhihu users

Content Focused	Identity Focused	Language Focused
1. "Big mac 汉堡本身还好，厉害的是碳酸饮料和薯条。" (Hamburgers from Big Mac are fine. Sodas and fries are worse.) 2. 请问有没有好的黑客社区推荐一下？在中国这些东西很缺少。(Could you please tell me if there is any good hacker community that you will recommend? We really lack [this kind of information] in China.)	1. "你好可爱啊，想和美国人做朋友！美国学霸！" (You are so cute. I want to make friends with Americans. Talented American students!) 2. "活捉外国妹子一枚～23333" (I caught a cute foreigner girl!)	1. "总体上写的很好，只是有一些不严重的拼写错误，但这些都不是大问题，随着学习的深入这些你都可以自己改正过来。" (Generally speaking, you wrote well. You just have some typos, not a big deal. As the learning continues, you will be able to correct them.) 2. "哈哈，为什么感觉这文章像是先写好英文再通过翻译软件翻成中文的？" (Haha, why do I have the feeling that this article was first written in English and then translated into Chinese using translate machine?)

requesting elaboration or clarification. Expressions of gratitude for sharing perspectives such as a simple 谢谢 ('thank you') or 谢谢分享 ('thank you for sharing your idea') were also categorized as content focused. Identity-focused responses were comments about the writers' foreign identity, which was either explicitly revealed in the posts or inferred by the Chinese readers. These comments varied from admiration of the great effort taken to communicate with Chinese people in their own language to suspicion over the students' non-Chinese identities, labeling them *jia lao wai* (fake foreigners). Similar to the identity-focused responses, the language-focused responses showed preoccupation with students' erroneous or unconventional linguistic expressions and included both harsh criticism and warm encouragement. Some cruelly mocked students' foreignism and their grammar mistakes while others patiently revised students' writings word for word. Thus, the last two types of comments completely ignored what was said and instead focused exclusively on who said it and how it was expressed.

In order to answer the second research question on what underlies students' successful and unsuccessful experiences on Zhihu, it is necessary to identify the most successful and unsuccessful cases for further analysis. Three successful cases of advanced-level students and three unsuccessful cases of upper-intermediate-level students were identified for further analysis (see Table 6.4).

These students' scenarios were identified as focal cases because the differences and the similarities in their engagement with Zhihu represent the experiences of the larger group of participants. Jane, Mike and Tina stood out as the most successful because their answers generated almost 100% content-focused responses. It is also important to remember here that Mike and Tina are two of the three advanced-level students who had also taken upper-intermediate-level classes before. Their posts identified here as successful cases were produced in their second semester of using

Table 6.4 Representative successful and unsuccessful cases for focal data analysis

Topics	Student	Total Number of Responses	Content Focused	Non-content Focused
Successful Cases				
What is the fundamental cause of the serious obesity in the United States?	Jane	19	19	0
How does a computer science professional get started with network intrusion? Are there any professional books to recommend?	Mike*	13	11	2
What do you think of Democratic Senator Dianne Feinstein's being asked by a group of students to support the Green New Deal?	Tina*	7	7	0
Unsuccessful Cases				
What is Chinese food culture like?	Jake	11	2	9
What are the existing disadvantages of American democracy?	Mike*	108	30	78
	Lynn	3	0	3

* indicates that the student has participated in Zhihu tasks at both upper-intermediate and advanced levels.

Zhihu in class. As for unsuccessful cases, Jake's post on Chinese food culture and Mike's and Lynn's posts on American democracy were identified because they received the fewest content-focused responses. Interestingly, Mike was identified for both successful and unsuccessful cases. His writing on American democracy as an "unsuccessful" case was accomplished five months before his writing on Internet security received nearly 100% content-focused responses. Although the identification of successful and unsuccessful cases was based on a thorough review of all the 16 focal participants' posts, the result seems to suggest that students' language proficiency level has played a big part in determining how their performances on Zhihu are received by other Chinese members. A detailed analysis of these cases is presented in the next section.

Findings

CFL learners' interaction on Zhihu

A statistical analysis of the 613 responses received from other Zhihu users reveals that more comments focused on students' foreign identity or their non-native use of Chinese, while the content-focused comments is fewer than half (42%). The specific percentages of each type of responses can be found in Figure 6.1. Apparently, Chinese Zhihu users were more attracted by the participants' revealed foreignism,

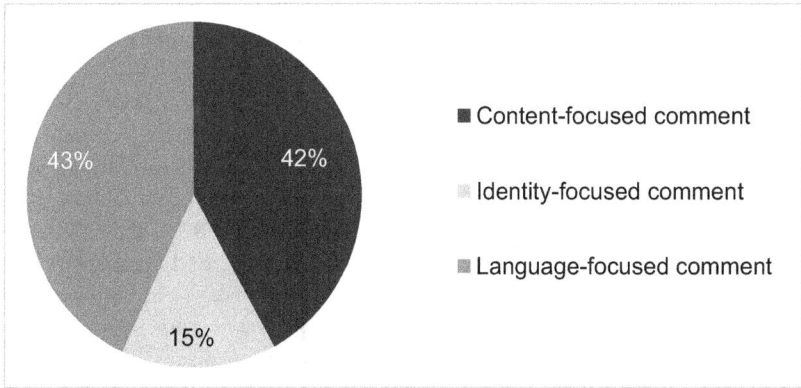

Figure 6.1 Percentages of three different types of responses from Chinese

which always diverted their attention away from the content of the discussion. No matter how students revealed or hid their identities, comments unavoidably focused on criticism or compliments with regard to their Chinese use, appreciation of their efforts and enthusiasm about learning Chinese and their potential value as native-speaking English tutors. This seems to echo a previous study that revealed the harsh reality that for English-speaking students participating in activities abroad, the most valuable asset they have to offer may be their English skills (Dewey, Belnap, & Hillstrom, 2013).

Most of the non-content-focused comments centered on students' use of Chinese (43%), and a few were simply attracted to students' foreign identity (15%), which was either disclosed by the students or inferred from their writing. Sometimes, these two types of comments converged and appeared simultaneously. Language-focused comments range from "Wow, your Chinese is awesome!" to "Reading your Chinese is painful. Why don't you just speak English?" The most common type of language-focused responses was relating to one's own English learning experience. This, however, can either be presented in an encouraging way (e.g., "You are talented. I was just wondering whether I was able to write as well as you did after studying English for three years in college.") or can sound like an implied criticism (e.g., "HAHA. . . . Your writing made me understand my English teacher's feeling when she read my English essay"). Interestingly, although language-focused comments occurred most frequently, a few debates could be observed among Chinese netizens themselves on whether or not they should concentrate on foreigners' non-native uses of Chinese. One was concerned that correcting their Chinese too much would discourage foreign users from participating in the community, and the other argued that it was disrespectful to ignore the contents they wrote while exclusively focusing on the expression.

Compared to the comments on language, comments focusing on students' foreign identity are more diverse in terms of their tones and expressions. Positive comments include a warm welcome and excitement over seeing a foreigner joining a Chinese community. Negative ones usually involve doubts questioning students' purposes of participating in this community. For example, one Chinese netizen questioned, "怎么一夜之间那么多老外来知乎上发言，是你们老师布置的功课吗？" (Why do so many foreigners post on Zhihu all of a sudden? Is this an assignment your teacher gave to you?) Another comment seemed to contain more hostility: "美国人准备攻击、攻占知乎了吗？" (Are Americans ready to attack and occupy Zhihu?)

Although explicitly negative comments like these occupied less than 2% among all the comments (and around 9% of the non-content-focused comments), what underlay these comments was a clear indication of anti-West or anti-American cyber-nationalism reflected in the tension between *laowai* (foreigners) and Chinese. The frustration of the netizens seemed come from two places: First, American students' utilizing the platform of Zhihu to practice Chinese as a school task has deviated from the nature of Zhihu as a knowledge-sharing community, which made some Chinese netizens feel that they are being taken advantage of. As one Chinese netizen harshly criticized, "一个老外胡诌几句, 哪来这么多赞？媚外！" (How can a foreigner's nonsense receive so many praises? Blind faith in foreigners!) CFL students' unpolished writing has disqualified them as legitimate knowledge contributors. Second, this particular harsh comment also highlighted another emotional factor underlying such hostility, which is the strong anti-West cyber-nationalism prevailing in the Chinese online community. This became especially noticeable when the topic was about America, such as American democracy (answered by Mike, Cara, Melisa, Lynn and John) and American people's prejudices about China (answered by Helena). As Wu (2007) observed, "in China's online discourse, if the topic is about Sino-U.S. relationship, you can always encounter two opposing points of view, one pro-American and one anti-American" (p. 210). When the nationalism starts, calm discussion is hard to sustain. Zhihu is considered then as Chinese territory, and no matter what Americans said, they were just intruders. Chinese netizens' using wartime vocabulary such as *gongji* (attack) and *gongzhan* (occupy) to interpret American students' intention are good examples of such thinking.

In the meanwhile, the statistical data also shows that less than 5% of the responses were able to elicit further interactions between the author and the commenters. In other words, the chance of American students and Chinese netizens sustaining a complex conversation on Zhihu was very low, and the anticipated negotiation of intentions and meanings between the two parties rarely took place. During the interview, Tina's response more or less explained why students were reluctant to respond to the comments:

> One time I made a post that got a lot of responses. At first, I felt good about it, but then I got discouraged because I didn't have enough time to look at and respond to all of them. I ended up feeling overwhelmed. I don't even like to post my thoughts onto American social media outlets, so posting on *Zhihu* in Chinese was something I got anxious about sometimes, especially if I got a lot of responses. In general, getting feedback from people I don't know always made me feel kind of worried.

In addition to the concerns towards getting involved in the public debate, Lynn also explained why she never looked at those comments:

> I do not use *Zhihu* unless it is for something related to Chinese class. It was interesting to use *Zhihu* because it is an authentic Chinese media. However, our assignments did not require us to use *Zhihu* in an interactive way. Sometimes, people would correct me, which was helpful. It will be a lot more helpful if the teacher corrects it every week.

What we can conclude from students' performance online and their explanations is that in most situations, students came to Zhihu without seeing themselves as knowledge contributors either. They stayed in their identity as Chinese learners using Zhihu to complete whatever tasks assigned to them. What they were anticipating from this activity, as Lynn suggested, was some native Chinese speakers' correcting their grammatical errors rather than a bond to the community or inspiration from further discussion. Furthermore, the community also presents obstacles to them. For various reasons as mentioned earlier, Chinese members of Zhihu tend to invalidate students' attempts to establish a legitimate persona of a knowledge contributor through those non-content-focused comments. Their invalidation could be gentle or harsh, friendly or hostile, conscious or unconscious.

Another tentative observation from the data is that the proportion of content-focused responses to non-content-focused responses is related to the activity design. In general, students' writings on self-determined topics received far more content-focused responses (50%) than those on curricular topics given by the instructors (34%). Such differences may lead us to consider the next question: What factors underlie the success and failure of maintaining a legitimate membership within a community of practice?

Factors underlying CFL learners' successful and unsuccessful engagement with the community

Three major themes emerged from a further study of the six identified cases, all of which correlated to each other and played a vital role in determining whether or not the CFL learners can meaningfully engage with the Zhihu community: (1) Identification with the community; (2) familiarity with the shared repertoire among community practitioners and (3) expertise in a well-defined domain.

Identification with the community

One factor standing out immediately from the data to distinguish the successful cases from the unsuccessful ones was students' willingness to identify with the community. Although CFL learners have been actively producing posts on Zhihu, most of them, as Lynn previously pointed out, rarely continued to participate in the conversation initiated by the "artifacts" they produced. Those physical and conceptual artifacts that students produced on Zhihu, in Wenger's (1998) word, are a form of *reification*. As Wenger emphasizes, reification must interplay with other forms of personal *participation* in the social contexts to make the meaningful learning happen, since "artifacts without participation do not carry their own meaning."

In those successful cases identified in this study, CFL learners have demonstrated both participation and reification. Mike had the time to make over a dozen Chinese friends on Zhihu who became long-term readers of his posts. Gradually, those Chinese netizens were no longer attracted to Mike's ability to communicate in Chinese. Instead, as they became knowing Mike more personally, most were fascinated by Mike's intelligence and humor as a person and his expertise in Internet security, particularly his familiarity with the frequency of hacking in the United States. Mike said he had received many personal messages from other Zhihu users; although the requests to become a language exchange partner still exist, many also consulted him on topics related to studying computer science in America, joining the Western hacking community and so forth. Similarly, Tina also shared changes that took place during this long journey. Describing herself as being "very anti-social media," Tina recalled how anxious and overwhelmed she was when she first started posting on Zhihu. She even asked her instructor to excuse her from posting on the actual website. However, she decided to push herself out of her comfort zone at the beginning of her fifth year of Chinese class. She reactivated her Zhihu account and began to reply to some private messages she had received from Chinese netizens. Similar to Mike, Tina soon developed a network with some Chinese netizens who read her posts weekly. She believed that these people's very positive responses to her posts influenced other Zhihu users' impressions of her. The more time Tina spent on Zhihu, the more confidence she gained in distinguishing between constructive suggestions and irrational curses, which allowed her to easily ignore the latter types without feeling overwhelmed.

Certainly, from these cases, we can also see that the amount of time that students invested on Zhihu has affected how much they are able to identify with the community. For both Mike and Tina, their previous semester of participating on Zhihu became the key to being able to socialize in this online knowledge-sharing community. Undeniably, Mike and Tina's posts may have been better received on Zhihu due to their more advanced writing proficiency in Chinese. However, aside from their superior writing performance, interviews with both students also clearly revealed that investing substantial time with this community provided them with critical access to local social networks, which offered significantly improved opportunities for sustained interaction. The dimension of *time* is, in fact, an important element in the community of practice framework, especially to the form of identity. In a later interview after Wenger proposed the community of practice theory, he added that identity is "a time/space concept" because "you become a person out of a whole series of experiences over time" (Farnsworth, Kleanthous, & Wenger-Trayner, 2016, pp. 11–12).

Familiarity with the shared repertoire

As discussed before, the shared repertoire consists of resources accumulated through the history of social learning within the community, which in the current context particularly include verbal expressions, ways of addressing, ways of using the website, symbols and genres that Zhihu members have developed and adopted. However, there exists no instructional manual that a new member can refer to about how they are expected to talk in this community. As Wenger (1998) pointed out, the shared repertoire is just "inherently ambiguous" (p. 83).

The Zhihu community shares a distinctive linguistic repertoire known as *Zhihu ti* ('Zhihu style'). Although such discourse style is not a prerequisite for joining the discussion on Zhihu, skillful application of it in one's writing can clearly index one's epistemic stance and social status, which will be easily recognized by all the experienced members of the community and increase the credibility of one's writing. For example, one typical Zhihu-style opening to start one's answer can be formed as "谢邀。人在XX, YY就职。" (Thank you for inviting me to answer the question. Located in XX and work for YY). Here, XX indicates where the author is located, which is always expected to be a highly developed country or city. YY indicates the name of the workplace where the author works, such as a Global 500 company. Such a template-like opening can be seen everywhere on Zhihu, signifying the author's educational background, professional experiences, economic and social status and so forth. According to a recent article (Pan Guan, August 2019) analyzing the current state of Zhihu, this distinctive opening style is so popular that some people even faked their identity so as to fit in this template, which is called to "build one's artificial character set" (打造虚拟人设). On a side note, this phenomenon also explains why some students were questioned about their true identity and considered to be fake foreigners, as one comment goes: "Is it no longer popular to say that you are a foreigner or a foreign-born Chinese? The current trend is to say you are a foreigner" (说留学生或者华裔已经不流行了吗？这年头已经开始说自己是外国人了).

Despite the popularity of revealing (or constructing) one's background at the beginning of the answer post, a close analysis of the CFL students' posts reveals that their writings on Zhihu are nothing similar to this preferred character setting. For example, instead of "showing off" their educational background and working experiences, the three students in the unsuccessful group constantly performed a humble student identity in the writings. Specifically, they disclosed their humble but real identities at the beginning, apologized for their "not-so-good Chinese" and expressed concerns about not being able to discuss the topic thoroughly. The three selected openings from the unsuccessful group are shown below:

1 我是学中文的美国学生，对不起，我的中文可能有一点错。 (I am an American student studying Chinese. Sorry, my Chinese might have some errors.)
2 大家好！我叫xxx。我是xxxx大学一名二年级的学生。 (Hello everyone! My name is xxx. I am a sophomore student from university of xxxx.)
3 我是美国大学生，我的专业是中文。我们最近学习这个话题。下面大概有很多的错误，请你们给我评论告诉我写错的地方。 (I am an American student. My major is Chinese. We have studied this topic recently. My writing below probably contains many mistakes. Please tell me where I made mistakes through comments.)

Such introductions not only appeared in these representative cases but also commonly occurred in most students' online posts, especially among the students who used Zhihu during their first semester to discuss curriculum-related topics. When asked why they decided to adopt such discourse styles, Jake attributed them to his Chinese teacher, who told the students that acting modestly and revealing one's American identity would inspire the Chinese netizens to easily forgive their linguistic mistakes. Other students interviewed, however, did not particularly associate this style with the instructions given by their teachers; rather they considered it to be a subconscious continuation of the speech-type discourse with which they were most familiar when giving oral presentations or leading class discussions. Without explicit guidance on how to adopt the typical Zhihu style through close observation, students do not even have the genre awareness to adjust their discourse styles.

In addition, students' lack of shared repertoire prevented them from being treated seriously as legitimate community members. Instead, whether they were welcomed or not, most American students on Zhihu were locked into the student/Chinese learner identity, which always required special accommodations. Some Chinese netizens made fun of students for revealing their real identities (e.g., "哈哈, 哥们, 你也不用把你的名字什么打出来啊, 太耿直了。Ha, ha, buddy, you don't need to type out your names and etc. You are too honest."), while others questioned them for being overly polite or formal (e.g., "可为什么你每个回答都是大家好大家好的呀, 这又不是在演讲。But why did you have to start with 'Hello everyone' in each of your answers? You are not giving a speech, are you?"). Although there is no "rule" that has ever been explicitly spelled out anywhere on the website, there is obviously a set of "dispositions" that generates practices and perceptions among its members and orients their actions and inclinations. Such shared dispositions are what Bourdieu (1991) calls habitus, which "incline[s] agents to act and react in certain ways" (p. 12). Lacking the habitus necessary to fully participate on Zhihu resulted not only in a devaluation of students' writing but also in an invalidation of their identities as legitimate members of the community.

All the three students in the successful group, on the contrary, do not easily reveal their "Chinese learner" identity unless necessary. In another word, in those posts they do not see themselves as CFL students completing a task on Zhihu but as knowers who feel it is necessary to say something on that topic. For example, Tina also revealed that she significantly changed how she composed her posts. At the beginning, like those students shown above, she took a preventive strategy of being humble, hoping to avoid criticism. However, she later realized that the more she acted like a humble student, the more attention would be focused on her foreign identity, which just discounted the message she was attempting to communicate. From then on, she tried to appear "more decisive" in her writings as she observed that Chinese people online seemed not as modest as those presented in her textbook. As a keen observer of her environment, Tina gradually discovered the repertoire shared by the online community and continued to base her behavior around it. Tina's case again highlighted the significance of the temporal element in forming the community of practice. In the meanwhile, it is again difficult to say whether this is a rhetorical strategy they intentionally adopted or it is just a natural manifestation of their strong identification with the community as legitimate members, as revealed in the previous section. These two factors apparently interplay and contribute to each other.

Expertise in a well-defined domain

A community of practice is not simply a network of connections among members. Its membership is defined by a shared domain of interest and a commitment to the domain and the "learning partnership" (Wenger, 1998, p. 12). As previously mentioned, students' writings on self-determined topics generated far more content-focused responses than their posts on curricular-based topics. Despite the fact that advanced-level learners' higher writing proficiency usually allows them to better articulate their thoughts, what underlies their success is also the demonstrated expertise related to the domain of the topic. Since self-determined topics are always from the domains that students are knowledgeable about, their experiences and expertise on these topics have made them more of an asset to the community. For example, posts that have received almost 100% content-focused responses are Jane's discussion on obesity in America (100%) as a student specializing in biological chemistry, Tina's discussion on Democratic Senator Dianne Feinstein and the Green New Deal (100%) as a student majoring in American politics and Mike's recommendations of books on hacking (85%) as an experienced hacker and computer science major.

Within the unsuccessful group, the topic Jake and a few other students answered ("What does Chinese cuisine look like?), in general, did not result in productive conversation but rather mocking responses. One Chinese netizen's comment more or less sums up a general lack of interest among the Zhihu users in carrying out further conversations on their answers: "离题。为什么这里的答案都有一种老师布置的作文的感觉" (Please allow me to diverge from the topic. Why are all the answers here giving me the impression that these writing compositions are assigned by teachers?) It is not difficult to pick up on the thinly veiled distrust and disappointment when reading between lines, though this post does not contain any intended outright hostility. To the Chinese netizens, the only reason that American students would post on Zhihu was to make use of this platform to practice their Chinese, which obviously was not aligned with the goal of the website and was considered as an insincere commitment to learning partnership as anticipated by the community. In fact, this commenter is not the only one who was bothered by a group of Americans responding to the same question around the same time with very similar answers (which they did not know are paraphrased from their textbook). Two other commenters posted parodies of American students' discourse style in answering these questions. One example can be seen as follows:

> 大家好，我叫彭狗蛋。我是中华人民共和国人，我上的是某某大学; 我的专业是中文和国家研究。如果我写错的, 请你们告诉我为了帮我提高

我的中文水平。谢谢你们。最近我在学习关于中国的食饭文化, 希望大家能教我怎么吃。

(Translation)Hello everyone, my name is Goudan Peng. I am a Chinese. I go to university xx; my major is Chinese and national studies. If I made mistake, please tell me so as to help me improve my Chinese. Recently, I am learning Chinese food culture and I hope you can teach me how to eat. (The original Chinese version of the last two sentences contain several grammatical mistakes, which seems an intentional imitation of American students' commonly made mistakes in their posts.)

Certainly, on one hand, American students were mocked by such parody because of the lack of shared repertoire as discussed in the previous section. Nonetheless, on the other hand, the distrust of Chinese netizens may also come from their entitled native speaker ownership of the target language and culture (Zeng, 2018; Zhang, Chapter 2 of this volume). As Zhang's (2016) study pointed out, "regardless of whether ownership is real or simply imagined, it has actual, concrete influences on people's practice and perception" (p. 147). It is such entitled native speaker ownership that motivates Chinese to always perceive a lack of cultural capital in American students in discussing such topics, whose foreign identities prevent them from being experts on such topics.

However, when American students made contributions to topics on which they had certain insider perspectives or expertise, the interaction looked very different. Tina's mention of a current event—a group of young climate activists confronting Senator Dianne Feinstein over the Green New Deal—had inspired a heated discussion with the Chinese netizens. As the original post asked people's opinion about this incident, Tina, as a senior college student specializing in international politics, was motivated to provide her perspectives. By quoting a previous comment, Tina first expressed her agreement with this Chinese netizen, who strongly opposed the actions of the young students. Following her expression of agreement, Tina strategically took a middle-ground position by trying to explain the motivations of the students, which hinted an indirect criticism of Senator Feinstein's refusal to support the Green New Deal. At the end of her post, she also acknowledged the positive aspects of the Green New Deal by calling it "a complete economic approach" (完整的经济方案). Although Tina thought she was taking a middle-ground position, most Chinese netizens still recognized her taking the young students' side, which therefore resulted in almost exclusive disagreement. However, these comments focused on nothing but her opinion and were expressed in a calm and serious manner. These comments were intriguing to Tina and provided her a window to learn more about Chinese netizens' attitudes towards American politics. They also motivated her to further negotiate what she meant by engaging her in a respectful conversation. For example, when Tina responded to this Chinese netizen, she first thanked them for teaching her a new Chinese expression 气候变化 ('climate change') to replace her original expression 全球变暖 ('global warming') and then re-asserted her middle-ground stance. She also asked the Chinese netizens for their opinions about the young students' confrontation, which eventually inspired a discussion involving more Zhihu users on how political topics are handled in K–12 schools in the United States.

Discussion: the sporadically emerging Third Space

As defined earlier, Third Space in this study not only refers to a static location where the intercultural communication takes place, but it is also conceptualized as a practice to actively engage a dialogic communication between the interlocutors within this intercultural space. Specifically in the context of a social Q&A site like Zhihu, such communication leads to learning through transforming perspectives rather than achieving agreement among the interlocutors. Based on the findings as discussed earlier, it is clear that although Zhihu as an online knowledge-sharing community may hold the potential to facilitate the emergence of dialogic communication, its existence is ephemeral. The anticipated negotiation of meaning cannot occur until CFL students are considered to be qualified knowledge contributors of the community. Students were observed to engage in the identity negotiations on Zhihu, which, as Bourdieu (1991) suggests, are struggles over the power to be seen and believed. They attempted to carve out a space where they could escape from being framed as incapable non-native speakers and become cross-cultural mediators. However, such negotiations were not successful and, in most cases, led to the end of conversations between the two sides. As a result, when mutual intentions of the two parties were not fully recognized and addressed, the anticipated Third Space only sporadically emerged and was difficult to sustain.

Two major factors have impeded CFL learners from negotiating and sustaining a productive Third Space with other Chinese Zhihu members: Sticking to the "self" and ignoring the "other." First, the pedagogical design of these learning activities utilizing Zhihu seemed optimistic, assuming that as long as students voice their opinions in that community, the intercultural communication between the CFL learners and other native Chinese Zhihu members will naturally happen. Although the instructors' intention was to incorporate authentic target-culture artifacts into the CFL curriculum without fully addressing the knowledge-sharing nature of the Zhihu community, some learning assignments were in fact just inauthentic tasks performed in an authentic target-culture community. For example, assigning American students who just read one introductory article on Chinese food culture to help Chinese netizens achieve a deeper understanding of Chinese cuisine has altered the nature of their participation in the community. Those writings were exclusively filled with self-expression rather than addressing the needs of the "other," resulting only in disbelief and invalidation. CFL learners' blind continuation of their familiar speech-type discourse on Zhihu is another illustration of such adherence to the self, and their being unobservant also led to the ignorance of the "other."

Second, students participating in discussions on Zhihu had very little knowledge about this community of practice in terms of its shared practices, repertoire and objectives. Without a full understanding of the cyber-nationalism against Western values such as American democracy, students were not able to recognize what underlay those hostile and irrelevant comments, let alone to initiate a dialogue with them. Lacking the shared linguistic repertoire to signify one's epistemic and social status within the community has prevented many students from conveying their messages with credibility and authority, which has led to few serious conversations. Such "ignorance" about the "other" made them perceived as complete outsiders who had demonstrated little commitment to the learning partnership or even as unwelcome invaders with ulterior purposes.

Conclusion and pedagogical implications

The Zhihu tasks were designed to encourage the students to contribute their perspectives and expertise as skillful users of Chinese and to connect with other members of the identified community. However, students' actual experiences examined in this study resulted in both alignments and misalignments between reality and imagination. On the one hand, attracted by the exotic nature of American students, the Chinese Zhihu users always diverted the focus of the conversation away from the content of the discussion and interrogated students about their purposes of participating on Zhihu. On the other hand, being eager to practicing what they have learned in class on this authentic target-culture online community, American students easily overlooked the special knowledge-sharing nature of Zhihu, which rendered them as complete outsiders who were perceived as intruding into this special community.

Three factors are identified from this study, determining students' success in engaging with the Zhihu community, which have significant implications for the design of pedagogical activities that take place in knowledge-sharing communities. First, students who had more successful experiences on Zhihu have demonstrated stronger identification with the community. On the one hand, it takes time to become accepted and to legitimately participate in a community, moving from the periphery to the center, especially within a knowledge-sharing community that emphasizes socializing. On the other hand, students' interpretation of this learning activity has also affected their motivation to identify with the community. Instructors who want to utilize the Zhihu platform to design such learning activity needs to explicitly articulate what are the expectations for becoming a Zhihu member if their goal is to design authentic reading and writing tasks using Zhihu. Socializing with other members of the community should be built into this learning activity with concrete requirements, such as being responsive to meaningful interactions.

Second, a lack of familiarity with the shared repertoire of the community prevents CFL learners from being treated seriously as legitimate community members. Therefore, instructors should more explicitly articulate the broader context of Zhihu, including its goals, the nature of the interactions taking place on it, and the demographic characteristics of the community. More scaffolding activities should also be provided to students in this line before having them join the thread and answer questions. These activities can be analyzing discourse styles of a group of posts selected by the instructor, making brief comments on other members' answers, and imitating the discourse style in more practice writing before posting online.

Third, in order to successfully engage with the community, students need to demonstrate their expertise in whatever domain they identify with. Therefore, when assigning topics to students as writing tasks, instructors should carefully choose topics about which students truly have expertise or insider perspectives that will benefit most Chinese Zhihu users. The Zhihu platform should not be considered simply as an online space to showcase students' Chinese writing. Whatever students produce, however, needs to demonstrate a commitment to the social learning as anticipated in the community of practice. After all, the pedagogy of incorporating target-culture online space into foreign language classes should be aimed at equipping learners with a set of strategies to "maximize the acquisition of symbolic profit" (Bourdieu, 1991, p. 76) online and eventually to be seen, heard and believed.

References

Bhabha, H. K. (1994). *The location of culture*. London: Routledge.
Bourdieu, P. (1991). *Language and symbolic power*. Cambridge: Polity Press.
Da Hua Yun Ying. (2018, August 29). 七个知乎用户的人群画像特点, 这些决定知乎运营的成败 (*Seven characteristics of Zhihu users who determining the success and failure of Zhihu's operation*). Retrieved from https://vvbig.com/hlw/1760.html
Dewey, D. P., Belnap, R. K., & Hillstrom, R. (2013). Social network development, language use, and language acquisition during study abroad: Arabic language learners' perspectives. *Frontiers: An Interdisciplinary Journal of Study Abroad*, *22*, 84–110.
Farnsworth, V., Kleanthous, I., & Wenger-Trayner, E. (2016). Communities of practice as a social theory of learning: A conversation with Etienne Wenger. *British Journal of Educational Studies*, 1–22. https://doi.org/10.1080/00071005.2015.1133799
Flores, N., & García, O. (2013). Linguistic third spaces in education: Teachers' translanguaging across the bilingual continuum. In D. Little, C. Leung, & P. Van Avermaet (Eds.), *Managing diversity in education: Key issues and some responses* (pp. 243–256). Clevedon: Multilingual Matters.
Gutiérrez, K. D., Baquedano-López, P., & Tejeda, C. (1999). Rethinking diversity: Hybridity and hybrid language practices in the third space. *Mind, Culture and Activity*, *6*, 286–303.
Hogarth, H. K. (2013). The Korean wave: An Asian reaction to western-dominated globalization. *Perspectives of Global Development and Technology*, *12*, 135–151. https://doi.org/10.1163/15691497-12341247
iClick Zhihu Research. (July, 2017). Retrieved from https://walkthechat.com/zhihu-chinas-largest-qa-platform-content-marketers-dream/
Kramsch, C. (2009). Third culture and language education. In L. Wei & V. Cook (Eds.), *Contemporary applied linguistics: Vol.1. Language teaching and learning* (pp. 233–254). London: Continuum.
Lave, J., & Wenger, E. (1991). *Situated learning: Legitimate peripheral participation*. Cambridge: Cambridge University Press.
Lee, K., Liang, H., Jiao, L., & Wheatley, J. (2010). *The Routledge advanced Chinese multimedia course: Crossing cultural boundaries* (文化纵横观). New York: Routledge.

Norton Pierce, B. (1995). Social identity, investment, and language learning. *TESOL Quarterly*, *29*, 9–31. https://doi.org/10.2307/3587803

Norton Pierce, B. (2000). *Identity and language learning: Gender, ethnicity and educational change*. Essex: Pearson Education.

Pan Guan. (2019, August 14). 谢邀, 知乎刚下神坛 (*Thank you for inviting me, Zhihu just stepped down from the altar*). Retrieved from https://zhuanlan.zhihu.com/p/78202683

Smith, J. D., Wenger, E., & White, N. (2009). *Digital Habitats: Stewarding technology for communities*. Portland, OR: CPsquare.

Soja, E. W. (2009). Thirdspace: Toward a new consciousness of space and spatiality. In K. Ikas & G. Wagner (Eds.), *Communicating in the third space* (pp. 49–61). New York: Routledge.

Toohey, K. (1996). Learning English as a second language in kindergarten: A community of practice perspective. *Canadian Modern Language Review*, *52*, 549–576. https://doi.org/10.3138/cmlr.52.4.549

Wenger, E. (1998). *Communities of practice: Learning meaning, and identity*. Cambridge: Cambridge University Press.

Wu, X. (2007). *Chinese cyber nationalism: Evolution, characteristics, and implications*. Lanham, MD: Lexington Books.

Zeng, Z. (2018). Striving for the third space: A U.S. professional's experiences in Chinese workplaces. *Foreign Language Annals*, *51*, 658–684. https://doi.org/10.1111/flan.12352

Zhang, X. (2016). *Four-character idioms in advanced spoken Chinese: Perception and reaction of native speakers and a pedagogy of C2 expectations*. Doctoral dissertation, The Ohio State University, Columbus. Retrieved May 1, 2020, from https://etd.ohiolink.edu/

7 Why we perform

Galal Walker

Introduction

An adult determined to learn how to communicate in Chinese as a foreign language and culture is on an extreme humanistic exploration. Succeeding in this venture requires a learner to agree to a persistent engagement with another culture long enough to gain the ability to co-construct meaning with the natives in that culture. That includes knowing what to do and what not to do in establishing intentions in familiar interactions done in unfamiliar ways. Knowing how to say something in a new language is not sufficient. That can easily result in dueling declarations focused on the declarers' intentions rather than the hearers' understandings. Conversation is the required method for realizing the agreement to communicate, emerging from a recognition of a new culture and in cooperation with owners of that culture. If the role of language is to convey messages, the messages are necessarily co-constructed by speaker and hearer, by writer and reader. Before American learners can begin to communicate with Chinese, they must perceive that assuming American English strategies for co-constructing conversations will often fail, and from awareness of those failures they become conscious of another possible way to socialize. This view of consciousness is not the mind on or off, but rather the ability to focus on the intention to communicate, to adapt communicative moves and judgment and to act on memories of successful communication events. This ability can be engendered early in the process of learning Chinese, a bit at a time, starting with enough knowledge and desire to get into the game and to continue participation over a long enough time. A new CFL consciousness is not perceived as an abstraction in the mind but as observable behavior in communicative events. The process is an extensive program of performances, presented by and required by designed Chinese instruction and realized by learners enacting what they know. Among a long humanistic tradition of observations of this aspect of the human condition, Wallace Stevens identified the appeal of this understanding in the case of Susanna and the Elders:

> Beauty is momentary in the mind
> The fitful tracing of a portal
> But in the flesh it is immortal.
>   (from "Peter Quince at the Clavier")

A language program

Every fall term we meet around 200 students in our first-year Chinese as Foreign Language (CFL) classes. Most of these students have chosen that course because they eventually intend to communicate in Chinese with people in and from China. The student who has chosen this course primarily to meet a language requirement is rare and is usually quick to exit the course once she or he understands the amount of time required to succeed there academically. The overwhelming majority of students in these classes have no prior experience with the language and not one of them in the classroom has had any experience communicating with Chinese people in Chinese-culture environments.[1] What we as teachers ask them to do to reach their goals reveals how we regard the process of getting to those goals in an academic environment without a surrounding Chinese society. A young adult in Columbus, Ohio, is engaging first-year Chinese as a very foreign language.

Our program at Ohio State University is designed and operated for beginning learners who in good time intend to communicate their individual interests in Chinese-speaking environments. That means our goal is for young adult learners from the American Midwest to reach observable advanced-level communication skills in Chinese before they graduate. That commits us to consider time as our most precious resource and the management of time our biggest problem. Compared to government institutes and programs that set their programs and budgets according to the resources required for individuals to reach institutionalized, mostly in-house proficiency ratings,[2] university programs must have more open-ended goals—namely, to prepare our learners to be astute acquirers of Chinese both during and especially after leaving our academic programs.

Lacking the resources and classroom time of a federal government program, universities can only afford pedagogical strategies for devoting the maximum amount of instructional time toward developing the capacity to engage Chinese native speakers who are not paid to engage foreigners in developmental communication. These pedagogical efforts strive to focus on providing practice and guidance in social interactions in the early stages and research skills in chosen areas of academic exploration at the later stages. The pedagogy, which simply put is the study of what humans do and make to assist learners to recognize and perform an identified body of knowledge, is based on a concept of "culture," which requires attention to the expectations of Chinese-speaking interlocutors, and "domain," which engages the intellectual interests of the learner and explores these interests in Chinese language and society. We focus on culture and domain in terms of actions that we can describe, execute and observe. Assessment is based on observing these designated behaviors. Our pedagogy for Chinese as a foreign language (CFL) is situated in an understanding of language as a function of culture, a view succinctly put by Daniel Everett (2017):

> A theory of culture underlies an understanding of language evolution. In fact, there can be no adequate theory of language evolution without a sound theory of culture.
>
> (p. 67)

Language is underspecified for meaning. Without culture, whether for *sapiens* or *erectus*, there is no communication.

(p. 256)

Taking culture per se as being necessary for communicating in a language, if a CFL pedagogy is not specifically designed for making meaning in Chinese culture, throughout the duration of a course of any study meaning will default to the available base-culture of the learners. For example, for our students elements of Chinese language and socialization would be assigned the meanings corresponding to English elements gleaned from American contexts.

Being in another culture

It is not uncommon for learners of a foreign language to protest that if they do not act in a certain way in an understood cultural context, they are being dishonest or untrue to their own selves. Young American adults are insistent about their social identity because they are basically unsure about it, so in a CFL class we avoid equating issues of identity with conventions of social behaviors in Chinese language and culture. We direct their awareness away from themselves and on to those real or imagined to whom they are speaking. We repeatedly point out instances where even in our base language and culture, we regularly behave differently from occasion to occasion, acting and choosing language one way in social groups and another way in formal rituals, business meetings or classes—this in order to appeal to those with whom we communicate. The difficult thing for some Americans to realize is that how we are known or regarded is determined by those with whom we are interacting; that is, our audiences determine who we are in relation to each group with which we associate. As teachers, we realize what we know of our students consists of only what they are willing to reveal in a class or in rather strained personal encounters. What an instructor can know about a student, then, is the student's revealed persona. If students stay with us long enough in their college careers, their personae as perceived by us will change considerably over time. Over time in our program, we want each learner to be able to develop at least one persona that will be effective when he or she is communicating in Chinese social contexts. As participants in social encounters, we too often choose to overlook that it is our audiences who characterize our various personae in the various social groups we infiltrate and occupy.

In presenting Chinese culture to our students, we have a working understanding of the steps involved when humans construct and perceive individuals through culture: (1) The culture provides contexts; (2) the contexts permit meanings; (3) meanings reveal intentions; and (4) intentions enable individuals (Walker, 2010). Encountering a new culture repeatedly presents learners with unfamiliar contexts. If they continue to communicate successfully in Chinese, they eventually create versions of themselves among those who participate in the communication events. Hopefully, the new versions will prove to be successful personae for forwarding the new learners' intentions when communicating with different groupings of Chinese people.

At Ohio State University, the base culture would be American culture as experienced by young adults. The majority of Chinese programs in the United States are implemented in the students' and the institution's base culture (i.e., using Chinese to respond to American English expectations). Situating Chinese language study solely in the learners' base culture works well if the students stay in their language program and are tested for their proficiencies with standardized (largely bilingual) tests and procedures based in their language program. For example, if the main role of a person proficient in CFL is to interpret Chinese back to English-speaking Americans—either in their language programs or in their employment environment—then it is reasonable to conduct language training in which the tests or anticipated requirements of employment are to report Chinese "meanings" to English-speaking Americans.

Alternatively, we seek to create programs that put our individual CFL learners in situations where they need to participate in sustained purposeful communication (e.g., work) in Chinese cultural environments. In our program, we have striven to create work opportunities for our students by arranging internships in organizations in China where at an appropriate time in their CFL career each student has the opportunity to work in a Chinese social group with an identifiable purpose (e.g., a job). We prepare and hope for successes, but those are not guaranteed. In our records, successful interns are identified by their hosts' descriptions of the many ways the young American adjusted to working with young staffers who were roughly the intern's age. Generally, they were praised for their ability to learn and to assist the host organizations' efforts to reach collective goals. These interns' respective abilities to progress in using Mandarin effectively were uniformly praised.

Our students were not always judged to be successes. As a program—students and teachers—we learned from our failures. To dismiss criticism of our students and thereby attribute failures to their host organizations would be equivalent to taking such criticism as opportunities to assist in the reform of Chinese office staff and managers by expecting them to meet some of our students' expectations rather than the obverse. We find it more productive to recognize that failures in the field are the fault of our program. Internship placements in Chinese firms and non-governmental organizations have been of high value to our various programs. We have expended extensive portions of our resources and charm in securing places where our students could go and work in Chinese environments as a first indication of their capacity to negotiate "serious" non-classroom relationships. It is hard to overestimate the importance of these experiences to the assessments of our graduates and our work. So, we were sure to follow up on the lessons learned.

All of us who set out to learn to communicate in another culture are travelers, either by physically relocating to other persons' piece of Earth or creating a space in our minds where the natives determine what we intend without first checking with us. When engaging persons and organizations in a foreign culture for the first time when things are not what we would expect, we have noticed that the most common thought to cross a traveler's mind is that they (the natives) are generally getting it wrong. After all, they are doing things that the traveler perceives as familiar, albeit in perversely unfamiliar ways. This is noticeable both when Americans first engage in China and when Chinese first engage in the United States. Successful travelers between cultures are adventurous and are sooner to learn to dismiss this concern about how natives act in their native spaces—some travelers learn this much quicker than others and some not at all. Our programs over the years have accumulated tales of successes and failures. While the successes reflected well on our students and programs, the failures were more instructive in identifying our needs to make changes in our pedagogy as the program changes over time. We explicitly decided that the successful interns demonstrated they knew something that the failed interns did not. The successes seemed to be specific, if somewhat unpredictable. On the other hand, failures were based on a relatively few modes of perception that we have striven to train our students to avoid in their social interactions in Chinese workplaces. This process led to the stark conclusion that our successful interns realized that their Chinese colleagues had reasons for their behavior even though it departed from the students' initial expectations—a possibility of which our failed interns did not show any awareness.

Admittedly we have been reluctant to use the examples of workplace failures from our own files, since the protagonist of each story is obvious and sure to be recognized by fellow participants in a program. Fortunately, we found an already published account of a young American doing a common job in China that reflected both familiar American-in-China failures and a distinct obliviousness to alternative interpretations. Such obvious failures often become stories that we innocently offer as positive reflections on the failed American and conclude with positive views of ourselves engaged in such experiences. This is where our program began noticing that the individuals who we observed as successes demonstrated a consciousness of systematic differences in Chinese and American cultures, whereas our obvious failures did not seem to have this awareness that the other exists. An insistence that all interpretations are for our base culture is understandable; otherwise, the reflection of the blame for our lack of success would shed light on us. Not everyone quickly recognizes the benefits of developing an additional cultural consciousness in addition to one's own.

Being yourself there

Fortunately, over 20 years ago, an accomplished US congresswoman and mother published an account of her daughter going off to China after majoring in Chinese in a prestigious American university (Schroeder, 1998). In referring to this published account, I do not risk seeking fault from a weak example. The author, the protagonist of this adventure, and the institution of higher education are clearly recognized as being American elite.

> Jamie went to Princeton majoring in Chinese, and then taught for a year at the University of Dalian, in northern China. True to her outspoken self, she

was running her own little Tiananmen Square revolution—showing movies that she wasn't supposed to show, assigning books the students weren't supposed to read, pushing the envelope of what the Chinese called "spiritual pollution." The military police in charge of that region would send an order that any student who donated blood would be excused from their midterm, and Jamie would respond. "It would be very nice for them to give blood, but I'm the teacher, and they are not excused from the test." Or the local prefect would declare that any student who helped to harvest the cabbages would be excused from class for a week, and Jamie would say, "They can harvest all the cabbages they want, but they have to make up the schoolwork." She went all through China, to Manchuria and Tibet. A friend from Princeton who traveled with her, a young Chinese-American woman, felt even more pressure than Jamie. While local people called Jamie a word that translated as "big nose." They acted as if her friend descended from some lowly Chinese who were dumb enough to leave the motherland. Together the women were a traveling novelty act—Dalian wasn't like Beijing, which has Dunkin' Donuts and McDonalds. They often encountered some unpleasant, even hostile behavior. But Jamie found a clever method of protection: She got an eight-millimeter video-camera, and if she encountered any guff, she'd whip it out and say in perfect Chinese, "Do that again for the police." A ballsy act. Boy, I was glad when she came home. It's hard to see your genes reincarnated in your children. You cheer and cry simultaneously. Jamie decided to get a master's degree in education at Cambridge University and is now studying for her Ph.D., eventually hoping to work in educational television. But she spent a summer training dolphins in Hawaii and sadly says she knows she will never have a job that good again! Jim was also thrilled with that line of work. He used to say, "She can't marry a dolphin, and she can't bring one home, so how bad can it be?"

(pp. 149–150)

This is a narrative about conflicts between American and Chinese perspectives on a personal, day-by-day basis in China. Despite all the possible contrasting considerations available to people in Dalian, the congresswoman is pleased to relate the daughter's refusal to consider any effort to encourage her students to engage in local community service, such as donating blood or harvesting cabbage. She praises the daughter for exposing her students in Dalian to books and movies not approved by local administrators and authorities without the slightest awareness that this activity might put the students in jeopardy, or that it would be unusual that unauthorized material would be available unless somehow smuggled into the country. The awareness of any actual local need for blood donations or help with the cabbage harvest (at that time a staple of the winter diet) is not present. The young American protagonist, instead of grasping an opportunity to play a contributory role in the local community, insists that her being a teacher excludes any efforts to benefit the people of Dalian other than that she and her students remain in the classroom. The option to give her students the experience of encouraging blood donations or harvesting cabbage in English is nonexistent in the daughter's approach to her pedagogy.

In addition to teaching at Dalian University, the daughter travels widely to Manchuria and Tibet with a Chinese American schoolmate, who is a target of insults by the natives. The adventures of most young foreigners traveling across China in those days mainly encountered difficulties that included resisting excessive offers of food and drink; however, these young American women are called names and mistreated because they are not natives. The daughter is called "big nose" and the friend is regarded as being from a defector family. For many Chinese, a "big nose" is not grotesque and having family living abroad is a point of pride. Chinese, at least those for whom fashionable appearance is important, often pay a substantial sum for an enhanced nose. And emigration has been a social feature for most of recent Chinese history—undertaken with the assumption that their Chinese culture would must accompany any such relocation by necessity. The young American women defended themselves against the natives by carrying an 8 mm video camera (a rather spectacular travel accessory in those days) and threatening in "perfect Chinese" to videotape any behavior of which they disapproved and then show it to the police. While it is amusing to imagine how that scene of two young Americans seeking the cooperation of the police to exact revenge against fellow travelers on the railway would work out in a Chinese police station, it is distressing to see that the result of earning and paying for a Chinese major at a prestigious American university ends in constant conflict between Americans and Chinese—even when the Americans are there in China.

If educational failures are reflected in this brief narrative, they certainly do not arise from the lack of resources. Also, the narrative is a mother's perspective. We do not suppose that the perspective of the young woman protagonist is completely represented here. However, her mother, who elsewhere reports herself having studied Chinese in university, reflects a perfect lack of awareness that her daughter's experiences in China could have another possible frame of meaning. The mother, an accomplished politician of national stature, is surprisingly not conscious of any contrasting perspective concerning the reported events and actions. She does not allow room for the people of Dalian to have a different account of the young American woman's time in Dalian. Without perceiving an alternative view of these experiences, she betrays a monocultural view that is indifferent to any other side of the story. This norm assumes that folks in China are simply bad humans, at least in American terms.

It is significant that her story does not report the daughter participating in any conversation with people in Dalian. All reported communication is declaration, and the story reveals no awareness or curiosity about unexpected events that invite closer inspection. The daughter has spent the time and effort to earn a degree with a Chinese major from her university. She then travels to the country and culture that is the subject of that study: A China in the midst of societal transformations of historic proportions. Having experienced university Chinese classes long enough to get a degree within a singular American culture perspective, all the reported communicative events reflect only perceptions and interpretations of events that could have occurred in some version of American culture, which is assumed to be the universal or at least the only one worth consideration. As reported, the people in China are deemed ill-behaved—but without any hint of inquiry or suspicion on the Americans' side for cause or reasons. There is no consciousness of another way of apperceiving these relationships and events, which leaves no opportunity for alternative interpretations.

Being yourself in other peoples' cultures

Although consciousness is most often discussed in terms of "self-awareness," here the concept requires the awareness of "other-awareness" or self in relation to others, leading to the ability to have subjective social experiences outside the boundaries of one's prior life. Here we can consider some alternative ways of successful CFL learners becoming aware of a new way to perceive and respond to doing and knowing in Chinese culture: Perhaps the act of refusing, or developing a new taste for an unfamiliar food, or to express time in a way that is not possible in English or another base language—all of which would require individuals to accept at least one alternative way to make meaning using a learned language and a newly experienced culture. Once in place and accepted as a possibility, this seed of "other-awareness" affects how individuals and groups develop the apperceptions that follow and shape individual and collective cognitions and expressions through subsequent communicative events over time. These awakenings of consciousness are more a matter of quality of actions than quantity of information. Even within our native culture we are continually presented with unexpected plights of others to which we can either act to develop a consciousness previously outside our experiences or avert our attention and remain oblivious. As a professor for a few decades, I have unexpectedly encountered previously unexplored worlds among students, colleagues and foreign encounters along the way: Extreme poverty beyond any way to remedy, family abuse, career ambitions, playing in a music group devoted to Holocaust survivors and university governmental relations. Such encounters provided me with options where decisions to engage or ignore were made and consequently potential kinds of consciousness were developed or declined. If the former, then I have seen things of the world I could not thereafter unsee or experience sentiments I could not unfeel; if the latter, then I remained calm and carried on as before.

Our minds make these forms of consciousness possible, but consciousness does not inform us of mind. Rather the consciousness referred to here is a capacity for ready awareness that provides us a way to direct attention to what is most important, make instantaneous decisions, take unpremeditated actions, and recall and predict from what we can remember or believe. However, such consciousness can also trick us into seeing and hearing what is not there, as demonstrated by common optical illusions that we cannot unsee and auditory illusions such as the McGurk effect, where we hear what we see and can only perceive the actual auditory signal when we close or avert our eyes.[3]

Formulating a new consciousness of this sort occurs when individuals become aware of new possibilities to socialize. For most individuals going to new cultures with the intention of communicating with the people they encounter there, the creation of a new awareness of preferred expressions and behaviors and perceptions requires training to implement and extensive repetition to inculcate. Practice may not make perfect, but it does make permanent. We accomplish the enaction of this consciousness by using instruction which focuses on culture for content and performance for action and assessment. To think about how adults can begin to perceive a new culture, we do not have to fret over 21st-century efforts to bring consciousness into cognitive studies, neuroscience, artificial intelligence or any other trending discipline. Many of these efforts seek to understand the origin and instruments of self-awareness, whereas we seek to see consciousness as awareness of others. This usually occurs as a sensitivity toward the social interactions between individuals and the contexts of communication.

Nearly two centuries ago, Thomas Carlyle (1831) described this condition in a way that is recognizable to most people in communication between two cultures, where mistakes in expectations and intentions are frequent and possibly costly or at least embarrassing. This homely concept is based on the perception that something is working wrong in social interactions that we value:

> The healthy know not of their health, but only the sick: this is the Physician's Aphorism; and applicable in a far wider sense than he gives it. We may say, it holds no less in moral, intellectual, political, poetical, than in merely corporeal therapeutics; that wherever, or in what shape soever, powers of the sort which can be named vital are at work, herein lies the test of their working right or working wrong.
>
> (Carlyle, 1831, p. 344)

The consciousness assumed here develops from Carlyle's forced change of perception, as when the body begins to hurt or functions wrong. When students of CFL realize that their intentions for communicating in Chinese are not being realized time and again, they may begin to recognize how others—namely, native speakers or more advanced CFL learners—realize that particular intention in similar contexts. If the learner is lucky, this happens early in instructional settings in preparation for a future of self-managed learning.

Over an academic career engaged in communicating with Chinese in my limited abilities in the language, I have often observed in myself as well as other Americans a lack of a conviction that Chinese with whom I engage can depart from an event with a story that differs considerably from my own, only to later become aware of myself: "The test of their working right or working wrong" that often leaves me disappointed for being unaware of the obvious. The congresswoman's narrative is not an outlier in our society. After all, Americans recognize with general approval when Popeye proudly proclaims: "I yam what I yam and that's all what I yam." A popular personality insists in the media the popular if dangerous conviction that you must be true to yourself no matter what other people think.[4] The congresswoman showed us one perspective and she stayed with it throughout the narrative, perhaps because she had no alternative.

If you know it, it is easy. If you don't know it, it is impossible

I overheard this comment when a student was asked if Chinese is a hard language. We can think of this doing something well or doing something not at all in terms of a "game consciousness" (Li C., 2018), as when a basketball player is introduced to volleyball and begins to realize new ways to make points, to win, to pass the ball, to foul or to impress others. If our player at some point decides there is a benefit to becoming proficient in volleyball and begins to perform the moves and with enough persistence in the game gains the ability to make the right moves at the right times without premeditation, the basketball player becomes a volleyball player and is a bi-gamer, if not a multi-gamer—perhaps even becoming expert in a game that was previously outside the player's consciousness. This potentially impressive knowledge begins with simple and probably awkward actions that later become a flow of purposeful gamesmanship. The prelude to expert ability in volleyball is obliviousness to volleyball as a possible game, just as an astute learner of Chinese can begin to communicate in ways previously unknown.

When challenged by having to reconstruct common aspects of our world in different ways, or accomplishing social interactions using different strategies, or realizing that the meaning of an expression is determined by context and intention, the amount of time and resource required is immense. Using game—whether as metaphor or as psychological reality—is a most useful concept for adults to begin learning to communicate in a foreign language and culture.[5] Learning a game assumes a new awareness of ways to behave and putting that awareness into actions intended to achieve a purpose. The intention to learn a game assumes that learning one thing leads to learning another in a conceivably unending process. Combined with the development of computer games and the small handheld devices that put games in individual players hands—as did Gunpei Yokoi, who combined Sharp instruments with Nintendo games in the 1970s (Epstein, 2019)—the acquisition and playing of human versus machine or human versus human with computer games has spread throughout the world. With the popularity of computer games, online and handheld, individual and team sports, autonomously learning to play games has become the most widespread mode of functional learning across the globe.

When games develop an economic structure, we think of them as sports. American football, basketball, tennis and soccer are sports. Such games have a wide variety of participants—players from the casual player to the sincere amateur to the high-earning professional to institutional stakeholders such as club owners. Certain sports have a discernable impact on American expectations and patterns of behavior. Over 20 years ago I asked a Chinese businessman with an international portfolio to comment on doing business with Americans compared to people from other countries. His response was given readily as if he had put some thought into it: "America is an 'olive ball' (American football) country in a soccer world." He went on to explain how putting together a project with Americans went better if he segmented the process in repeating periods of planning, implementation and measurement. He was sure Americans would never be comfortable with the continual flow of strategy and tactics expected in a game of soccer (football).

When it comes to learning a new language, we have choices—learning how that language reflects the world we know or how it permits us to learn to communicate in new ways. Learning to communicate our native culture in conversations in a new language limits us to conversing with only people who have knowledge of our culture. This does not seem to be sustainable for ordinary people, even though it exemplifies the young American woman in Dalian. Learning to communicate in the culture of the language you are studying can be slower in the early stages of a course of instruction when you are learning what you do or do not do to communicate successfully; however, knowing cultural strategies is increasingly effective once you know the reasons you learn new expressions and communicative moves. Once you develop this practice, you will ultimately have access to an inexhaustible exploration throughout a lifetime.

No matter where you go, you are in *their* there

Years ago there was a too oft repeated expression used at the point of a departure: "Remember, no matter where you go, there you are." This did not make any sense to me for a few years, until I considered the necessity of paying attention to the people involved in my conversations and the realization that understanding my intentions and observations was not entirely up to me. After realizing the need to understand my interlocutors' expectations (i.e., *their* there), my attempts at communication improved substantially, although I still regularly fall short of assurance that my messages achieve my intentions. But wherever I find myself, I can accept that their comprehension is largely my responsibility—come success or failure.

The significance to a CFL teacher of the Dalian narrative is that it is a story of someone who is almost certain not to continue studying and living in Chinese long enough to develop a functional consciousness of interactions and communication with and in Chinese culture. There has to be a recognition of place and audience and some expressed desire to react effectively. From the perspective of an under-endowed university program, precious resources and opportunities are wasted if this is happening to our students. We seek to avoid this waste by not assuming that the top goal of a student of Chinese is to report about things Chinese to fellow Americans, but to seek understanding from and with and among people in China. We do this by beginning the study of the language with a focus on communicating in Chinese culture and ending it years later with a focus on an individual domain of interest. Over a sufficient amount of time, our students will have encountered China with a growing consciousness of its culture and attain the ability to research and discuss topics of their own interest.

Learning to communicate in a foreign language is a formidable challenge. It starts with accepting the possibility of regarding other humans on this planet in unfamiliar ways. It enters into interactions that have built-in capacities for cultural and social change over time. Conversations are the main means of co-constructing meanings and memories, and stories are the elements by which memories are replicated through time. Stories reflect what we do with language, how we adapt language to places we are familiar with and people we know and the values that define societies and individuals with whom we interact. Communicating by language has recognizable structures and patterns of behavior that emerge through performances, individually and cooperatively, through speech and written language. Conversations and compositions reveal what is important to the participants in and bearers of a culture: For example, what is to be noted about individuals, what set expressions occur in which contexts, what colors are to be identified and what they mean in references to people and events, how food is to be used for social purposes and all things that are to be considered, recognized and noted in daily intercourse. Grammar is a device used to identify describe sequences of language elements, but most importantly we rely on grammar as a way to complete the expressions we begin. We start expressions, sentences and discourses and complete them without premeditation. Our knowledge of grammar allows us to unconsciously finish an element of language even if doing so may reveal errors of fact and judgment that can result in a noticeable disadvantage to the speaker or author of a piece of language. Grammar can save or savage an individual reputation while demonstrating adherence to a group of people with whom we can share a consciousness, allowing varying levels of linguistic and cultural communication.

Some examples of communicating in American culture might illustrate contrasting intentions between cultures in common interactions: I grew up in the mountains of Colorado and teach university in Columbus, Ohio, which always seems to be quintessentially "Midwestern" to me. Offering greetings between strangers is a commonly experienced phenomenon as I walk across the campus, and being greeted by people I do not know and will probably never see again seems normal to this American Westerner adrift in the Midwest. Although I work on a university campus, which is a sophisticated environment compared to some others, the only people who are unnerved by this practice are foreigners and the occasional refugee from New York City. Chinese students and academics find this practice disquieting and curious, and they mostly ignore friendly greetings from people they do not know and will probably never see again. This often results in Ohioans detecting a sense of unfriendliness on the part of Chinese students.

Our beginning CFL students must be taught to forgo the friendly greeting when they have a chance encounter with a Chinese person with whom they are not acquainted. Even though they learn perfectly good Chinese greeting phrases and gestures, they are instructed and tested on their ability to forbear putting them to use if they do not recognize the individual they meet (or are pretending to meet), because it causes discomfort. Our students are incredulous to learn that the Americans who greet strangers are probably the global outliers when it comes to this practice. And often our students protest when told that the objects of their smiles and greetings in Chinese likely have different interpretations among the non-Americans on the receiving side of their goodwill—for example, this person is up to no good, smiling and greeting strangers for no conceivable reason implies a disturbing lack of sophistication, or (according to personal experience when I walk through Chinese airports) the desire to provide me with an overpriced taxi ride.

Our reason for pointing this out early in the learning process is to give our students time to get used to the idea that our intention for engaging in a social event is not as important as the interpretation of the recipient (i.e., audience) of that action. It takes time to realize this result and make this adjustment and then start looking to identify and respond to a recipients' expectations. When designing a program of study for beginning CFL learners, we need to heed the time it will take them to attain the ability to communicate effectively in the language and culture. Therefore, we do not assume we are guiding them to communicate with students of their current age in China. By the time they can interact with people in China, typical CFL learners will be looking toward careers and find themselves amid the expectations of adulthood. At this point, they will benefit from knowing how people in China expect to be addressed as adults by adults.

Different language, different reality

Perceived different realities are observable in some of the commonest elements in social interactions. American names generally consist of common given names and unusual surnames. The situation is reversed in Chinese. (Note that referring to first and last names in this situation is just confusing.) So while the given name is the first convenient item to remember in American English, the opposite is true in Chinese. For adults, in Chinese an even more important term in addressing another person is the title (generally occupational but also generic). When addressing someone you know in America, depending on the situation, acquaintances can be addressed by given name (informally) or title plus surname. In Chinese, you address or refer to a person by title (only) or surname and title. English titles tend to refer to broader categories of social roles: For example, "president" is used for the leader of a government, the highest-ranking person in a college or university, the leader of a company, the head of the PTA or a leader of a student organization. In Chinese, all these social ranks will have different terms. Titles as terms of address generally are more fixed over time in Chinese culture than in American culture. The prominent American exception in this regard are titles associated with political offices: It seems anyone who has attained political or politically appointed offices expect to be addressed by the title associated with their highest office. So a person who has been elected senator expects to be addressed as "Senator" to the end of his or her days, unless he or she picks up an even more prestigious position and title afterwards. When communicating in Chinese, other people are regarded differently than when communicating in American English. When regarding others in Chinese, the feature about them to prioritize is social standing; in American English, it is name.

The contrast between referencing others with pronouns also exists: In Chinese it is number, singular or plural (*ta/tamen*); in English it is gender, number, subject or object (he/she, him/her), number (they/them). When native English-speaking persons speak Chinese, they rarely have problems with pronouns; when native Chinese-speaking persons speak English, problems with he/she and him/her distinctions can persist among the most skillful communicators. This, perhaps, is the result of not performing a focus on gender in early stages of learning to speak English and failing to develop the habit of automatically prioritizing gender without conscious premeditation.

In American English, teachers, professors and even preschool teachers often encourage students to use first names when referring to their instructors. Some do; some do not. Calling a teacher by first name is negotiated in English; not so in Chinese. Over my decades of managing Chinese language programs, the most common complaint from Chinese teachers about American students concerns terms of address: A student may simply greet his Chinese teacher with *Ni hao* or *Laoshi, ni hao* instead of the expected *Laoshi hao* or *Laoshi, nin hao* (polite). Even though CFL teachers are accustomed to American communicative behaviors, when students fail to meet this expectation in Chinese, even long-serving teachers seem to find this irritating. Paying attention to these contrasting behaviors is more beneficial in terms of good feelings and productive relationships than an American is prepared to expect.

The contrasting representations of our worlds permeates the apperceptions of those who communicate across languages and cultures. Aside from referring to others in contrasting ways, common social interactions are structured differently, and Americans learning Chinese have to learn new ways to accomplish these actions without premeditation, just as a basketball player beginning to play volleyball learns to avoid catching and throwing the ball that needs to be passed to a teammate. The volleyball player has learned to hit the ball to a teammate without thinking about it. Forgetting to do this and catching the volleyball means he suddenly is no longer playing the game of volleyball.

Accepting an offer provides another common example. When Americans make an offer, we generally expect a direct response. Americans offer a beverage and expect the person receiving the offer to immediately inform us whether they want to accept it or to decline. American hosts are aware that a guest may have sincere reasons for not accepting an offer: The beverage may be proscribed by the guest's religion, or it may contain a substance to which the guest is allergic. An American host is not inclined to insist on the guest imbibing the proffered substance, even feeling it rude to persist in the offer. American hosts assume their responsibility is to provide guests with choices and are willing to leave the choice to accept or to decline to the guest.

A Chinese host offers hospitality to guests who do not wish to appear too eager to indulge in the host's largesse. A Chinese host makes offers and repeats them until the guest accepts. Guests refuse offers repeatedly, and rarely the refusal stands. A host's job is to repeat offers at least one more time than the guest refuses.

Americans initiate an acceptance by accepting; Chinese initiate an acceptance by refusing. This phenomenon causes issues when Americans and Chinese play in each other's social events. American guests, who assume that the guest's choice is supreme, can complain that Chinese hosts are "bullying" them into accepting what they do not want. One saving feature of Chinese hosts (as far as American guests are concerned) is that once you have accepted an offered item to eat, your plate is never commented on. You can leave the food untouched or enjoy it. Your host will seem not to notice at all. When Americans learn of this, there is a general feeling of relief and an enhanced chance to enjoy the hospitality.

An alcoholic drink is a different matter. Chinese hosts pour the guests' drinks and continue to "toast" until the event times out. A guest playing a defensive game tries not to empty a glass—which will be filled immediately—or will seek out ways to slow down the consumption. If all else fails, such guests claim a medical reason for abstaining from alcohol or ply any other gambit that might appeal to the host's sympathies; relying on advanced years becomes an increasingly effective tactic after a guest reaches an obvious seniority.

In addition to constructing our social worlds differently in persistent if subtle ways such as prioritizing gender in English and ignoring it in Chinese, language will simply mislead an unsuspecting outsider by reserving a special meaning for an otherwise unsuspicious expression: In this case we can consider "other peoples' children."

Chinese sentences can be analyzed into topic and comment. The topic is an expression that the sentence is about and the comment is a question or statement about the topic. Here are examples with "ticket(s)" (*piao*) as the topic:

票是谁买的. *Piao shi shei/shui maide?* Who bought the tickets?
票是我买的，*Piao shi wo maide.* I bought the tickets.

Meanings of expressions are generally determined by the context in which they occur. We recognize contexts that predictably occur in the society and culture in which we live. We understand what someone means because we generally know the intentions of someone in that context and are familiar with the language we hear or read. Chinese has sufficient syntactical resources for making explicit comparisons between phenomena and physical entities. However, Yawei Li directed my attention to the phenomenon of implied comparison in Chinese (Li Y., 2018). She pointed out that adjectives occurring in positive sentences are comparisons: For example, the adjective *gao*.

她高。*Ta gao.* She is taller (or the tall one).
她很高。*Ta hen gao.* She is tall.

If you want the topic pronoun *ta* ('he, she, it') to be described as "being tall/high," you need an adverb (e.g., *hen*), which only signifies that you are describing the topic. To make things more complicated in this situation, if you want to indicate gender or animate versus inanimate, you must visually indicate the she, he, or it anticipated by English prejudices by writing *ta* in *hanzi* (characters: 她, 他, 它) or by pointing out a visual representation of *ta*. Understanding this syntax, we can argue that making comparisons is less marked for meaning in Chinese than is description. Yawei Li's notice that the expression 别人家的孩子 *bie renjia de haizi* ("Other peoples' child[ren]") as a topic always implies a negative comparison of the children in the speaker's family in the favor of the ever-superior children in other people's families. Suspecting that Li Yawei was wrong, I spent months creating numerous scenarios where sentences beginning with this topic would show the children of the speaker's family in a good light, offering faint praise instead of withering criticism. In every case, Li Yawei's hypothesis withstood, and the interpretations of my native speaker informants in and outside China always left the speaker's child on the short end of the comparison. We can conclude that growing up in a Chinese family creates the realization that any child in another family is better than you, no matter how many medals and approbations you have garnered in your few years. Americans tend to vastly overstate the achievements and positive impressions about our own children. Thus when communicating in Chinese, an American must either avoid this expression altogether or attend to its intent and practice placing value in a manner that does not appear to be overly obvious and overbearing when referring to one's own child. Despite the tendency to consider your native culture to be the human standard, I have a strong conviction that Americans do not value their children more than Chinese do.

Third Cultural Space

When learning to communicate in Chinese as an American, there are always two cultures involved in the meaning making—the American base culture and Chinese culture. An individual does not possess or represent a culture: A culture is an overwhelming flow of the intentions and expectations of a discrete part of humanity. A culture is a mighty flow into which some dive deeply and over which some transverse broadly, while some just float as they will on the surface. I suspect the idea that an individual represents a culture is itself a cultural phenomenon. For decades in the course of conversations, I have referred to unsuspecting persons with the following statement in what I considered the appropriate language: "You are a typical American/Chinese." 你是代表性的美国人 / 中国人. In the vast majority of instances when I volunteered this observation to an individual, the Chinese person was flattered or at least untroubled, and the American was offended. My sense is the different reactions were focused more on the term "typical" 代表性 rather than the nationality.

If as Daniel Everett observed, culture is necessary for communication, then at least one culture will be present in a social exchange. In communications between Chinese and Americans, both cultures are available for making meaning. In the Dalian story, we can assume the declarative statements and the behaviors between the Americans and the locals were made in the Chinese language and culture, but the interpretations of these exchanges were presented in American culture. A culture can be operational in a social event even when the consciousness of that culture is not. Declarative statements across cultures do not require consciousness of both cultures, but conversations do. Conversations are social exchanges that are constructed by two (or more) speakers in a back-and-forth exchange of information within a specified period of time. When this involves people from two different cultural and linguistic backgrounds, co-constructing meaning has recourse to the contexts of at least two cultural spaces. When the conversationalists are aware of both cultural spaces, it forms what we regard to be a Third Cultural Space[6] where the conversationalists have access to the meaning-generating contexts of both cultures. The Third Cultural Space is a dynamic combination of the available contexts that change according to where the conversation takes place and the cultural experiences of the participants. Depending on the recognized intentions and expectations of the conversationalists, either Chinese or American culture will dominate the balance of the cultural influence.

This view was articulated in detail over a quarter century ago by the anthropological linguist Michael Agar, who carefully pointed out that

> different languages aren't just alternative ways to talk about the same reality. Alternative languages carry with them a different theory of what reality in fact is. A shift from one language to another is a shift between two different worlds.
>
> (Agar, 1994, p. 66)

Agar is mostly right, but the story about the young American girl in Dalian has described a situation where the language is Chinese but the reported meaning appears to be strictly from American culture. It is possible to be in China while demonstrating no consciousness of Chinese culture. The obverse of this is not difficult to find among the students in English programs in China or even among some older Chinese in America. To avoid learning a foreign language without leaving the comfort of the native culture, foreign language programs can provide the opportunity to learn to communicate in the foreign culture. In the early stages of a CFL program, a Third Cultural Space is designed into the pedagogical encounter with the language. Chinese culture is introduced to students as a series of "performances" of functioning in Chinese culture. Students learn that these performances have five critical elements—place, audience, roles, time and script (PARTS). Changes in one element of PARTS will trigger changes in one or more of the other elements. Early in the process, they learn to recognize and acknowledge the social status of the persons they encounter through video, audio, graphic illustrations and text. From there, through materials and personal instruction and a consistent program of instruction, American learners daily construct a new consciousness of social communication in much the same way a dedicated player becomes a successful participant in a game. Successful instructors know the culture of their learners and guide them as they learn to communicate effectively in Chinese culture. Encounters with a world previously invisible to them leads to an extensive series of short-term explorations, acting first and thinking later. Over time they realize where they are and who they are in that place. Some may even come to understand why this is so in theory; but if they can recognize the expectations of Chinese conversationalists and respond effectively, theoretical understanding is not necessary for an individual's success.

Knowing and doing is the same thing (知行合一)

Wang Yangming (Ming dynasty, 15th–16th centuries), without a discernable intention to do so, provides us with a principle for learning and teaching a language along with any other type of performance-based discipline. This principle

156 *Galal Walker*

is obvious when talking about dancing and sports, where physical strength and coordination are on constant display; however, it is not so obvious when language is considered to be an academic endeavor and is explicated by interpretation or translation, especially in assessments where the learner is awarded more for analysis than for performance. Dominating the design of textbooks and characterizing classroom presentations, the common image we have of students being introduced to Chinese is the study of listable items such as dialogs, vocabulary items, English glosses, sentence patterns, syntax and rules that are applied to create meaningful expressions. When language is regarded as a list of sentences and understanding is primarily demonstrated by translations into the students' base language or analyses of sentences through completion or transformation drills, thinking of learning a language as schoolwork is reasonable.

When the goal becomes learning to communicate in the language, the focus is on culture, context and performance—either in place of the sentence-based study or accompanying the item-based study. The Performed Culture Approach in Chinese is usually arranged in Act and Fact sessions, the former being organized for learner performance in Chinese and the latter being bilingual or English coaching sessions toward improving learner performances in Chinese. While we assume that how different people learn is mostly the same, how people study can vary considerably. Gaining the ability to communicate in a studied language is done more by the performance of culturally appropriate events than by the application of rules. That effective communication has important components that are learned through performance can be demonstrated by pointing out examples of these components in everyday usage. N. J. Enfield wrote an important book about these,[7] providing detailed analysis of the uses of elements of English that have never been "taught" but rather learned through exposure and performance.

In a sad effort to avoid working on this chapter, I have watched an embarrassing amount of television (American and British). To justify this shameful behavior to myself, I hastily took notes on the underground grammar of spoken English that is obviously learned through performance, because no self-respecting teacher of English would attempt to teach such things to their cherished students. I shall choose three unavoidable examples of underground English grammar and try to be brief.

"So, . . .": The beginning of a sentence following a question or signaling turn-taking. "So, . . ." conveys the intention to tell someone something in a multi-sentence narrative. When Alex Trebek, the host of the game show *Jeopardy!*, at a designated pause in the answering and questioning asks a contestant to say something about themselves, many of the responding sentences begin with "So, . . ." as in: "So, Alex, I'm a clogger. I spend a lot of time working on my moves and timing. It takes a lot of time and effort on my part, but it just seems to irritate most people."

"Like,": Used to introduce the subject of a sentence or to indicate a pause for emphasis or hesitation:

> Like, there he was in Tokyo in the midst of a heat wave. It was not a place for a tall blond Swede. He was like sweating profusely in a crowded train with

no air conditioning. He was like worried he would offend other riders. It was like 42 degrees and he was late.

". . . to my colleagues and I"*: When a nominative pronoun displaces an objective pronoun, "it sounds better," according to the few people who seemed irritated when I remarked on this aspect of their speech. No native speaker of English would utter the phrase "You honor I"*, but I recently wrote down the words of a leader of an organization at a formal occasion: "You honor me tonight with this award, but you honor my colleagues and I more with your continued interest in our work." The replacement of the objective pronoun with a nominative pronoun in a (proper) noun plus pronoun combination following a verb or preposition is never taught. There is no "rule" that determines this "honor my colleagues and I . . ." structure, nor has any student been directed to create such a structure in a repetition or transformation drill. Still, this type of replacement of a standard English objective singular pronoun (me) with the nominative singular pronoun (I) regularly occurs in the spoken (and sometimes written) expressions of native English speakers in a wide range of communication events: In formal speeches, by professional communicators in the media, in the movies, in American and less frequently in British English. When this is brought to a culprit's attention by a tiresome quibbler on minor points of grammar, expect to experience their annoyance and sometimes outright denials. I have an unproven idea about why people do this, and why I have caught myself doing this, but that is not interesting. The interesting thing here is that this practice has permeated contemporary American English through the sole influence of hearing and performing this structure continuously since the latter half of the 20th century. I have not observed a non-native English speaker in China using this grammatical alternative, probably because explaining the transformation rules required to teach someone to do this is much too troublesome. Lacking exposure to the incessant repetition of the substitution of the objective pronoun by the invasive nominative pronoun and the need to perform it, it is easier to use the pronoun "me" in this structure.

We keep track of what students learn by typifying their experiences as personal memories of doing things in Chinese. We simply refer to these memories as stories. Stories about doing things in Chinese culture (e.g., shopping, flattering, using large numbers) are classified as Cases. Stories about specific places or people (e.g., classrooms, offices, members of a club, dorm mates, a television series about charming and entertaining groups of attractive people) are deemed Sagas. Many of the media-based materials are in this category because that is the nature of how stories are presented in movies and television. Stories about actions that convey cultural values (explicitly recognizing social hierarchy, appreciating the roles of host and guest in social events, initiating acceptance by refusing) are Themes. CFL instruction consists of an extended period of purposeful engagements with prepared materials, trained teachers and willing learners. We arrange for these to all be in a specified place—either in a prearranged physical space or a space formed by electronics and minds.

Then, we perform.

Notes

1 The OSU Chinese program offers individualized instruction, an option chosen by nearly every student with previous exposure to the language—whether through heritage exposure or academic experience.
2 The US government's Interagency Language Roundtable and Defense Language Institute ranks languages by groups of difficulty based on the amount of instruction required to attain certain levels of "proficiency" determined by in-house standardized online tests and oral interviews. The primary use of these data is to make budgets, not to prepare for work.
3 See common optical or visual illusions online, and the McGurk effect as well (McGurk, H., & McDonald, J. (1976). Hearing lips and seeing voices. *Nature*, *264*, 746–748).
4 Katy Perry, a recording artist, in promoting a new product, "Daisies" (2020).
5 Psychological realities determine how we make meaning from symbols we see and vocal sounds we hear. Sapir (1949) explains the phoneme (the minimal unit of sound that distinguishes meaning in a particular language) as a psychological reality. Our perception of phonemes identifies certain sounds that influence meaning when we speak or hear that language. For example, /θʌm/ (thumb) can be distinguished from /sʌm/ (sum) for English native speakers, because /θ/ and /s/ are two phonemes in English. Not so for Chinese speakers, who cannot hear the difference. Tone is a phonemic feature of Chinese, clearly evoking different meanings to sounds like *mā* and *má*, where English speakers fail to perceive any difference in sound or meaning (Cong Li, 2018, pp. 45–46).
6 See previous chapters where the concept of Third Space is discussed in terms of learning to communicate in a foreign language.
7 N. J. Enfield (2017) richly demonstrates the elements occurring constantly in conversation that are never taught in school.

References

Agar, M. (1994). *Language shock: Understanding the culture of conversation.* New York: William Morrow.

Carlyle, T. (1831). Characteristics. In T. Carlyle (Ed.), *Carlyle's complete works* (Vol. 5). Boston, MA: Estes and Lauriat.

Enfield, N. J. (2017). *How we talk: The inner workings of conversations.* New York: Basic Books.

Epstein, D. (2019). *Range: Why generalists thrive in a Specialized World.* New York: Riverhead Books.

Everett, D. I. (2017). *How language began: The story of Humanity's greatest invention.* New York and London: Liveright Publishing Corporation (Norton).

Li, C. (2018). *Gamification in foreign language education: Fundamentals for a gamified design of institutional programs for Chinese as a foreign language.* Columbus: Ohio State University.

Li, Y. (2018). *Other people's children: Implicit comparison in modern Chinese conversation.* Columbus: Ohio State University.

Sapir, E. (1949). The psychological reality of phonemes. In D. Mandelbaumn (Ed.), *Selected Writings of Edward Sapir in Language, Culture, and Personality.* Berkeley: University of California Press.

Schroeder, P. (1998). *24 years of housework and the place is still a mess.* Kansas City, MO: Andrews McMeel Publications.

Walker, G. (2010). Performed culture: Learning to participate in another culture. In G. Walker (Ed.), *The pedagogy of performing in another culture* (2nd ed.). Columbus, OH: National East Asian Languages Resource Center.

Index

advanced-level: CFL learners 48–49, 51, 99, 101–102, 103–105; curriculum 14, 88–89, 105; *see also* program, at Ohio State University
aesthetics 21
Agar, Michael 155
American in China: as heritage Chinese speaker 31–32; as *laowai* 30–31; story 143
audience 49–51, 53, 60–62, 141

Bakhtin, Mikhail 15, 69, 86
Bhabha, Homi 3, 7, 69, 73, 118
boundaries 13–16
Bourdieu, Pierre 132, 135
buer/don't see/do two 10–12

C2 receptivity of learner 26, 34–35
Carlyle, Thomas 147
cases 157
categories 13–14
chengyu 30, 39, 83, 87, 89; *see also* conventional expressions
co-construction: of intention 45; of messages 139; of Third-Space persona(e) 38; *see also* Third Space; Third-Space persona(e)
common ground 46, 62
communicating in American culture 150
communicative repertoire 86
Communities of Practice: joint enterprise 119; mutual engagement 119; shared repertoire 119, 129–136
consciousness 143, 146–147; of culture 149–150; game 148
construction 13–14, 16–17; of personae 20
constructive 7–8, 14–15, 20
context 48–52, 55–56, 62, 65, 88–89, 141, 154–155; and intention 148

conventional expressions 83–84, 90; *see also* formulaic expression
conversation 139, 149; as co-constructed 154; and compositions 150; and declaration 154–155
cooperation 7, 15–16
creativity 79–82, 84–85, 87, 90; and boundaries of being creative 89
culture 8, 140, 154; base culture 33, 70, 142, 154; and individuals 141; target culture 37–38, 39, 70, 85, 89, 100, 102; theory of 140–141; *see also* Performed Culture Approach; target-culture(C2) expectation
cyber nationalism 128, 135

Dalian, University of 143
dichotomous: "cultural differences" 14; ideologies, perception, interests 117; opposition between learner and environment 36
discourse analysis 41, 51, 71, 73
domain 122, 133, 140; domain expertise 5, 72, 73, 75, 77–78, 84–86, 88–90, 99, 105–106, 112, 122, 129, 130, 133–134, 137; -general 103; -specific 100–102, 103–106, 110, 112; *see also* expertise

ecological approach to SLA and SLS 35–36
emergent 3; agent(learner)-environment dynamics 36; expectation 40; intention 46–47; Third Space 3, 117; Third-Space personae 19, 36, 39
Enfield, Nick 156
Everett, Daniel 140–141
expectation 1–2, 28; conflicting 33–34, 142; from meeting to negotiating 14;

160 Index

see also native speaker's expectation; target-culture(C2) expectation
expectation game 37; "judges" and "players" 37–38; winning 38–39
expertise 78, 86, 88–89, 91; in communicating in Chinese 102

foreigness 84, 103; performed 39
formulaic expression 56, 59, 61

game: autonomously learning 148; of C2 expectations 37; consciousness 148; as psychological reality 148
gazing 7, 14
global: cooperation 1; globalized workplace 26, 73; glocal (global-local) 7; professional 26, 70, 82, 84, 85, 89; qualities 83, 90
goal: -based 13, 20; of foreign language education 1, 7, 26, 40, 89, 140; of learning Chinese/foreign languages 35, 36, 140, 149, 156; -oriented 13; shared 3, 4, 5, 38, 69, 113, 118; short-term and long term 105–106, 109; *see also* vision
grammar 69, 87, 101, 125, 150, 156
greetings (in the Midwest and China) 150

huayi 29, 31, 38
hybridity 3, 7, 15, 69, 117, 118

identity 4, 20–21, 28, 33, 39, 82, 124–125, 130–132, 141; foreign 84, 125–127
index 38, 72, 78, 79, 81–82, 86; and affective stance 87; linguistic 30; and social stance 82
intention 1–2, 28, 34–35, 38, 45–48, 55–62, 69, 86, 128–129, 139, 141, 147–150, 154–156; intentional hybridity 15; situated act of 41
interculturality 16; intercultural communication 3, 36, 38, 45, 47–48, 61, 106, 118, 135; intercultural conversational interactions 45, 48, 60; intercultural cooperation 1–2
internship 72, 75, 142; successes and failures 143
interpersonal communication 46, 48, 61
interpretation of recipient 151
intracultural communication 47

Kramsch, Claire 3, 8, 16, 28, 29, 35–36, 39, 68, 69, 70, 71, 73, 89, 90, 119

language ideologies 27, 37, 41
laowai/waiguoren 29–31, 32, 33, 38, 83, 128
legitimate peripheral participation: identification with the community 129–130, 133, 136; legitimacy 120; and legitimate knowledge contributor 117, 121, 128
linguistic appropriation 29, 79, 87, 89

message 19–20, 149; as co-constructed 139; and messenger 19–20
metacommunication 56, 60, 62; metapragmatic activities 49–50; metapragmatic comments 49–50, 52, 56, 58, 61, 65
monocultural view 145
monolingual 17, 19, 34
motivation: language learning motivation 5, 99–100, 103, 109; motivating factors 108–111, 113; sustainable learning motivation 100, 111
multilingual 2–3, 7–8, 15, 19; subject 39–40, 68–69, 70–71, 89

native speaker effects 26–29, 35, 37, 40
native speaker/non-native speaker dichotomy 27–29, 37, 40, 70; power dynamics 27
native speakers 45, 48–49, 51, 61–62; nativespeakerism 27–28; native speaker's expectation 68, 70, 72, 73, 82–85, 87, 88, 89, 90–91; *see also* target-culture(C2) expectation
negotiation: of intention and expectation 1–2, 15, 26, 35, 40, 37–38, 48, 57, 59–62; of meaning 47, 68–73, 128, 135; of Third Space 7–8, 14–16, 21, 36, 85, 90, 99, 103–105, 111, 113, 119, 128, 135

obvious-two 8, 10–12
online knowledge-sharing community: linguistic repertoire 121, 131, 136; social question and answer site 117; Zhihu 117–121, 126, 136
open role-play 50, 62
other: one and other 12–13, 16, 19, 27–28, 118; *Othering* 30–31, 87; self and other 8–9, 21, 32, 46–48, 69, 86, 135–136, 146–147; *see also* Third Space

pedagogy 140; Chinese language 6, 51, 69, 70, 73, 88–89, 140–141; foreign/second

language 2, 14, 16, 19–21, 26–27; see also target-culture(C2) expectation
perceived different realities (Chinese and American) 151
performance 13, 20–21, 37, 39, 41, 49–50, 71, 85–86, 155–156; five elements of 155; perceived by C2 34, 86–87, 90; perform beyond proficiency 106
Performance Watch 41
Performed Culture Approach 41, 156; see also program
persona(e) 4, 8, 19–20, 33, 36, 114, 141; see also Third Space
personal memories (stories) 157
perspectives, American and Chinese 144
Popeye 146
proficiency 102; and expertise 89, 105, 109; level(s) 8, 20, 31, 35, 74–75, 82; Oral Proficiency Interview (OPI) 75, 102; ratings 140
program: Chinese/foreign language 8–9, 14, 16, 20, 26, 39, 40–41, 49, 74, 121–122; failures and successes 142; Midwest US-China Flagship 105–108, 140, 112; at Ohio State University 140–143

sagas 157
shared experience 1, 3, 20
socialization: with native speakers/in a foreign culture 28, 38–39, 99, 100–101, 107, 110; second language socialization (SLS) 35
speech act 49–50
symbolic competence 69, 70–71, 88, 89

target-culture (C2) expectation 4, 29, 34–35, 119, 140, 151; of "foreigners" in mainland China 29–33, 102; a pedagogy of 17, 26–27, 35–41
themes 157
Third Cultural Space 154–155
third culture 3, 16
thirdness 16, 69
third place 3, 8, 28, 36
Third Space 1–3, 7–8, 10, 14–15, 16, 19, 26, 33, 69–70, 113, 118–119, 135; co-constructed 2–3, 8, 19, 21, 70, 89, 91, 104; deliberate engagement 118; location 117, 119, 135; personae 4–5, 19–20, 27, 33–35, 36, 39–40, 68, 103, 104; practices 119; productive 7–8, 10, 14–15; subversive potential of 70, 89
time, management of 140
titles (terms of address) 151
transcultural 2, 7–8, 15–16, 18–19, 20; transculturalism 15

underground grammar 156

values 21, 38, 83, 87, 149, 157
vision: construction 38, 104, 107, 111–112; of domain-specific self 100, 104; role model as a vision construction 107

Wang Yangming (Ming dynasty) 155
working right or working wrong 147
wuer/no-two 8, 10–12

Yokoi, Gunpei 148